Y0-BDO-673

Ideologues
and Presidents

Ideologues and Presidents

From the New Deal to the Reagan Revolution

Thomas S. Langston

The Johns Hopkins University Press
Baltimore and London

© 1992 The Johns Hopkins University Press
All rights reserved
Printed in the United States of America on acid-free paper

The Johns Hopkins University Press
701 West 40th Street
Baltimore, Maryland 21211-2190
The Johns Hopkins Press Ltd., London

Library of Congress Cataloging-in-Publication Data

Langston, Thomas S.
   Ideologues and presidents : from the New Deal to the Reagan
revolution / Thomas S. Langston.
      p.   cm.
   Includes bibliographical references and index.
   ISBN 0-8018-4361-8 (alk. paper)
   1. Presidents—United States—Case studies. 2. Ideology. 3. Roosevelt,
Franklin D. (Franklin Delano), 1882–1945. 4. Johnson, Lyndon B.
(Lyndon Baines), 1908–1973. 5. Reagan, Ronald. I. Title.
JK518.L35   1992
353.03′13′0922—dc20   91-45013

LIBRARY
ALMA COLLEGE
ALMA, MICHIGAN

For My Parents

Contents

Acknowledgments

I am indebted to the Massachusetts Institute of Technology and the Lyndon Baines Johnson Foundation for support in the early stages of the research and writing of this book. The manuscript was completed during a year as a John M. Olin postdoctoral fellow at the Institute for the Study of Economic Culture at Boston University (ISEC). Under the direction of its founder, University Professor Peter L. Berger, ISEC was a most congenial and stimulating environment in which to finish this project and begin another. Tulane University made it possible for me to accept the fellowship at ISEC by granting me a year's leave, and I am most grateful to Robert Robins, then chairman of the Department of Political Science, James Kilroy, provost, and my departmental colleagues at Tulane for making this possible.

It is also a pleasure to acknowledge my debt to the dozens of men and women who consented to be interviewed for this book. The archivists and librarians at the Franklin Roosevelt and Lyndon Johnson presidential libraries were also extremely helpful, as were their counterparts at the Library of Congress and the libraries of the following institutions: the United States Treasury Department, the Department of Housing and Urban Development, MIT, Harvard, Yale, the State University of New York College at Geneseo, Tulane, and Boston University.

For their unstinting efforts to improve the original version of this book, I wish to thank especially Walter Dean Burnham, Joshua Cohen, and Richard Pious. Thomas Berger, Sonia Floriani, Frank Heuberger, Ronald King, Paul Lewis, Michael Lind, Cesar Mavratzas, Nicol Rae, and David Steiner also shared with me their time, expertise, and advice as I worked on successive drafts. The reviewer commissioned by the Johns Hopkins University Press provided insightful and detailed comments and suggestions, for which I am grateful. Henry Y. K. Tom, executive editor at the Johns Hopkins University Press, provided valuable editorial suggestions that caused me to improve, I believe, not only the felicity of my prose in this work but the clarity of my argument as well. None of these individuals, of course, bears any responsibility for whatever flaws remain.

In addition, I would like to thank several individuals for their more personal contributions to this effort. For introducing me to the worlds of science and scholarship, I owe a great deal to Professors William B. Stavinoha and Carl Leiden. For reinforcing the hopeful lessons absorbed from my association with these two men, I wish to acknowledge Professor Lucian Pye, whose example and encouragement have meant a lot to me, as well as, I know, to a great many other graduate students over the years at MIT. To my wife Mary I owe the most of all, for I cannot imagine having begun this book, much less completed it, without her. For her inspiration and delight, finally, I acknowledge my daughter Jessica, whose own vastly more significant beginning coincided with the genesis of this book.

Introduction

"The ideologues are coming!" "Thank Heaven, the ideologues have gone." These stylized but all too typical reactions to the Reagan administration's arrival and passing are, I argue in this book, ill-considered. To begin with, if the Reagan administration brought us James Watt, David Stockman, and William Bennett, Franklin Roosevelt's New Deal and Lyndon Johnson's Great Society brought to Washington scores of other idealistic and dedicated men and women who exhibited equal fervor in the logical certainty and comprehensive explanatory power of their social and economic theories. As to whether or not the latest batch of ideologues to descend upon Washington has gone, that question deserves a careful answer. It is true that Ronald Reagan's successor is innocent of ideological intentions. But a president draws advice and personnel from where he finds them, and increasingly, presidents find the people and theories they need to direct the activities of government from ideologically committed think tanks, university research centers, interest groups, and congressional and editorial staffs.

Jack Kemp, for instance, a former member of Congress and for a brief time a senior fellow at the Heritage Foundation in the interim between his retirement from the House and his selection for President Bush's cabinet, may or may not have a correct philosophical understanding of the obligations of the well-off to the poor. But he and his allies in the Bush administration, many of whom have deep ties to the network of conservative policy entrepreneurship, know a great deal about their subject and are incessant in their offers to "help" their president, whether he really wants that assistance or not.[1] And when the next president comes along who—like only Franklin Roosevelt, Lyndon Johnson, and Ronald Reagan since conditions in executive branch politics have been favorable to ideological influence—has both the ambitions and the resources to attempt a major redirection in the course of domestic policy, he (or she?) will likely turn in earnest to yet another assortment of "people of ideas." If, then, when we look at the Bush presidency in light of its predecessor, it seems that the ideologues have largely left town, we need only be patient (my research permits me to speculate) to witness their return in force.

If the ideologues do return in force, we should be prepared. For people of ideas have not simply appeared and disappeared since the New Deal but have exerted a more profound impact on our politics each time since the 1930s that our nation's implicit social compact has been opened for renegotiation. In the chapters that follow, I seek to demonstrate that the increasing leverage that people of ideas have periodically exerted in presidential politics is attributable to some long-term trends affecting the polity. Such trends would include the decay of partisanship and the subsequent partial decoupling of elite political thought and action from what passes for political participation beyond the Washington Beltway. My research implies that if these are not checked (and I do not see any hope or threat that they will be), the administration of the next president with a streak of great ambition is likely to be even more ideologically saturated than was Ronald Reagan's. The potential ramifications for national politics are decidedly, though not exclusively, negative. True, a president who pursues an ideological strategy benefits from a surplus of new ideas and may achieve a level of control over the bureaucracy that otherwise would not be possible. But such a president does nothing to restore the democratic linkages that established the boundaries of more "old-fashioned" party-mediated efforts at policy realignment. Also, the programmatic ambitions of people of ideas—of whatever philosophical hue—embody systematic, if unintended, distortions of social reality. As a consequence, presidential policy achievements that are based upon the designs of ideologists are not likely to provide satisfactory solutions to the problems of domestic policy. If people of ideas now are indispensable for presidents of exceptional programmatic ambition, they clearly are not irreproachable. But simply to disparage without trying first to understand a newly powerful force in our politics accomplishes nothing. In this book I attempt to provide a foundation for reasoned debate over the influence of ideology in American politics.

That there have been *ideologues, ideologists,* or *people of ideas* (the precise meaning of these terms, used interchangeably throughout this work, will be explained later) in the three modern "presidencies of achievement" to date,[2] those of Franklin Roosevelt, Lyndon Johnson, and Ronald Reagan, is not itself a novel observation. By definition, such administrations come into being at moments in "political time" during which bold departures from past policies seem most possible.[3] Roosevelt and Reagan, of course, came to office aligned against the repudiated party of the incumbent president and after several years of intense economic turmoil. Roosevelt also came into office at the start of a critical partisan realignment, which provided him with an extraordinary legislative opportunity. Reagan, though he had of necessity to rely more upon his rhetorical skills than upon his abilities as a party leader, was buoyed his first year in office by the appearance of a prescriptive mandate and sustained throughout his two presidential terms by his skill at communicating directly to the American people. As for Lyndon Johnson, the new president was at first a trustee for his slain predecessor. But after winning the office in his own right in an overwhelming victory for himself and his party in 1964, Johnson eagerly set out to achieve a legacy of his own by reorienting domestic policy about emerging issues of the *quality* of life.[4] It is during just such presidencies that the interests of presidents and people of ideas can be expected to converge. Presidents with ambitions and resources to attempt major redirections in domestic policy need ideas about what ails the country, as well as detailed blueprints to help reconstruct the polity. These are the products that people of ideas stand ready to provide.

Thus, it is not surprising that a plethora of specialized accounts looks at these individual presidents and their ideological helpers.[5] There are, for example, numerous books (many of them written by the subjects themselves) on the exploits of such people of ideas as Rexford Tugwell and Felix Frankfurter in the New Deal, Richard Goodwin and Bill Moyers in the Great Society, David Stockman and James Watt in the "Reagan Revolution." Systematic and comparative explorations of the ideological character of recent presidencies are far fewer in number. Most exemplary in this latter category are the articles by Joel Aberbach and Bert Rockman, and John Kessel.[6] And in the related field of public policy studies, there is growing interest in "the power of public ideas," to appropriate the title of a recent collection of articles.[7]

My work differs considerably from these studies. The principal differences stem from (1) my method for identifying people of ideas as members of a cast of political actors distinct not only from pragmatic professional politicians but also from the nonideological "experts" with whom ideologues compete for power and (2) my effort to relate the influence of ideology in presidential politics to the ongoing transformation of the American party system, an absolutely central theoretical and practical concern in the study of American politics as a whole. My method, explained in detail in chapter 1, permits the sort of comparison across several decades that has for the most part been lacking in treatments of ideological influence in presidential politics.[8] This method further differs from that employed in prior work on the subject in treating ideology not simply as a particular set of policy preferences or values but as a distinct way of thinking about the world,[9] with significant implications for politics and policy making. My effort to relate the issue of ideological impact on the presidency to one of the central concerns in the study of American government permits me to argue that people of ideas are not a sideshow in our politics. They have, indeed, become central actors, filling some of the vacuum left behind in Washington in the wake of the secular transformation of the American party system since the 1930s and all that this has entailed.[10]

As recently as the 1930s, and to a lesser but still significant extent in the 1960s, presidents were heavily tied to the logic of a nonideologized system of partisan political contests. The logic of party politics (especially as it existed in the early decades of this century) essentially differs from the logic of ideological politics. While ideologues in politics work toward the principled and comprehensive control of the powers of the state, party politicians typically pursue contrary ends, such as the maintenance of ideologically inchoate coalitions through the promotion of distributive policy making. Presidents who emerged out of the political environment of, roughly speaking, the first half of this century were not likely to favor ideological over partisan ways of thinking about policy and politics.

By contrast, presidents today are less indebted than before to old-time party leaders and the panoply of particularistic political issues that once defined the national government's agenda.[11] Thus they possess greater latitude than their predecessors did in pursuing policy agendas with universalistic, ideological objectives. Furthermore, the greater reliance of modern presidents on public opinion has in this respect been liberating, not restraining. Today's presidents still need the approval of the electorate, of course, but they can win this in many ways, only a few of which have much to do with the changes in domestic policy sought by their administrations.[12]

In other ways as well, the apartisanship of the presidency has been strengthened over the past several decades. The list of familiars here is lengthy: the virtual "eclipse of the official party in the politics of presidential selection";[13] the transition from anomaly to norm of divided party control of the government; the emergence in the persons of Jimmy Carter and Ronald Reagan of the first twentieth-century presidents with no prior Washington experience; and the incapacity of newly strengthened national party organizations to exert an influence over presidential (or congressional) politics commensurate with their recently acquired professionalism.[14] In such an entrepreneurial, "frontier" environment, the person of ideas should be in an advantageous position.

A priori, an argument can be made that the opportunities provided people of ideas by the weakening of partisan ties affecting the president would not have been squandered, for both motive and means have also been present to bring about an increase in the impact such people might reasonably be expected to enjoy in presidential politics. From the White House point of view, presidents since Roosevelt might be motivated to rely more on people of ideas in their approach to governance for two reasons. First, presidents of exceptional ambition and resources in domestic policy, including the two most recent such men, Johnson and Reagan, feel in need of a comprehensive program to call their own. Their parties are poorly suited to provide them with one, and the electorate is poorly structured to demand one of them. By contrast, ideologues are always ready for action and indefatigable in their offers to help. Second, modern presidents want to reach out for control of the executive bureaucracy. Again, party ties in the 1960s were too weak to be the building blocks of a successful effort to coordinate the thousands of workers for whom a modern president is ultimately responsible. And insofar as the partisan homogeneity among appointees increased in the 1980s, this reflected not simply an old-fashioned raid on the Treasury by former "outs" but also the convergence since the 1970s between the Republican party, partially shorn of its liberal eastern establishment wing, and the conservative ideological movement.[15] From the viewpoint of the person of ideas, the motive for the pursuit of influence in presidential politics is transparent: the power to change the world so as to conform to and thus validate his or her beliefs.

As for means, the raw material necessary for an ideological strategy in presidential politics—a stock of people of ideas—has always been present to some degree. From the president's perspective, however, the necessary means for such an approach to office are more accessible today than in the past. People of ideas are better organized and possess more of the expertise modern administrations desire than in the days of the New Deal. From the ideologue's perspective, the means necessary to peddle his or her wares at the White House have increased as a consequence of several factors. There has been, first, a proliferation in the past two decades of politically oriented think tanks, which provide support and employment for people of ideas.[16] There has also been a tremendous increase in the communication and computational technologies useful to the dissemination of ideas over roughly the same time period.

Tying together means, motive, and opportunity in the emplotment of this "mystery," ideology needs to be understood as a response to social and intellectual stresses, which have been abundant in American society in the sixty-plus years since the Great Depression. And since the redrafting of the people's social contract with their government resulting from the actions taken by Roosevelt during the Great Depression, what has been abundant in our society becomes abundantly relevant to our politics in short order. Thus, even though this is not a work in intellectual history, it seems clear that a pattern of ideological response to societal tensions characterizes the period 1933–90 and that such tensions and efforts to resolve them have peaked during the three administrations under study.

In the 1930s, two pivotal concerns raised by the Great Depression and the new administration's response to it were the relation of the government to the economy and the extent to which the federal government would enter into direct coercive relationships with individual citizens. The ideologues of the New Deal responded imaginatively to these two troubling concerns, as will be evident in chapter 3. In the 1960s, a confluence of historical events brought about the perception, among certain intellectuals at least, of a "crisis in the cities" and in the "quality of life" enjoyed by all Americans. The ideologues of the day offered theories to make these concerns intelligible and programs designed to address them. And in the 1970s, in the aftermath of the Vietnam War and Watergate, a generalized crisis in public authority was proclaimed in academic and lay forums and, finally, from the bully pulpit of the White House itself, in Jimmy Carter's infamous "malaise" speech. Ronald Reagan and his ideological helpers eschewed Carter's pessimism but responded to the same sense of crisis.

People of ideas, to be more specific about the claims of this book, have become over the course of the three presidencies of achievement, beginning with that of Franklin Roosevelt, more systematically integrated into White House operations and more closely tied to the defining domestic interests of these administrations. They have, in short, become increasingly indispensable to presidents of achievement. People of ideas have also become increasingly organized and ambitious to influence presidents on their own terms. In short, they have become increasingly irresistible, especially to presidents with great ambitions for domestic policy.

My principle of analysis, then, is largely structural. It is the *relationship* of a particular cast of political actors—present in all of the administrations under study—to the political system that is at issue. Thus, for example, the people of ideas in the New Deal found themselves at a serious disadvantage when they sought influence in a heavily partisan environment. But perhaps the most paradoxical claim I make about the New Deal period is that the realignment of the party system in the 1930s (the last "classic" realignment of its kind), though it permitted ideologues to draft and implement a great deal of innovative legislation, did not provide a firm foundation for the influence of such people in shaping policy. Rather, it served as a useful check to their zealotry. By the time of the Reagan administration, the linkages that had tied together the polity in the 1930s had greatly dissipated. Despite the renewed vigor of the national parties at the organizational level, parties today do not bind together a people and their government as they once did. Ronald Reagan was consequently freer than previous presidents to integrate systematically people of ideas—for the most part an elite stratum of political actors with few ties to the vast electorate—into his administration. Also by the time of the Reagan administration, an ideological "counterestablishment" had achieved expansive proportions and was eager for a part of the action in Washington. For its part, the Johnson administration was closer to the Reagan than to the Roosevelt model in its reliance on integrated networks of people of ideas for personnel and policy initiatives. But in choosing partisan over ideological modes of policy implementation, Johnson revealed his truer self: an old-fashioned party "pol." The result was the overwhelming partisan frustration of an otherwise impressively ideological agenda.

Finally, in each administration, the presidents themselves were important in either aiding or obstructing the work of people of ideas. Presidents Roosevelt and Johnson were principally obstructionist when it came to implementing ideologically conceived policies, while President Reagan was generally (though by no means always) helpful to the ideologues who labored under his aegis. That the presidents differed in this way is itself explicable, I believe, in terms of a structural argument. Each period produced a president of ambition capable of sustaining its principal dynamics. In the chapters that follow, these arguments are developed and substantiated through the analysis, based on archival materials, personal interviews, and the vast pertinent secondary literature, of pivotal domestic policy struggles in each of the three modern presidencies of achievement.

People of Ideas and the New Deal

In the case of the Roosevelt administration, I will show how people who spoke from various and irreconcilable ideological positions—planners such as Rexford Tugwell and Adolf Berle, corporatists such as Raymond Moley and Hugh Johnson, and "Brandeisians" such as Felix Frankfurter[17] —were permitted to compete behind the scenes to influence personnel and policy decisions. Though the president himself oversaw the recruitment to his government of a number of these and other highly visible people of ideas, in managing executive branch operations he seems not to have paid the slightest attention to the potential net influence of his ideological helpers. In fact, in his relationship with the people of ideas brought into his service, Roosevelt, like Johnson after him, was notable for the barriers he seemed instinctively to erect to the organization of ideological influence in administrative struggles.

Roosevelt's ad hoc, partisan approach to personnel selection and management was dramatically illustrated in the effort to establish the Tennessee Valley Authority. The legislation establishing the TVA gave the chief executive and his board of three supervisors extensive authority to define for themselves the mission of the agency. Because Roosevelt habitually shied away from defining priorities, the task was left largely to the board. Because the president, as was his habit, appointed men of conflicting visions to serve on the board, a tremendous battle ensued within the TVA between a devoted advocate of planning, board chairman Arthur Morgan, and a disciple of Brandeisian principles, the board's co-director, David Lilienthal. This battle ended in the defeat of the more ambitious ideological alternative, planning, and became a significant political embarrassment to the president.

The roots of this debilitating battle within the TVA, I will argue, lay in the strong party system of the 1930s. The issue decided in the shift of partisan balance in the Congress and the presidency in 1932 was whether to pursue government activism beyond precedent. The cues thereby given to legislators and other policymakers stopped far short of defining the appropriate course of action to be taken in even the most talked-about areas of domestic policy. Thus, in the legislative phase of the New Deal realignment, the ideas of social planners, dam builders, utility battlers, and fertilizer experts could be merged speedily yet haphazardly into dramatic new configurations, one of which was the regional authority. But whether the innovative TVA corporation was to be primarily a supplier of electricity to the valley, and thus a competitor against the power trust in the South, or a cooperative social planning agency eschewing competition in all aspects of its mission was not any clearer after its creation. The New Deal realignment —the crucial occurrence making possible the passage of the TVA bill— provided a mandate for neither planning nor trust busting and, thus, could be (and in fact was) construed to support either.

People of Ideas and the Great Society

In the Johnson presidency, the struggle of mainstream liberal people of ideas such as Eric Goldman, Robert Wood, Charles Haar, and Bill Moyers to assert influence was considerably better structured at the front end of the policymaking process than in the Roosevelt administration. People of ideas were consciously sought out by the new president and his closest aides. And because of the expansion of incidentally ideological institutions, in this case the humanities and social science faculties of the elite universities of the Northeast, from which the Johnson White House preferred to recruit its intellectual talent, and because the White House by this time was a fairly rationalized bureaucratic structure capable of conducting systematic talent searches, the available pool of people of ideas was large and easily accessed. As a result, the Johnson administration was able to commission nearly two hundred task forces, with a strong ideological presence in many of the most prominent ones, and to pursue vigorously the appointment to full-time jobs in the executive branch of people with impressive ideological credentials. Under Johnson, the White House personnel director even maintained separate files on "BYM"—the "Bright Young Men" of Camelot and, Johnson seems to have hoped, hill country lore.[18] In bringing people of ideas into the government, then, the Johnson presidency represented a step forward from the 1930s. Despite these "gains" (whether or not they were gains for the polity, they *were* gains for ideological impact upon government), there were still a number of barriers to the influence that people of ideas could have upon policy making, as becomes clear in a study of the effort undertaken by the Johnson administration to build Model Cities.

By the time the Model Cities program was proposed in late 1965, the formerly stalled agenda of the post–New Deal Democratic party had already gained passage. The Great Society, of which Model Cities was to be the keystone, was to be a grand departure from this past. The Model Cities program, consequently, was written from the ground up, not—like the TVA bill—on the skeleton of former legislative proposals. The deeds of the task force that designed the Model Cities program, directed by MIT political scientist Robert Wood and Harvard Law School professor Charles Haar, were to be constructed therefore, not upon the distributive principles of party politics, but upon the twin pillars of Reason and Affluence. The idea was to spur the creation not merely of new physical communities but of new *total* communities, racially and economically integrated.

In implementing Model Cities, the mainstream liberals who had designed the program ran up against considerable obstacles. When the time came to select locales to receive grants to plan and then implement programs, partisan politics clearly predominated over the rational, technocratic interests of the people of ideas ostensibly in charge of the program at the Department of Housing and Urban Development (HUD). From an ideological viewpoint, this was an outrage. To Lyndon Johnson, it was just good politics. Johnson, after all, was wed strongly to the system of partisan exchange and only weakly to the philosophies espoused by some of the people he put to work for him. Johnson, furthermore, in old-fashioned political terms, had already gotten a great deal out of the Model Cities project before a dollar was actually spent in the field. In simply getting Model Cities off the ground, Johnson had performed a favor for an important backer and had brought into his debt a number of his former colleagues in the Congress.

The history of the Model Cities program will serve to highlight the transitional nature of the Johnson administration in the developing integration of people of ideas into the work of modern presidents of achievement. The policy shift represented by Model Cities was not the result of any realignment of the parties. In classic realignments such as that which ushered in the New Deal, emergent political demands were channeled into partisan conflicts that pitted the two polarized parties against each other. In the New Deal, such a realignment was necessary at least to initiate an ideological effort to shape federal domestic policy (just as classic realignments were the apparently necessary precursors to the Jacksonian revolution, the Civil War, and the consolidation of Republican dominance in the "System of 1896"). By the time of the Johnson administration, ideological input into government was sufficiently organized and routinized to proceed in the absence of a New Deal–type realignment.[19] As a partial consequence, the Model Cities legislation was not superficially as philosophically incoherent or ambiguous as was the legislation that created the TVA. The

Model Cities legislation was drafted in a task force that met, with staff assistance and White House support, for several weeks. The TVA Act, by contrast, was drafted virtually overnight with ad hoc input from contradictory groups of people of ideas. Yet in the Johnson case, forward movement in the systematic promotion of ideological initiatives as government policy was balanced by the still impressive loyalties of an executive to a system of personalistic and partisan rewards and coalition building. Twenty years later, some (though certainly not all) of the frustrations that characterized the efforts of people of ideas in the 1960s were absent.

People of Ideas and the Reagan Revolution

Despite the laments from conservatives over the "missed opportunities" of the most explicitly ideological presidency of the century, the record of conservative influence in the earliest, most productive phase of the Reagan administration is considerable. As we will see, in the Reagan administration, ideological commitment to the president's agenda was formally sanctioned as the highest priority in selecting presidential appointees. At the subcabinet level in particular a pattern emerged after several months of appointments being awarded to some intensely conservative people of ideas, who could be counted upon to go about their anticipated tasks without arousing the level of public scrutiny routinely attached to the actions of their superiors. And in appointments to the federal judiciary, the Reagan White House displayed a similarly intense ideological dedication.

Reagan's ideological appointees were "managed," furthermore, in a style appropriate to their comparative advantage within the bureaucracy. Derisively called "trained seals" by some in the White House, Reagan's more conservative appointees were exhorted and expected to do the "right" thing.[20] How this all worked out in practice will be investigated with reference to the central feature of President Reagan's agenda when he entered office: the enactment of complementary "supply-side" budget and tax bills. Among the points to be made are that Reagan's tax-cut proposal was based on the work, prior to 1981, of ideological supply-siders such as Congressman Jack Kemp, journalist Jude Wanniski, congressional staffer Paul Craig Roberts, and economics professor Arthur Laffer; that the budgetary changes Reagan desired were in accord with his basic antistatist philosophy of government; and that in translating the ideological propositions of supply-siders and antistatists into law in 1981, a handful of people of ideas—led at that time by David Stockman—were indispensable.

The significance of bringing ideology into long-term focus in the study of the presidency should become most clear in examining the Reagan presidency. For although no partisan realignment worth its name provided Ronald Reagan with his initiatives or the resources to pursue them, he attempted and partly achieved the sort of broadly encompassing innovations in domestic policy that historically had been associated with such mass reorderings of partisan dominance within the government and among a highly mobilized electorate. Perhaps, then, the increasing integration of people of ideas into the central work of presidents of achievement indicates a way in which the oft-lamented policy deadlock of our contemporary, nationalized yet fragmented, and probably nonrealignable government may be overcome. But the price is high. Social engineering on a wide scale, only weakly constrained by democratic fetters, promotes governmental and societal instability. It does not so much call for sacrifice as commit sacrifices—of the very people it intends to help, be they the working poor, urban blacks, or the residents of the Tennessee River Valley—all in the service of a world-view elaborated by unelected and unaccountable ideological cadres.[21] People of ideas, as people, do not deserve our disapproval. But this should not prevent us from offering a critique of their growing influence within our polity, as a group or indeed, as shall be explained, a New Class of political actors.

The plan of this book is simple. In chapter 1, I provide my definition of the term *person of ideas* and demonstrate its operational content. Also in chapter 1, I elaborate on what is at stake in the ideologization of our politics. I do this by analyzing the contrasting paradigms of governance implicit in the old-fashioned partisan-based strategy and the emerging ideology-based strategy of presidential attempts at major domestic policy redirection. Exploring the costs (as well as occasional benefits) of the unfolding of ideological influence in presidencies of achievement will be a major theme of this entire work. Chapter 2 is intended to do a couple of things. First, it substantiates the claim that there is a family resemblance among the people of ideas associated with the three presidencies examined here. The principal task of the chapter, however, is to describe the manner in which ideology became a formal concern in the selection and management of the president's top appointees. Chapters 3–5 form the empirical, historical core of this work. In these chapters I explore the experiences of people of ideas in the effort to define a mission for the TVA, build Model Cities, and launch the Reagan Revolution. Finally, in chapter 6 I discuss the significance of the preceding analysis and description, and in a brief epilogue I bring the story up to date with an analysis of the status of people of ideas in the Bush administration. Though George Bush, heading into the contest for reelection, shows no signs of being another "president of achievement" in the sense in which that term has been defined by political scientists, there are still lessons to be learned from observing the way that conservative ideologues fight for input in the aftermath of "their" administration.

Ideologues
and Presidents

Chapter One
Ideology: Attributes and Significance to Presidential Politics

Many people *have* ideas, but only a few are people *of* ideas. These people of ideas form a particular subset, presumably just one of many subsets of people active at an elite level of national politics. Such men and women have been present, and the object of much comment, in the three presidencies under study here—Franklin Roosevelt's, Lyndon Johnson's, and Ronald Reagan's. Many observers have noticed that in these administrations (not exclusively, of course), significant numbers of people surrounding the president stood apart for their absorption with ideas, especially for their devotion to comprehensive theories about what ails America and how to set things right. But what exactly distinguishes individuals such as Rexford Tugwell and Adolf Berle from Daniel Roper and Harold Ickes, or Eric Goldman and Bill Moyers from Joseph Califano and H. Barefoot Sanders, Jr., or William Bennett and David Stockman from Terrel Bell and Donald Regan? It is not expertise: everyone named here was an "expert," certainly, in his respective field. Nor does education distinguish them. How, then, can the differences between these elusive though notable "idea men" and their nonideological colleagues be studied?

The Ideologue: An Ideal Type

There are many plausible ways to distinguish these persons of ideas, or ideologues (for that is how the dictionary would define men and women with an intense allegiance to a set of ideas), from other experts. My way is to use an ideal type,[1] according to which a person whose thought is "ideally" or purely ideological

  1. makes claims to logical certitude, absolute truth, and comprehensive explanation;

2. ascribes value to different states of being; and
3. displays an imminent historical consciousness.

In addition to these three core attributes, we may add

4. approaches the generation of knowledge in a characteristically set way; and
5. is likely to affiliate with like-minded individuals in clubs, organizations, journals of opinion, think tanks, or similar institutions.

To elaborate a bit more on (4) at this point, while conservative ideologues generally respect tradition and sometimes revelation as a guide to knowledge applicable in public debate, liberal ideologues are likely to advocate experimentation or some other form of rationalistic inquiry.[2] This trait, I explain below, is a correlate of the ideologue's claim to logical certitude.

Many political leaders and activists in the United States, including those already named, who embody the traits listed above possess what we commonly call a "world-view" or "philosophy." Most basically, what makes such persons exceptional in American politics is their claim to a widely encompassing, principled perspective on the nation's alleged ills and the dogmatic way in which they announce their diagnoses and seek to implement their cures. Such people have been abundant in American politics since the 1930s because of the rise of the administrative state and the expansion of nonindustrial services as a component of the economy. One consequence of these historical trends has been the emergence of the so-called New Class, a segment of the broad middle class which produces and distributes symbolic knowledge. The people whose ways of thinking approximate the ideal type sketched above are among the primary producers and principal disseminators of symbolic knowledge in our society and thus correspond to an "upper crust" of this New Class.[3]

The differences, therefore, between "liberal" New Dealers and Great Society architects, on the one hand, and "conservative" Reaganites, on the other, real as they are, may not be as profound as they are typically held to be. In fact, the "class" interests of most ideologues are far more compatible than their ideas. For example, the choice between a conservative war on poverty through economic empowerment and a liberal war on poverty through the rational design of comprehensive community development plans, though real, does not involve a choice of the primary interest of one class over that of another. Both choices would empower elite members of the New Class to shape society. And both policy options would take the American voter farther away from party-mediated politics and decisions and closer to a future of rapid, unstable shifts in policy directed by competing cadres of unaccountable social engineers.

An ideal type, Peter Berger reminds us, is not intended to be a "photographlike rendition of social reality." "This implies," Berger continues, that the categories of an ideal type "cannot be falsified or supported by data—they can only be shown to be more or less useful in the interpretation of data."[4] As a first step toward demonstrating the usefulness of this characterization of the "ideal" ideologue, I wish to clarify the meaning of the core components in the above list of traits and indicate their likely relevance to the past six decades of American presidential politics.

Relevance to Presidential Politics

The first cluster of traits is especially relevant to the employment of ideologues as presidential appointees. To take the claims that people of ideas make for their beliefs in reverse order: Because of the presumed comprehensiveness of ideology, every problem that an ideological appointee or ally of a president might encounter in his work should be amenable to ideological analysis. Thus, ideology can provide cues to action valid for an extremely wide array of issues. The claim to absolute truth as well as logical certitude suggests that the person of ideas will be steadfast in his actions, even under pressure from interest groups, the permanent bureaucracy, or the media to compromise his principles. And because logical certitude, along with comprehensiveness, implies an exceptional degree of coherent order, an ideologue's beliefs should be highly predictable. Because an overriding problem in presidential politics since the creation of the modern welfare state, with its behemoth administrative apparatus, is how to achieve control of appointees in an environment where confusion is part of the job and oversight a losing battle, the ability to work independently yet with steadfastness of purpose and predictability of decision makes the person of ideas with just this first cluster of traits a potentially influential force in the post–New Deal presidency.[5]

In addition to making these claims, all ideologies allege to provide insight into the worth of particular individuals or groups. This is one way an ideology helps its adherents make sense of their surroundings—a functional attribute of any integrated body of knowledge, including the ideological. For example, in Ayn Rand's "objectivism," the poor, by virtue of their poverty, are ascribed negative values such as laziness and unworthiness.[6] To Claude Brown, by contrast, the poor are not simply impoverished but, paradoxically, enriched by their experience.[7] As a consequence of the internalization of such ascriptive norms, ideologues tend to interpret social reality in terms of polar opposites, "us" against "them."

This trait, too, should help the person of ideas to be an efficient filter of information and, consequently, a predictable and independent decisionmaker. Specifically, ascriptive thought might help a person of ideas to distribute consistently the costs and benefits of his actions, rewarding "us" and punishing "them." It might also contribute to the esprit de corps of people working within an administration. This might be important in maintaining the morale of ideological cadres within the Washington Beltway.

Finally, as a consequence of their aspiration to efficacy, those who subscribe to an ideology display an imminent historical consciousness. Ideology not only projects into the future an ideal society; it tells those who can decipher its messages how to achieve it in the near future. There is, therefore, a highly directive, program-oriented side to ideology. For presidential politics this means that the employment of a comprehensive, far-reaching ideological program might permit a president to short-cut history by guiding a realignment in policy in the absence of a prior thoroughgoing realignment of the political parties. For the ideologue, this means that utopia is always just over the horizon and that extraordinary efforts to realize it are justified.

Concrete Referents

To illustrate further the sort of referents that can be isolated for each of the core attributes as well as the subsidiary traits in the ideal type, I offer extended examples below. Examples come from the writings and biographies of self-proclaimed ideologues and leaders of what are commonly taken to be ideological movements in recent American politics. To make these examples as accessible as possible to readers who are not specialists in the history of the New Deal or the Great Society, I shall focus on persons prominently associated with the Reagan administration, the most recent and most familiar presidency of achievement.

Logical Certitude

An ideology, unlike a political culture, does not contradict itself. Scholars such as Philip Converse, Gabriel Almond, and Sidney Verba have already commented on this aspect of ideology's compunction for logical orderliness.[8] What has not received as much attention is how ideologues view their beliefs as logically compelling or certain. This unshakable belief in the soundness of their ideas is a fundamental part of their inheritance from their historical predecessors. The original *idéologues* were in fact a cultural by-product of the ruthlessly logical French Revolution. Self-proclaimed "scientists of ideas," the ideologues of the French National Institute were eager to apply *analyse* to all "natural" phenomena, including politics. The guiding assumption of the *idéologues* was, in the words of Richard Cox, that "the root cause of civil discord was the prejudicial quality of men's ideas about the nature and objects of political life."[9] From the ideological believer's point of view, religious, irrational faith has always been for the other person; the ideologue's truths would surely be perceived by all who honestly and rationally studied the issues. These points can be illustrated with

4

reference to David Stockman, Ronald Reagan's first director of the Office of Management and Budget (OMB) and a self-proclaimed ideologue.

Stockman began his young adulthood reading Marx, Ginsberg, and *Ramparts* and signing his letters "Comrade." Looking back, he described himself as an undergraduate at Michigan State University as a "full-fledged (if half-baked) neo-Marxist."[10] Stockman changed his ideological leanings while still a student because he was disillusioned with what he perceived to be the hypocrisy of the student Left. It was later, as a graduate student in divinity at Harvard, that Stockman began his movement toward both Washington and a Republican world-view.

While working as a staffer on Capitol Hill, Stockman emerged from a study of economics a disciple of the economist Friedrich A. Hayek. To Stockman, this was no conversion experience. When he read *The Road to Serfdom,* Nixon's wage and price controls had just been put into effect. As far as Stockman could tell, they failed in just the ways that Hayek had implied any such intervention into the market must fail. In describing this penultimate shift in his world-view, Stockman does not speak of truth being revealed to him mysteriously or of truths so powerful that they would deny rational or logical investigation. In his own words:

> Finally, as the futile bureaucratic apparatus of control mushroomed, caprice became endemic. The lottery of windfall gains and losses multiplied throughout the economy. Forms and red tape proliferated, got lost in the mail, and lost contact with the English language. . . . These investigations [undertaken as part of Stockman's job as executive director of the Republican Conference] also demystified the projects of government. Until then I had tended to take the stated policy objectives of government to be actually altering the societal status quo with earnest seriousness. . . . The Nixon wage and price control program shattered nearly every one of these illusions.[11]

To understand more fully what was happening in the political economy, Stockman sought enlightenment in neither poetic nor sacred texts, but in a "text" of a different kind: Theodore Lowi's political science classic, *The End of Liberalism.* "Lowi's model was a welcome find. Just as I had discovered that the story of Noah's Ark wasn't all it had been cracked up to be . . . now I was finding that progressive government—rooted as it was in the mundane graspings of clientele politics—did not command belief, either." While campaigning for a seat in Congress, Stockman continued his self-education, arriving at a "profound principle that was to prove crucial in the final, impending phase of my own odyssey. Before the state can distribute wealth, the society must first produce it." What convinced Stockman more than anything else of these propositions was "the plain evidence I had encountered, down in the economic anthills."[12]

The last leg of Stockman's journey took him from Hayek to Wanniski. And again, in explicating the substance of his new beliefs, Stockman exuded confidence in the logical necessity and coherence of his views. Jude Wanniski's book *The Way the World Works* was given to Congressman Stockman in manuscript form by his colleague Jack Kemp. Stockman reports that the book "hit me with the force of revelation. It reordered everything I had previously known or thought about economics."[13] Despite Stockman's own reference to a conversion experience, he makes clear in his telling of the story that his enlightenment required no great leap of faith. Anyone willing to approach the subject with an open mind, Stockman suggested, would have to admit the truth and logic behind the supply-side message. What Stockman took on faith after this conversion, only to discard it after service in the White House, was not the supply-side's logical force but the belief that its logic, or that of any ideology's, could be enforced without compromise upon the American government and people.

Comprehensive Explanation

Stockman's supply-side mentor, Jude Wanniski, like many other people of ideas, claims to possess a key to understanding the entirety of human existence. Before becoming a supply-sider, Wanniski was a journalist in Las Vegas, where he did his own investigative research to see "the way the world really worked."[14] In Las Vegas, the world seemed to work through bribes, kickbacks, and other forms of corruption. This might have been obvious to a cynic, but to Wanniski it was an epiphany. Later, when he was introduced to the supply side by Arthur Laffer, Wanniski again felt that he had found the underlying principles of a system that fooled most people by its appearances. This time, the system was the global economy, and more. To set forth his latest discoveries, Wanniski wrote a book.

In *The Way the World Works*, Wanniski sought to interpret all of human history as a movement toward a collective global consciousness of the principles of supply-side doctrine. Actually, he felt that not only all of human history but each person's own history was explicable in supply-side terms. There is, in other words, not only a supply-side view of Byzantine agriculture and Chinese urbanization but a supply-side developmental psychology as well. Every child learned supply-side truths, as it were, on his mother's lap. The adult could be led away from these truths, but they were always latent and operating in the intuition of the "global electorate."[15] Furthermore, in its policy implications, the supply side, according to Wanniski, offers solutions to foreign, military, and social puzzles as well as to economic problems. Even abortion, Wanniski insisted in an interview, "can be resolved satisfactorily for the electorate through the implementation of a proper supply-side economic policy."[16]

Absolute Truth

When we say of an ideologue that his thought is "dogmatic," we speak, appropriately, in a religious idiom. For one aspect of ideological thought is the ideologue's assertion that his beliefs are true, not, like worldly truths or mere opinions, for some people some of the time but, like the truths of religion, eternally and universally. As a prime example, this absolutism is evident in the beliefs of former secretary of the treasury and contemporary conservative activist William E. Simon.

Simon is one of the most true-believing of contemporary conservatives. For him, the truths of conservatism are as absolute as human nature, and being a conservative, he does not believe that human nature can be transformed. In his book on conservative principles, *A Time for Truth,* after explaining that the capitalist miracle occurred in the United States as a consequence of its being the "politically freest nation in the world," Simon underlined the "true defense of capitalism," that "wealth is uniquely a result of *individual liberty.*" Simon went on to explain that "there is nothing subjective or biased about this view that political and economic freedom are inextricably linked."[17] As to why so many professional economists and researchers continue to doubt this, Simon suggested in an interview that there are plenty of "180 I.Q. idiots" milling about government agencies and college campuses.[18] Simon is certain about his truths because he deduces them from a distinct view of human nature. Man, he believes, should be known not as *Homo sapiens* but as *Homo faber.* It is man's unique ability to produce wealth that makes it a transcendent obligation of government to order society so as to promote the natural expression of man's essential being.

On the Left in contemporary American political discourse, James F. Lea, an academic with hopes of bringing about change through enlightenment, is Simon's mirror image. Lea believes that American culture is in need of radical change precisely because Simon's world-view has triumphed. (Simon, of course, would be surprised to hear this!) This is undesirable, according to Lea, because it is antithetical to the nature of man. Man is meant to find fulfillment in community and cooperation, not in competition. As is often the case in ideological writings, the author's fundamental assumptions are folded within a dense and angry jeremiad:

> If a governmental system upholds competition rather than coopera-
> tion, material acquisition rather than moral development, and self-
> interest rather than the public interest as the natural principles of
> human behavior, rewarding those most adept at advancing their am-
> bition, greed, and selfishness, that system will, logically, encourage the
> development of these very traits.[19]

In Lea's view, in clear contrast to Simon's, man's worth is uncovered only when he becomes part of a larger community, whose interests collectively are the proper objects of government action.[20]

Different States of Being

The ideologue ascribes value to persons according to their status within certain key categories of being. The categories are determined by the content of the particular ideology. For instance, to the conservatives Robert Carleson, John Svahn, and David Swoap, who rewrote for President Reagan the guidelines for eligibility in the Aid to Families with Dependent Children (AFDC) program, being welfare-dependent is almost always bad. A theoretician of the moderate Right, Nathan Glazer, explains the principle behind the actions of these men as a time-honored one: "Welfare is charity."[21] Thus, the recipients of welfare are to be either pitied (as widows, orphans, or invalids) or left to their own devices (as members of the "undeserving" poor). The social "safety net" is to catch the former when they fall, but the latter must not become the responsibility of the government.[22] The tendency to dichotomize people in this way, into a good group, "us," and a bad group, "them," is a manifestation of the ascriptive attribute of ideological thought and is not peculiar to conservative modes of analysis.[23]

Ralph Nader, writing of the Reagan administration's "callousness" and "greed" in opposition to his and his fellow liberals' sensitivity and compassion, manifests this same tendency to see the world through polarizing lenses: "The Reagan White House did not belong to all the people, just to what Mary McGrory [one of "us"] has called 'the deserving rich.' Such a description of some Administrations might be considered a normative statement. For the Reagan Administration, it was simply a statement of fact, reaffirmed day in and day out by its actions, inactions and profound absence of either a public philosophy or public compassion." "The top Reaganites," Nader continues, "are reluctant to mix with ordinary people —injured workers, consumers and afflicted elderly." "What is really at work here," consequently, "is the dismantling of government's traditional public role in defending victims abused by established private powers." In contrast to the enemies, Nader posits the category of common people— presumably victims of Republican greed. Also in contrast to the greedy few are Nader's selfless few—those leaders characterized by James McGregor Burns (another one of "us") as "transformative." Quoting Burns, Nader calls for "leaders, who, by boldly interpreting the nation's conscience, could lift a people out of their everyday selves."[24]

Imminent Historical Consciousness

Ideology, argues anthropologist Clifford Geertz, arises in times of stress as a type of societal or political poetry. It is an aspect of human thought,

Geertz asserts, that when social realities cannot be understood in terms of accepted norms or assumptions, men and women attempt cognitive as well as expressive leaps of "analogic figurative language." In such leaps, society's natural poets attempt to "transform sentiment into significance and so make it socially available." Like a metaphor in literature, then, an ideological formulation seeks to "extend language by broadening its semantic range, enabling it to express meanings it cannot or at least cannot yet express literally."[25]

In making their metaphorical associations, ideologues create "cognitive and expressive symbol-systems that work as extrinsic sources of information in terms of which human life can be patterned." In this way, ideology permits primitive societies to escape the confines of traditionalist politics and modern societies to make revolutions (both violent and pacific) in their politics and policies. Ideologies work, that is, by providing "maps," "templates," and "blueprints" for the analysis and resolution of problematic social relations. In the language of Anthony Wallace and Chalmers Johnson, such tools and guides constitute a key product of ideological activity: a "transfer culture." In highly developed ideologies, the transfer culture permits the routinization of a previously mysterious world-view. In the routinized working out of an ideology's imperatives, the person of ideas seeks to carry forward an agenda—to transfer ideas from one realm to another—to bring about imminent revolutionary change.[26] As one of the master ideologists of a previous era, Antonio Gramsci, observed, although "civil society has become a very complex structure and one which is resistant to the catastrophic 'incursions' of the immediate economic element," the "superstructures of civil society are like the trench-systems of modern warfare."[27]

As an instance of this trait of ideological reasoning, one need only recall, once more, Ronald Reagan. When Reagan and his more zealous aides spoke in the early 1980s of a return in domestic policy to the days of the 1950s, or in fiscal policy the 1920s, they might seem to have been more mythologists than ideologues. But Ronald Reagan and his supply-side advisers had a plan. Cut marginal tax rates, build up the military, and roll back government intervention, and their vision of a vastly better America would be realized. There were in the 1980s, of course, some conservative intellectuals who did not share in the Reagan administration's offering of a transfer culture. Such conservative luminaries as Paul Gottfried and Russell Kirk, who reportedly spends much of his free time walking about the physical ruins of the Middle Ages in the United Kingdom, thus cut themselves off from active engagement in political life (as well as from the scope of this work).[28]

Ways of Arriving at Knowledge

People of ideas claim to have special insight into the appropriateness of different ways of arriving at knowledge. In ideological thought, this "epistemological" close-mindedness often appears as a correlate to the ideologue's pretension to logical certitude. In American politics, the conservative ideologue is therefore able to be rock solid in his beliefs while holding *some* truths to be closed to discussion. William F. Buckley, Jr., in one noteworthy instance, proclaimed that the American right "is based on the assumption that however many things there are that we don't know, there are some things we do know; on the assumption that some questions are closed, and that our survival as a nation depends on our acting bravely on those assumptions."[29] Buckley thus rejected any attempt to inform further the basic moral principles of public life through rational inquiry. (That there are still a great many things to debate, however, is quite clear from Buckley's own frenetic example. People of ideas, it bears emphasizing, are neither stupid nor blind, though on particular points they are notoriously thickheaded.)

For the liberal Left, the idea that one can arrive at publicly useful political knowledge through revelation, or even with reference to the "way things have always been done around here," is illegitimate. This principle distinguishes, for example, the work of John Rawls. Rawls, an esteemed political philosopher, sought in his famous work to discover the laws of a just society through the extensive elaboration of a thought experiment. He implied, thereby, a belief that the reasoning faculty of man, independent of revelation and liberated from social convention, was sufficient to discover the foundations of social justice. His book *A Theory of Justice* provoked a strong reaction from more conservative theorists, some of whom answered with books of their own.[30]

An Institutional Criterion

As a consequence of his allegiance to a set of ideas, the person of ideas is often a member of a self-conscious movement of like-minded people. Career profiles can be particularly useful, therefore, in drawing distinctions among persons whose expressions of belief make them equally candidates for categorization as persons of ideas but whose political motivations and goals seem to be vastly different. Take, for instance, James Baker, Edwin Meese, and Richard Allen. All have at times spoken about such things as "encroaching governmental interference," "the power of the free market," and even the essential and immutable differences between the Free World and the Slave World. But in their common service for Ronald Reagan, Baker earned a reputation as the leader of the "pragmatists," while Meese and particularly Allen became known as ideological trench fighters.

Baker, the unofficial "Mr. Houston" until he left for Washington with Reagan, says he was "totally apolitical" before managing George Bush's unsuccessrul bid for the U.S. Senate in 1970. There followed a succession of management positions with other campaigns, including those of Presidents Nixon and Ford. After the 1976 election, in which Baker earned the enmity of the Reaganites for his work on behalf of Ford, Baker mended his fences with the conservatives. Consequently, in his own bid for the state attorney generalship in 1978, he chose for his campaign manager a Reagan loyalist and former head of the conservative Young Americans for Freedom, Frank Donatelli. And Baker sought and secured endorsements from Reagan as well as from Bush, Ford, and John Connally. In the campaign, Baker, who had wrongly anticipated running against the liberal Price Daniel, sounded very much like a Reaganite, railing against lax juvenile justice, soft-hearted parole boards, and federal "encroachment" through voting, environmental, and energy regulations.[31] Had Baker become a conservative ideologue? One indication that he had not was the absence from his résumé of affiliations with movement institutions. Baker had decided back in 1970 that he was, in his words, "absolutely, totally, pure Republican."[32] In the early 1990s he remains, furthermore, a quintessential party professional, serving as secretary of state for his old friend George Bush.

When Edwin Meese talks about getting tough on criminals, he speaks out of a conviction that is the result of affiliation with numerous conservative institutions. The most central of these "institutions," of course, is Ronald Reagan. Meese came to Reagan's attention when the former was deputy district attorney for Alameda County in the late 1960s. Berkeley is in Alameda, and when demonstrations there brought the sheriff's department out in force, Meese became the most prominent advocate of getting tough with the protestors. Meese, first as legal affairs secretary and then as chief of staff, helped then Governor Reagan establish a hardline policy to deal with campus unrest. Meese, now as then, blames the campus troubles on "a relatively few skillful manipulators on the campuses who got the rest of the students riled up." After Reagan left the governorship, Meese added to his credentials, helping to found two conservative institutions, the Institute for Contemporary Studies in San Francisco and the Center for Criminal Justice Policy and Management at the University of San Diego.[33] Despite this entrepreneurship, Meese is not a consummate movement man. His institutional affiliations are those of a mature man with ambitions for himself and his primary patron, an electoral candidate. Even now that Reagan has left public office, Meese's ties to the image of Ronald Reagan as conservative savior remain secure. At the Heritage Foundation, where he repaired at the close of the Reagan administration, Meese is the Ronald Reagan Fellow in Public Policy.

Richard Allen, in comparison with both Baker and Meese, exemplifies true movement conservatism. His affiliations with ideological institutions go back to his college days. After college, Allen held a Weaver Fellowship from the conservative International Society of Individualists. In 1962, Allen became the first staff member hired by the American Enterprise Institute's foreign affairs spin-off, the Center for Strategic and International Studies. From that base, he developed far-reaching conservative organizational credentials, sufficient to permit him to help Edwin Feulner, later a cofounder of the Heritage Foundation, attain a fellowship to study at the Hoover Institute. Going into the Reagan presidency, Allen expressed his loyalty to Reagan's ideas but not to Reagan himself. "What's important," he told a journalist in the summer of 1980, "isn't Ronald Reagan. . . . It's the set of attitudes he brings into office with him."[34] After he was forced to resign for accepting a gift from a Japanese newspaper, Allen became the first ex–Reagan administration official to become a senior fellow at the Heritage Foundation.

A Test of the Ideal Type

Now that we have examined each of the attributes of the ideal type, we shall establish the utility of the ideal type as a whole by comparing two prominent members of the Reagan administration, Donald Regan and William Simon. This comparison should be a worthwhile test because these two men are more than superficially similar in nonideological respects. Both have been associated with regular Republicanism. Regan was suspect to movement conservatives as a cabinet member because of such things as his membership in the Council on Foreign Relations and his published praise of regular Republican economics, including Nixon's wage and price controls. And Simon served in the cabinets of Nixon and Ford but not in Reagan's. In addition, both men have been associated with the conservative movement. Simon's connection in this regard is clear, and Regan was considered a supply-side convert by the media in 1981, the year he established himself as the leader of the Treasury supply-siders by doing battle with James Baker and Richard Darman in the White House.

Donald Regan

Donald Regan's entire professional life before he became secretary of the treasury in Reagan's first term was spent at Merrill Lynch. Having dropped out of Harvard Law School after one year to join the Marine Corps, Regan was left with "no training for anything but fighting" after his retirement from the armed forces.[35] Because he could not afford to go back to school, he entered Merrill Lynch's training program to become a broker. He spent the years 1946 to 1971 working his way to the top of the company, until he became the leader of what Walter Wriston, Citicorp's former chairman, once said was his vision of the future's dream bank.[36]

In the 1970s, Regan apparently began looking for a new ladder to climb. A private man, he went public in 1971, hiring a speechwriter and authoring a brief book about Wall Street and himself. In this book and in speeches, Regan went on record in defense of Nixon's wage and price controls, which put him clearly at odds with conservatism's fundamental defense of the free market. Regan compounded the distance between himself and the conservative wing of the Republican party when he grew close personally, professionally, and politically to members of the Republican party establishment in the East, particularly William Rogers, Nixon's first secretary of state. Rogers became a member of Merrill Lynch's board in 1974, and his law firm became Merrill Lynch's chief outside counsel. What was worse from the point of view of the Reaganites, Regan became a member of the Council on Foreign Relations (CFR). The CFR is not half as far from the Right as the Brookings Institution (which is not, after all, very far left itself) but is probably hated twice as much because it is associated with an anti-ideological style of Republican politics instead of being viewed (as is Brookings) as an auxiliary organ of the Democratic party. (When George Bush, as vice president, reflected upon what he had learned en route to the number two spot in the White House, he resigned his association with the CFR.)

How Regan came to be the secretary of the treasury in the Reagan administration is taken up later in this book. Here it is sufficient to note that once he assumed that job, he was more loyal than any other high-ranking "pragmatist" in the administration to the president's complete economic program. In fact, throughout the first term Regan was the person in his department who most frequently used the words *supply side*.[37] He was also known in the administration as the keeper of the Book of Promises, the statements on economic policy made by Reagan in the campaign. But was Regan really a person of ideas? In expressing his political beliefs, did he:

> *1. Claim logical certitude, absolute truth,*
> *and comprehensive explanation?*

The answer to the first part of this question is yes. Regan believed wholeheartedly in the logical force of his ideas. As the chief "salesman" (Reagan's word) for the supply side, though not at all associated with its development, Regan laid out for various congressional committees the integrated logic of Reagan's "bold and dramatic break" with past economic policy. His specialty, in fact, was explaining how the pieces of Reagan's economic policy fit together. Not having been involved in supply-side, monetarism, or traditional budget balancing, and dismayed by the president's laissez-faire management style, Regan studied the Book of Promises and put the pieces of the Reagan program together accordingly.[38] Thus, in his first congressional appearance, he sought to demonstrate that "a stringent budget policy," "a noninflationary monetary policy," "a regulatory reform program," and an "incentive tax policy" were "mutually reinforcing" and "unique" in their "long-term interactions." This became the Treasury Department's standard in testimony, followed by supply-siders, monetarists, and eclectics.[39]

Regan's logical certitude was not so great, however, that he was close-minded about challenges to his beliefs. The approach he took, appropriately, was neither ideologically liberal nor conservative in this regard. Unlike an ideological liberal, Regan did not reject tradition and common sense as guides to government action. In his words:

> Progress demands that we recognize one of the best and oldest principles of tax economics: that taxes enter decision-making and affect economic behavior at the margin. This principle is not only accepted by economists of all persuasions; it is also based solidly upon common sense. I was a "supply-sider," as were most of my associates in the business community, long before the term was invented. And I venture to say, so were the members of this Committee.[40]

And in contrast to traditional conservatives and most supply-siders, Regan also did not reject experimentation as a guide to knowledge about the aims and strategies of government. The slippage in Regan's adherence to the supply side over the course of his service in Reagan's government might, in fact, be partially explained by this pragmatic attitude.

The answer to the second part of the question, Did Regan claim absolute faith in his newfound economic program?, is no. There is no indication that Regan linked his economic ideas to any sense of the transcendent, absolute purpose of human existence.

Finally, concerning whether Regan claimed comprehensive explanation, the answer is twofold: of the economy, yes; of the whole nature of human life and history, no. Regan did, in a speech before a business group in New York City in 1981, describe Reaganism as a "Newtonian Revolution." He probably meant to say Copernican, but even if he had, the meaning of this statement would not have been clarified. The speech was devoted entirely to the economics of Reaganism. If Regan believed, along with the supply side's originators, that there might be a supply-side foreign policy, a supply-side abortion policy, and so on, he gave no indication of it in his public statements as secretary of the treasury.[41]

2. Ascribe value to different states of being?

There is no evidence of this attribute in Regan's articulation of Reagan's program nor in Regan's other public writings and speeches. It is instructive, for instance, that in addressing the subject of poverty in 1981,

Regan did not ascribe negative values to poor persons for being poor. Instead, he spoke, as a moderate liberal would, of their being victimized by a system, in this case a system of high marginal taxation.

> The intent of the President's tax proposals is to expand incentives and opportunities for socially productive efforts and saving for *all* taxpayers, not to try to redistribute a slower and slower growing amount of total income. Indeed, if we are to revise our tax system to give the poor greater opportunity to expand their future incomes, we must reduce the tax they confront for greater and more productive effort . . . by reducing . . . marginal tax rates.[42]

3. Display an imminent historical consciousness?

Weakly. Reagan, according to Regan, helped to set Americans on a course toward a more prosperous future, not to deliver them to the Promised Land. No great break with the past seems to have been anticipated in Regan's articulation of the promise of Reagan's policies.

4. Possess a movement background?

The brief biographical introduction to this examination permits a definitive negative answer. In the cabinet, and later in the White House, Regan's interest was clearly in serving a president, not in serving the cause with which this particular president was associated.

William E. Simon

William E. Simon rose to become a managing director of Salamon Brothers before being chosen as a subcabinet official in Richard Nixon's second term. Simon had let Nixon's staff know of his desire to join the government,[43] and when he received a call from the White House informing him that he was to go to Camp David the next day for an interview with the president, he thought he was being considered for the job of secretary of housing and urban development. Instead, he was named George Shultz's assistant in the Treasury Department and became the virtual "energy czar" of the government, a job he saw as arising from the predictable collapse of liberalism into tyranny. (Simon believed that Congress's regulation of the oil economy had destroyed the domestic industry and that as a result, after an exogenous shock, a dictator had to do the job of the markets, whose muscles had atrophied under liberal bedrest.)[44] Before leaving office, Nixon named Simon secretary of the treasury, and Ford retained him in that position.

While in service for these more or less regular Republican presidents, Simon did not act at all like a regular Republican or a presidential loyalist. During the Ford administration he even took to lecturing the Congress on its decadence.[45] Congress, he warned, was leading the country to the suicide that James Burnham had prophesied for liberal nations. When he left office, Simon returned not only to business but to conservative activism. He turned the John M. Olin Foundation into one of the wealthiest, most ambitious, and most professionally managed conservative academic funding organizations in the nation. He also wrote two brief tracts laying out his principles and policies, *A Time for Truth* and *A Time for Action*, both published by Reader's Digest Press. Based on a reading of these volumes, as well as personal interviews conducted for this study, it is possible to characterize Simon's thought in terms of the ideal type. Did he

1. Claim logical certitude, absolute truth, and comprehensive explanation?

Yes on all counts. On the first point, Simon's book *A Time for Action* is devoted entirely to prescriptions for comprehensively reshaping the nation's economic policy. Also Simon views liberalism as misguided largely by its lack of logic. He describes it and its adherents as "stupid." Liberalism, to Simon, is "a hash of statism, collectivism, egalitarianism, and anticapitalism, mixed with the desire for the results of capitalism. This murky conceptual mess renders even the most innately brilliant of men stupid."[46] Simon is not, however, as dogmatic epistemologically as are his social conservative peers. He believes sincerely that his ideas will be supported by scientific, rational inquiry and thus does not differ from his liberal opponents in this respect.

The second point has already been demonstrated with respect to Simon's perception of man as *Homo faber*. On the third point, liberalism, to Simon, is not only stupid about economics; it is "a fundamental assault on America's culture and its historic identity."[47] Though his ideology is not proactively comprehensive, it is proscriptively so. It tells him that government, indeed any public authority, should not extend any further than it must.

2. Ascribe value to different states of being?

Yes. Not only being habitually poor is morally suspect; being a bureaucrat is too. According to Simon, the civil service attracts and then further deforms people who are stupid and lazy and do not know how to "solve problems." As the head of the Treasury Department, he had always to go outside the bureaucracy to accomplish his tasks. "I ignored most of my bureaucracy," he writes, "and worked with only a handful of brilliant, mostly non-Civil Service staffers. I could discover no other way to accomplish anything."[48]

This trait is further demonstrated by Simon's analysis of the "secret system" through which the "liberal establishment" rules this country. To be a "ruling elite," part of the "secret system" of liberalism, linked by the media, the public interest groups, liberal think tanks, the bureaucracy, the courts, and even most large corporations, is, to Simon, to be not merely a political enemy but morally corrupt. "Egalitarianism," Simon says, "is the ruling value system of our urban 'elite.' And it is no coincidence that egalitarianism and despotism are linked." Thus he aligns the liberal leadership with "Hitler, Stalin, and Mao."[49]

3. Display an imminent historical consciousness?

Simon has a well-elaborated transfer culture. His propositions for economic betterment are listed in his second book point by point. Nowhere does he evoke mythic or utopian images of the future. Rather, his focus is consistently upon the present system and how to correct it. Simon is, however, rather fuzzy about the details of the good society we can hope to achieve through free enterprise's invigoration. Perhaps it seems obvious to him that in the good society, there would simply be more: more wealth for the wealth-producing and more freedom for everyone to acquire wealth. Still, though Simon's ideology directs him to see the future for the most part in terms of the past, only enlarged, his call to conservative activism implies imminent doom should the status quo be maintained.

If aid "by the multimillions" is not rushed to the intellectual defenders of capitalism, Simon believes, the consequences will be dire. The "secret system" will push America closer and closer to dictatorship. The "crisis," he writes, is "impending." In short, "if the Republic is somehow to be rescued from destruction, the people must reclaim control of their government, and of their destiny, from this determined band of zealots."[50]

4. Possess a movement background?

Although Simon came to conservative activism late by movement standards, he quickly established his institutional credentials. He engineered the conservative reincarnation of the Olin Foundation, founded (with Irving Kristol) the Institute for Educational Affairs, and spoke across the country, especially to business groups, about the necessity of creating a "counterintelligentsia." His efforts, in short, were intense. He said in an interview that this period of his life was "a bitch; it left me with no time for anything else, including my family."[51]

The points of difference between these two men in terms of the ideal typology can be summarized briefly. While Simon exhibits (though not fully in each respect) all of the core attributes of ideological thought, in addition to "passing" easily the institutional standard, Regan exhibits only two aspects of a single trait on the list. Regan does claim, specifically, logical certitude and comprehensive explanation for his thought. Even in terms of these two items, however, qualification is necessary. Regan is not so logically certain of his ideas that he is close-minded about what sort of evidence might be gathered to confirm or refute his beliefs. And the comprehensiveness of Regan's politically relevant beliefs does not extend beyond economics. Simon, for his part, comes as close to a perfect match with the ideal type as might be possible. Though his close-mindedness is in question, he exhibits the other traits with little or no need for qualification. If the match between Simon and the definition being tested were any greater, in fact, it would suggest that the list of traits is something less than it is intended to be, that is, an *ideal* type.

Interim Summary

A person of ideas, then, exhibits certain specific traits in his thinking. He believes that his ideas are logically certain and thus impregnable to criticism. Consequently, he often appears to be "close-minded." The person of ideas believes that his ideas are true not just conditionally but absolutely. He is certain, furthermore, that his way of looking at the world can help make sense of a wide array of phenomena that leave others fooled or confused. And in any situation in which a choice is likely to produce one group of winners and another of losers, the person of ideas knows what to do: reward "us" and punish "them." The person of ideas, finally, knows not only what he believes but what he wants to do. He has an agenda and believes that the world might be transformed by its implementation. A priori, it would seem that a person with these traits could be a force to reckon with in presidential politics. The following chapters will provide evidence that people with these traits have indeed become increasingly indispensable and irresistible to presidents who expect their administrations to bring about significant change.

To explain further the rise of people of ideas in presidential administrations, let me elaborate on the stakes involved in the ideologization of presidential politics since the New Deal and the changes in the structure of national government that allowed this to happen. Basically, the underlying cause has been the increasing difficulty (near impossibility) of a critical partisan realignment that would set the boundaries for ideological maneuvering and, within those boundaries, allow the president a free hand to redirect the national agenda. Given this limitation and the ambition of certain presidents to leave a large personal stamp on the life of the nation, the president has had to rely increasingly upon an elite suited to such an environment—people of ideas—to formulate change and innovation.

Contrasting Paradigms of Presidential Achievement

The American party system has never been consistently and intensely programmatic. But the American people used to care much more about parties and their own partisan identities than they seem to today. As a consequence of how people used to feel and think about the parties in relation to themselves, American political history was once punctuated periodically by critical partisan realignments. These realignments were not merely electoral phenomena; they profoundly affected national governmental policy outcomes as well. And the focus of such realignments was the presidency. For these reasons, the critical partisan realignment may be understood as occupying one pole of a continuum from partisan to ideological models of presidential achievement.

The Old-time Partisan Realignment

Most of the time in American politics, parties constrain coherent shifts in policy direction. Approximately once every generation, however, from perhaps 1800, and certainly 1828, to the 1930s, there occurred a critical partisan realignment that not only reordered the partisan identifications of significant groups within the electorate but provided the impetus for sweeping changes in the course of government policy. Such realignments as occurred with the election to the presidency of Andrew Jackson, Abraham Lincoln, and Franklin Roosevelt, according to Walter Dean Burnham, a leading scholar of the phenomena, "involve constitutional readjustments in the broadest sense of the term" and are thus "intimately associated with and followed by transformations in the general shape of policy." They "arise from emergent tensions in society," are "issue-oriented," "result in significant transformations in the general shape of policy," and "have relatively profound after effects on the roles played by institutional elites."[52] Realignments, in other words, are a matter of not just who votes for whom but to what ends.

The logic of realignments is purposive. Realignment theory, especially as propounded by Burnham, following the leads of V. O. Key and E. E. Schattschneider, begins with the observation that there is an enduring tension in American political development between, on the one hand, a relatively static and fragmented configuration of institutional structures and cultural biases and, on the other, an exceptionally dynamic economy and society. This disjuncture creates an unstable political mix. Rapid economic development yields changing sets of economic losers, who seek the government's help in recouping their losses and changing the rules of the game. America's constitutionally constrained government, however, cannot do much for these persons until their complaints are aggregated and articulated in the process of forming a newly dominant electoral coalition that can take control of the multiple strands of an intentionally fragmented national government. Tensions mount until there is a critical realignment. In the wake of a critical election—the starting point for a realignment episode—some of the major grievances of the newly dominant partisan coalition are addressed. It is in this way, Burnham, David Brady, Benjamin Ginsberg, and others have argued, that many of the most vital decisions about America's public life have been made: whether to fight for the Union or against it; whether to pursue a redistributive monetary policy in the wake of rapid industrialization; whether permanently to expand the police powers of the national government.[53] Without periodic critical realignments, in fact, tensions might conceivably mount to the point where no "substitute for revolution" (as Burnham has termed realignments) would suffice.[54]

Presidents of exceptional achievement have been intimately tied to these realignments. The list of presidential "greats" overlaps with the list of chief executives brought into office in critical elections: Thomas Jefferson, Andrew Jackson, Abraham Lincoln, William McKinley (and his successor, Theodore Roosevelt), and Franklin Roosevelt. The fit is not perfect. There is ongoing controversy over the appropriateness of designating Thomas Jefferson as the head of a realigned party system. Also, such presidents as James K. Polk, Grover Cleveland, and Woodrow Wilson achieved quite a lot but were not elected in the wake of a full-fledged partisan realignment. But they were the exceptions during the long course of America's history when the party system was subject to these episodic rejuvenations. In the past, critical realignments and exceptional achievement on the part of American presidents have gone hand in hand.

Because realignments were based upon a reordering of the partisan identities and voting habits of groups within a highly partisan and highly mobilized electorate,[55] policy redirections presided over by chief executives who came to office as part of a realignment episode tended to endure. Such redirections were based on laws passed by a newly dominant partisan majority within a Congress polarized by party and were locked into place, so to speak, by the intensity of partisan feeling that permeated the mass electorate.[56] After having their partisan identities forged in the crucible of civil war, for a stark example of this dynamic, voters were thereafter urged in election after election to "vote as you shot." That voters responded to such appeals is suggested by the low levels among the electorate of old of such antipartisan behavior as splitting tickets and voting only in presidential election years.[57]

Presidents who achieved significant policy shifts in the age of functionally strong parties could rely upon the partisan integuments linking people with their government, then, to sustain the newly dominant party's major accomplishments. After the Second Bank of the United States was demolished in the critical realignment of the 1830s, for example, the voters prolonged the ascendancy of the anti-Bank Democrats until other issues, namely, territorial expansion and slavery, obscured from view the economic questions raised in Jackson's original crusade against the "Monster Bank." And after the critical elections that placed into office Abraham Lincoln, William McKinley and Theodore Roosevelt, and Franklin Roosevelt, the newly dominant party maintained its control of the presidency, the Senate, and the House for at least fourteen years, during which time little backsliding on the formative issues of their respective regimes was tolerated by the partisan troops outside of Washington, D.C.

The American people were deeply implicated in changes made during realignments. Voters did not determine the details of the government's fiscal policy in the Jacksonian revolution, but they did provide their champion, President Andrew Jackson—who was running for reelection in 1832 in a campaign that was dominated by the issue of the president's veto of the Whig-sponsored bill to recharter the Second Bank of the United States—with a mandate to destroy the nation's central bank. Upon reelection, Jackson claimed his mandate and accomplished his task.[58] Similarly, the voters did not determine military strategy in the election or reelection of Abraham Lincoln to the presidency, but they did determine war, as another generation of voters would decide against waging a populist crusade against industrial interests, and yet another would opt for a radical expansion of federal responsibilities in the wake of the Great Depression. By placing in power in the presidency and the Congress a newly dominant party, in elections that focused upon particular constellations of issues and upon candidates' positions on these issues, voters at times set the outer bounds, so to speak, of *policy* realignments pursued by presidents of achievement and their partisan allies. The intense partisanship of the electorate, the necessary condition of the partisan realignment process, provided successful candidates for national office, especially presidents, opportunities to serve as the instructed delegates of electoral majorities.

An Emerging Model of Ideological Policy Redirection

Concerning the contemporary period, Everett Carl Ladd is right: waiting for a partisan realignment in the 1990s is like waiting for Godot.[59] The parties just are not what they used to be, and the realignment process depended upon the parties of old. The newer American political parties, with their increasingly sophisticated, national infrastructure, may in some ways be "stronger" in the abstract than the parties of old,[60] but they do not control the nomination of candidates for the presidency (or virtually any other post, for that matter), and they have utterly failed to maintain the loyalties of the voters. By some measures, in fact, the two most significant parties today are not really parties at all: they are the "party" of nonvoters, followed by the "party" of independents.[61] Not only do contemporary voters fail to give the Democratic or the Republican party their votes with any great enthusiasm or consistency; they withhold their affection as well. As a careful analyst of the parties, David Price, has observed:

> During the 1950s more than 60 percent of the electorate responded with a positive evaluation of their own party and negative words about the opposition. But since 1972, a majority of respondents—compared with some 30 percent in the fifties—have responded with a negative evaluation of *both* parties. Similarly, questions concerning the attentiveness of parties to people's opinions and their role in "making the government pay attention to what the people think" have drawn a steadily declining number of affirmative responses.[62]

And in a fascinating glimpse of the partisan sand in which modern presidents and other politicians must try to forge their governing coalitions, Seymour Martin Lipset, reporting on the rapid swings in partisan self-identification that were witnessed in the early 1980s, states: "To the 30 to 33 percent who have described themselves as 'independents' since the early seventies (up from a fifth in the early sixties) must be added at least another 20 percent who change their identification as they shift their voter [i.e., candidate] preference."[63]

Finally, the necessity of moving beyond partisan models of realignment in order to come to grips with how contemporary presidents of achievement might accomplish their tasks takes us to the example of the Reagan presidency. For a time, it seemed to Republican party hopefuls, at least, that Ronald Reagan was on his way to a successful partisan realignment. Newt Gingrich and a few others still seem to believe in the imminence of such a change. But Ronald Reagan, it is becoming clear in retrospect, was elevated to the nation's highest office, and kept there, not so much because the electorate wished for him to do some particular thing(s) for them, but because he seemed to be the sort of person that the public desired to have as their national patriarch at a troubled time in the country's history. Though Reagan did succeed during his first year in office in exploiting the popular revulsion against "big government" to persuade the Congress to join with him in significant redirections of domestic policy, his was an exceedingly soft "mandate."

When Jefferson, Jackson, Lincoln, McKinley/Roosevelt, and Franklin Roosevelt claimed their mandates, they could point to a reordering of party dominance in the legislature to bolster their claims. That Reagan's election did not herald a change in the minority status of the Republicans is becoming clearer each year. In fact, Republicans gained fewer than twenty seats net in the House from 1978 to 1986 and lost their short-lived majority in the other chamber in 1986.[64] And if Reagan's victory had behind it a mandate for self-consciously conservative government, it is difficult to find evidence for this in the opinion polls. While 37 percent of Americans identified their views as conservative in 1981, that percentage was down to 30 percent in 1985. The largest number continued through the Reagan years to consider themselves "moderate."[65]

Even in 1980, when Reagan's views on specific policy questions were closer to the middle of public opinion than were his opponent's, "this proximity," according to Martin Wattenberg, "was of far less importance than Carter's low performance ratings on matters such as inflation, unemployment, and Iran."[66] In accord with this analysis, Reagan chose a refrain for his 1980 campaign that invited not a prospective delegation of authority but a retrospective judgment. "Are you better off now than you were four years ago?" Reagan asked repeatedly. Four years later, Gallup exit polls suggested that Reagan's backers were still asking themselves that same nonideological, retrospective question, though to the benefit this time of the incumbent.[67]

In addition to appealing on pocketbook issues in his bid for reelection, Reagan demonstrated a master's touch when it came to the politics of persona and image. This was fortunate for Reagan, for on issue after issue, including support of the Contras, military spending, government aid to minorities and women, and abortion, Ronald Reagan and the American public parted company in 1984. In a remarkable reflection of the values emphasized during the tenure of such a president, Reagan's friend Senator Paul Laxalt observed heading into the reelection year that although people "have deep differences with his policies," they trust Reagan and are willing to "look beyond the issues to style and character."[68]

What, then, should be made of the apparent nonrealignability of the modern party system? Byron Shafer suggests that we stop talking about realignments and start talking about "electoral orders."[69] The contemporary electoral order, for instance, would be characterized by divided party control of the Congress and the presidency, by relatively low voter turnout, and by other facts of contemporary electoral life. From the point of view of understanding the evolution of the party system, however, Shafer is letting the tail wag the dog. According to what might be termed the "metatheory" of realignments, the electoral order is significant not just for what it *is* at any given time but for what it *does*. It used to permit the occasional democratic redirection of national government policies. The contemporary electoral order does not provide this foundation for attempted policy redirections of realignment magnitude.

Yet the *need* for some mechanism for the periodic adjustment of government policies in line with the emerging interests of a dynamic economy and society surely remains with us. The ideologization of presidential politics might best be understood in this light. Ideology can provide at least a simulacrum at an elite level of the bonds that partisanship offered more compellingly and more democratically in years past. Ideology offers cues for decision and a framework within which to forge alliances, enmities, and a personal as well as political identity. And in the elaboration of transfer cultures, ideologies offer an expansive supply of ideas—on ways to cope with pressing problems given only superficial attention, when not merely ignored, by the decreasingly structured electorate.

The implications of a partial substitution of ideological for more simply partisan strategies in presidential politics are troubling. The very logic of an ideological policy shift differs from the logic of partisan realignment. A contemporary ideological realignment in *policy*, with necessarily shallow roots in the electorate and uncertain partisan support and longevity in the Congress, to begin with, will likely be subject to more rapid displacement than an innovation institutionalized in an environment of partisan realignment. One consequence could be a pattern of significant policy redirections with unusually brief lives. The costs to the polity in terms of policy instability and confusion are potentially great. In addition and, to an extent, alternatively, the judiciary, the fiscal balance between revenue and expenditures, and the administrative apparatus of the state may become increasingly significant objects of political conflict, as presidents and their people of ideas look for nonpartisan ways in which to lock into place their innovations.[70] The consequences here would include the overt politicization of institutions that rely for their legitimacy on their reputation as neutral and autonomous repositories of competence and caution.

To overstate in the interest of clarity: While partisan politics is by its nature weak when it comes to providing detailed instructions for elected officials, it is (or more precisely, was) a useful way to check the power of elites and, periodically, to furnish before the fact a majority's support for a redirection in the deliberations and products of their government. The equation for ideological politics is reversed. Ideological politics, as I have defined it, as distinct from the opinions, regardless of their character, of a nation's people as a whole, is poorly suited to linking elite political activism with the concerns of a broad electorate. Yet ideology is all too effective at providing to those who are motivated to receive them detailed instructions on what to do with the powers of the state. Furthermore, while policy shifts associated with partisan realignments were durable, those that flow from an ideologized government are not as likely to be so, or are likely to be centered in the less visible and less democratically accountable realms of the government, such as the judiciary and the bureaucracy.

In comparison with the partisan model, the ideological model is not capable of promoting the democratic control of government. To make matters worse, it is not at all clear that there is a realizable alternative to the growth of ideological influence in national governance. To borrow from the conclusion of the famous Brownlow Commission, which advised the Congress and the public as to how they should treat their chief executive, the president and the people around him continue to "need help." Ideology and people motivated by ideology stand ready to offer their assistance at a time when other, older patterns of policy redirection have slipped upon their foundations.

In the chapters that follow, ideological and partisan approaches to policy redirection will of course be seen as they really exist: not as entirely separate "models," but as interacting patterns of association. An essential point to keep in mind about the historical trends uncovered in the remainder of the book, though, is that while ideologues were not unknown when parties were strong—as the extended discussion of the New Deal in a later chapter makes clear—the impetus for ideological impact in the New Deal was a democratic realignment of mass partisanship. Also, the party system's comparative strength in the 1930s and, to a lesser extent, the 1960s kept democratic checks on the utopian schemes of the most zealous ideologues in both the New Deal and the Great Society. Ideologues, one might say, are like poison: useful when used in measured quantities and under the direction of enlightened opinion. With the decay of the party system, we have lost both the enlightened direction of the electorate, who once were necessary to set the ideologues in motion, and the ability of the party system to establish the boundaries within which a president's ideological helpers vied for impact.

Conclusion

Karl Mannheim, one of the pioneers in the study of ideology, believed that it was possible to go beyond ideology, partisanship, and even class.[71] What lay beyond such parochial concerns was the promise of a truly "scientific" politics. Every group within society, Mannheim observed, speaks from a particular position. Unsophisticated political thinkers believe this is true only of their opponents. Sophisticated participants of political debate realized some time ago, however, that as truth is a human product, even one's own claims to knowledge are contingent and partial. Mannheim believed, finally, that the possibility would soon present itself for elite members of modern societies to move beyond even the latter perspective to attain a deeper wisdom about political life. By evaluating the circumstantial character of the diverse truth claims put forth in a political controversy, a true scientist of politics, Mannheim argued, should be able dialectically to transcend the biases of particularistic thought. The persons who might achieve this feat were the intellectuals, whom Mannheim thought in the 1930s to be on the way toward realizing knowledge of themselves as a distinct group within Western states. The self-knowledge of the intellectuals, significantly, would not be knowledge of themselves as a *class*, for the intelligentsia, Mannheim believed, was a meritocratic elite open to members of all classes who, in any event, by virtue of their many years of schooling, would generally leave their class affiliations behind them as they matured.[72]

Perhaps Mannheim's theorizing will yet prove to have been prophetic. In the countries of Eastern Europe, for instance, people Mannheim would recognize as intellectuals are among the burgeoning elite of their new governments. But in the United States, the idea of an ideologically neutral policy elite guiding politics along scientifically validated paths strains belief. It is not that the intellectual life is not possible; not all intellectuals, I repeat, are ideologues. But in the United States since at least the 1930s, there have been pressures toward the greater integration of ideological members of the knowledge class with presidencies of achievement. There have not been any comparable pressures exerted upon those American intellectuals who eschew the ideologues' certainty, absolutism, comprehensiveness, and blueprints. For these traits of the ideologue, which are antithetical to nonideological intellect, as Mannheim would have recognized, happen to be the very traits that make the ideologue influential in American presidential politics.

Chapter Two
The Recruitment and Management of People of Ideas

In Doctor Doolittle's menagerie there was a two-headed creature, the "Push-Me-Pull-You," that suffered from the same sort of contradictions that have only gradually and partially been overcome in the recruitment of people of ideas to service in presidencies of achievement. The contradictions between the president's fulfillment of nonideological responsibilities and the payment of his debts to people of ideas, between, in a larger sense, the pull of the weakly ideological past and the push toward the more ideological future, have beset each of the three presidents of achievement since the 1930s. But with each of these administrations, one side in this struggle has grown stronger, culminating in the systematic ideologization of presidential politics under Ronald Reagan. This chapter establishes the increasing affinities between particular groups of people of ideas and the campaign advisory structures and personnel recruitment and management strategies adopted by the Roosevelt, Johnson, and Reagan administrations during their crucial transitions to and early experiences in power.

Personnel Politics in the Early New Deal

Before he entered the general election campaign for president in 1932, Franklin Roosevelt's career ladder was constructed almost entirely of party planks. Party machinery, party rules, party professionals, party patronage, and party ties stand out plainly in his rise to power.[1] Roosevelt's ties to party encompassed even the legendary Tammany organization. Though Roosevelt had developed an antibossism reputation early in his career as a state senator, he mended his fences with the Tammany bosses after he failed to overcome their opposition and win a seat in the U.S. Senate in 1914. Three years later, Roosevelt was the keynote speaker at the annual Tammany Fourth of July "wigwam."[2]

By the time he assumed the presidency, however, Franklin Roosevelt had developed bonds of interest, respect, and affection for particular people of ideas. At the outset of his governorship Roosevelt had begun to introduce into his circle of advisers and administrators a select number of men and women who were either leaders in or allied with various liberal causes, such as Frances Perkins, whom he appointed industrial commissioner, and other future New Dealers, including Morris Cooke, Leland Olds, James Bonbright, and Harry Hopkins. His associations with people of ideas hardly made Roosevelt himself an ideologue, as the liberal press of the day made abundantly clear in their attacks on Roosevelt as a presidential candidate.[3] In fact, one might say that Roosevelt's gubernatorial dealings with such persons immunized him against ideological conversion on the presidential campaign trail. For it was the prospect of the presidential campaign, and the anticipated demands of the media for the candidate's opinion on any and all aspects of the crisis facing the country, that persuaded Roosevelt's trusted adviser Samuel Rosenman, in March 1931, that Roosevelt should recruit expert help from outside his Albany circle.[4] The group that Rosenman and Roosevelt assembled, with the assistance of "Doc" O'Conner, the governor's law partner, was of course the brain trust, which embodied two of the three ideological schools of thought that came to be associated with the Roosevelt presidency: the antimonopolist spenders; the industrial, agricultural, and social planners; and the proponents of voluntary business-government cooperation, the corporatists.[5]

The Corporatists

Raymond Moley has been castigated for decades as a backsliding or co-opted planner. According to Arthur Schlesinger, Jr., Moley went into the administration thinking along the same lines as his brain trust colleagues, but within two years he "was increasingly accepting the notion that business knew best."[6] Actually, Moley was a "corporatist" and had never made the planning philosophy his own. A criminal law expert and professor of political science before joining the government full-time after the election of 1932, Moley had had a more narrowly specialized academic career than had his brain trust colleagues.[7] Outside of the brain trust, the corporatist solution to the economic crisis of the 1930s was advocated by veterans of the World War I War Industries Board, including Bernard Baruch and, less consistently, General Hugh Johnson.[8] The organized intellect of segments of the business community as represented in the New Deal Commerce Department and in the Committee for Economic Development may also be categorized as corporatist.[9]

The corporatists believed that the nature of the economy was changing in a way that gave advantages to bigger, more efficiently managed enterprises. Conglomerates, trusts, and certain monopolies were thus accepted as fixtures of modernity. Because the economic system was evolving according to inexorable laws of efficiency, the corporatists saw no need to force revolutionary changes upon business. Certainly government, itself transformed by modernization, would have to take a more active interest in economic life in the future. But in the ensuing business-government dance, business would lead. The objective was not government domination or even leadership so much as the "harmonization" of public and private interests. As Moley explained early in the New Deal, the Roosevelt administration was working for "an architecturally more harmonious national life" in which the government would "supervise the ebb and flow of economic affairs more closely" than before to "assure every American citizen . . . that his general interest is not sacrificed to special interests."[10]

This line of thought possessed limited ideological attributes. Corporatists certainly made claims to logical certitude but did not purport to have tapped into transcendent meanings or to have a key to solving the entire range of problems besetting society. Even in terms of their ideological certitude, the corporatists were not so certain of their knowledge as to be dogmatically close-minded. Thus corporatists, though typically liberal in their epistemology—favoring hard-headed reason and analysis over tradition as guides to publicly useful knowledge—did not seek to extend this perspective to social policy or other areas of concern to planners and Brandeisians. Nor did corporatism have a strong dichotomizing principle whereby persons could be divided into a good group, "us," and a nefarious group, "them." Certainly planners were not to be trusted, but neither were "extremists" of any stripe. In terms of their historical consciousness, corporatists thought of the future more from an evolutionary than a revolutionary or imminent perspective. Overall, the corporatists were on the margins of ideological thought.

The Planners

Adolf Berle, Rexford Tugwell, Jerome Frank, and Arthur Morgan were among the planners active in the New Deal. Like the corporatists, the planners saw evolutionary movement in the economy. Unlike the corporatists, they were disturbed by what they saw. By 1932, economic concentration had already progressed, according to Berle's calculations, to the point that "some six-hundred-odd corporations . . . control two-thirds of American industry."[11]

Following the leads principally of Thorstein Veblen and Simon van Patten, Berle and the other planners sought to infuse the national government with sufficient directive intelligence and legal authority to outweigh that of the expanding private conglomerates. The idea was to create in the executive establishment not a *countervailing*, but an *overriding*, power, one that could ensure that complexity and size were separated from concentration.[12] In words that Adolf Berle penned for candidate Roosevelt in the "New Individualism" speech delivered at the Commonwealth Club of San Francisco on September 23, 1932: "Our task now is not discovery or exploitation of natural resources, or necessarily producing more goods. It is the soberer, less dramatic business of administering resources and plants already in hand; of adjusting production to consumption; of distributing wealth and products equitably; of adapting existing economic organizations to the service of the people."[13]

The market itself, if it could ever have been trusted to steer enterprise to a just end, was in any event disappearing in the modern world. Competition was rightly avoided by corporate managers, for it was wasteful and obsolete. As Tugwell stated in *The Industrial Discipline and the Governmental Arts*, published in 1933, "What is required in view of the nature of industry is a recognition of the desirability of large scale and of concentration. . . . Such a recognition would cause us to abandon attempts to prevent association and to enforce conflict."[14] Competition had been effective in piling up wealth, the planners conceded, but now that the economy was or would soon be "mature," the distribution and management of wealth were the pertinent issues of economic policy. In the words of the Commonwealth Club speech, "The day of the manager has come." Differences among the planners centered about the relative weight to be given to persuasive as opposed to coercive means of government leadership. Berle generally favored the former. Although he thought that public ownership of vital industries would in time become "irresistible," Berle hoped that in the meantime the government might instill a new morality among the business elite. If necessary, Tugwell was willing to err on the side of coercion. Because man is social, he argued in 1932, "the individual, to get anywhere himself, must subordinate himself, must sink or swim with others. He must consent to function as part of a greater whole and to have his role defined for him by the exigencies of his group."[15] That Tugwell took his ideas seriously is suggested by the fact that he saw the failure of the TVA and the National Recovery Administration (NRA) in terms of their inadequate concentration of power. Like Berle, Tugwell believed that public ownership of key industries, such as banking and utilities, was the way of the future. Unlike Berle, Tugwell at times prescribed action toward these ends in the New Deal.[16]

The planners were ideologues. They represented their ideas as being logically coherent and compelling. Any intelligent person could see that truth was on their side, for they had discovered, or paid homage to those they felt had discovered, the inexorable laws of progress. Their theories were based, furthermore, on a view of man's ultimate nature. Man was a communal being who could find fulfillment only in cooperative, as opposed to competitive, institutional settings. In Tugwell's words:

> Men are, by impulse, predominantly cooperative. They have their competitive impulses, to be sure; but these are normally subordinate. Laissez faire exalted the competitive and maimed the cooperative impulses. . . . Men were taught to believe that they were, paradoxically, advancing cooperation when they were defying it. That was a viciously false paradox. Of that, today, most of us are convinced and, as a consequence, the cooperative impulse is asserting itself openly and forcibly, no longer content to achieve its end obliquely and by stealth.[17]

Their thought, finally, putatively comprehended an enormous array of human affairs.

The planners, furthermore, ascribed negative value to categories of being associated with tradition; the past was to be swept away in the onslaught of modernity. Thus they castigated the family farmer, the southern aristocrat, the greedy banker, and the Republican civil servant as obsolete. Redemption was available but must follow conversion. Failure to repent would be dealt with either harshly, if Tugwell were to have his way, or magnanimously, if Berle's vision were to prevail. Their dichotomizing principle was typically liberal, however, in that it was intended to apply only temporarily. (Modern liberals typically take a proprietary view of the future.)

With respect to the remaining core attribute of ideological thought, the planners rate an equally solid mark. The historical consciousness of the planners ranged from solidly linear to categorically imminent, from Berle's hopefulness to Tugwell's secular revolutionary passion. As Tugwell wrote, "We have turned our backs on competition and have chosen control."[18] For since "we possess every needful thing for Utopia, and nearly everyone knows it," he wrote in 1932, "it is a quite simple conclusion in most minds that control ought to be taken out of the hands of people who cannot produce it from the excellent materials at their disposal." If planners were permitted to run things, Utopia might be just around the corner. "I believe that we are within a stone's throw of the end of labor—as labor, not as willing and cooperative activity. We know how to make machines do nearly everything. Only defective social mechanisms prevent the consummation of the trend toward the abolition of employment."[19]

The weak link in this profile is the institutional one, for the planners were an army of generals. Planning was to prevail not because it was popular but because it was necessary and right. There was, consequently, no concerted effort to disseminate the principles of planning in even elite circles, such as within a particular research institute, university department, or, as in the case of the similar-minded Fabians overseas, an informal but tight-knit circle of friends in high places.[20]

The Brandeisians

The Brandeisians were weaker in some of the core ideological attributes than the planners but had more of the appearance of a movement. They were organized and instructed by Louis D. Brandeis and Felix Frankfurter. As Bruce Murphy, the most thorough chronicler of their association, has written, these two were on a "crusade for securing government action." Together, they sought not only to "redirect the focus of a number of executive departments and agencies" but to "convert the administrators of the already collectivist agencies."[21]

Brandeis and Frankfurter had been secretly working together ever since Brandeis had become a justice of the Supreme Court. Brandeis had even helped to place Frankfurter on the faculty of the Harvard Law School, where he could be of outstanding service to Brandeis. As a law professor, Frankfurter conveyed to a set of elite students destined for prominent roles in business, finance, and law the social philosophy he imbibed from his elder mentor. Frankfurter also used his seminars to research topics of interest to Brandeis and sent a stream of bright young men to serve as his clerks. In addition, as a professor of law, Frankfurter had time to devote to public affairs. He could spare that time, finally, because Brandeis not only guided him in his public service but paid him as well, at a rate reflecting the opportunity cost to Frankfurter of thus neglecting a potentially lucrative part-time private practice. As the Roosevelt presidency got under way, this team applied its considerable skills and experience in behind-the-scenes maneuverings to the selection and education of high-ranking members of the executive branch.[22]

In addition to influence over personnel, Brandeis wanted some specific things from the national government in the early 1930s. First, he desired massive public spending to support employment. This spending, he argued, should be directed toward public goods such as "control of waters" and "wholesale afforestation." Second, he wanted to pay for this spending (he was, after all, neither a Keynesian nor a supply-sider) through a steep inheritance tax on the rich. Finally, to prevent or mitigate the effects of future economic downturns, as well as to decrease the relative influence and status of financial barons in the nation's affairs, he advocated the comprehensive reform of the financial industry and comprehensive unemployment compensation.[23]

The overriding principle motivating Brandeis's policy advocacy was his insistence that increasing size and the spread of organizational hierarchy did not represent laws of history. Rather, it was possible, Brandeis believed, to preserve a sense of community in the American culture—

a sense of fellowship that he associated with life in the small and stable communities of the American past. (Brandeis himself was born in a small city in the American heartland, Louisville, Kentucky, in 1856.) Brandeis's detractors, such as Tugwell, deprecated his philosophy as an almost pathological suspicion that "bigness is always badness."[24] To Brandeis and his friends, however, the issue was not simply bigness but its deleterious effects, especially the impact of industrial concentration upon the working class. The solutions they favored contrasted sharply with those proposed by the planners. In Justice Brandeis's own words, men should "seek for betterment within the broad lines of existing institutions . . . by attacking evil *in situ*." "Remember," he cautioned, "that remedies are necessarily tentative; that because of varying conditions there must be much and constant inquiry into facts."[25]

What was at stake in the dispute between the "facts" of the planners and the "facts" of Justice Brandeis was not merely who had the better statistics. Rather, man's freedom and "perfection" were up for grabs. "The object," Brandeis once explained to one of his law clerks, who was then instructed to circulate a memorandum on the subject to the justice's circle of allies and followers, "is to impose limitations in order to achieve" the object of freedom.[26] Furthermore, "success in any democratic undertaking must proceed from the individual," Brandeis wrote in 1922. "It is possible only where the process of perfecting the individual is pursued."[27]

Brandeis thought that limitations on bigness and concentration served the freedom and perfection of the individual because he was certain mankind has but limited capacities and judgment. As one of his young law clerks, Dean Acheson, explained the justice's views with regard to the League of Nations in 1920: "People haven't the intelligence for that sort of thing. They have only the intelligence to operate in small personal groups which deal with the things with which they are intimately acquainted."[28] Or in the words of Felix Frankfurter, speaking for himself: "The Lord doesn't create people sufficiently capacious in wisdom and detachment . . . no matter how disinterested . . . to run these vast organisms, whether of government or of finance."[29]

The ideological attributes of "Brandeisianism" were several. Claims were made to the possession of a logically compelling and consistent explanatory framework. This framework, it was maintained, could comprehend the full range of domestic functions properly to be assumed by the federal, state, and local governments. Though it did not give as many positive cues to decision making as did planning, it instructed its adherents to block a considerable range of activities in the domestic arena. Absolute knowledge was claimed in the negative terms of the mainstream twentieth-century American liberal.

Justice Brandeis and his followers were not ideological, however, in the sense of ascribing value to persons in accord with a dichotomizing principle related to their world-view's sense of priorities. The ideological verve of this group was also weak with respect to its historical consciousness. The Brandeisians, in fact, evidenced at times an anti-ideological, mythical conception of the ideal future as a time when life would once again center about small personal groups.[30] In this regard, however, Felix Frankfurter parted company with his mentor: Frankfurter believed that with advances in scientific knowledge, all manner of fundamental societal transformations were presently attainable. Even "human nature" might be changed, he once wrote to a friend.[31] As for the secondary quality of institutional affiliations, the "Brandeisians" were organized about their leaders and Harvard Law School.

When Franklin Roosevelt entered office, then, reasonable odds might have been obtained that the new president would seek to break somewhat from his past, choosing to be guided in his personnel policy by his relatively short-lived but intense bonds to various idealists rather than by his extensive partisan debts. Roosevelt might construe his inaugural, that is, as an opportunity to move toward ideologically coherent planning, or to resume a War Industries Board approach to government-industry cooperation, or to enact the program of Justice Brandeis. He might even renounce some of the well-documented party-building trades he had made at the convention. But in the strongly partisan environment of the 1930s, not many people viewed the world in terms that would have made any such decision plausible. Even Roosevelt's brain trusters were wary of claiming in their chief's election a mandate for the empowerment of people like themselves.[32]

Roosevelt, of course, became famous, once he assumed office, for the ideological conflict, not harmony, that he fostered through his appointments. In the NRA, Hugh Johnson was often at odds philosophically as well as temperamentally with his high-profile deputy, Donald Richberg; in the Department of Agriculture (DOA), Henry Wallace and his undersecretary, Rexford Guy Tugwell, were opposed daily by George Peek and Chester Davis, the first two men chosen by Roosevelt to oversee the vital Agricultural Adjustment Administration (AAA); while within the AAA itself, Peek was so horrified by the ideas of his appointed counsel, Jerome Frank, that the conservative agriculturalist personally paid the salary of a substitute, since he could not persuade Roosevelt to fire Frank.[33] By failing to provide coherent leadership for government operations, Roosevelt left the field open to competitors. Thus patronage specialists and ideologists battled for control of the personnel process left uncoordinated by the president. The party professionals, especially, or so they hoped, had things all worked out for their chief.

To James Farley, Roosevelt's postmaster general and chairman of the Democratic National Committee, patronage was the "true watchword of government," the "democratic way," and even "the most democratic way of all and, in the long run the best way of getting competent people" in the government.[34] As both a cabinet member and party chairman, Farley had unique visibility and resources with which to influence appointments. While the White House itself had no single person assigned to the job of personnel selection or management, Farley had several assistants and worked closely with the president and members of Congress on appointments. What is perhaps most important, Farley enjoyed excellent access to President Roosevelt, seeing him three or four mornings a week in his bedroom before the president went to his office.

Farley had competition from several quarters in influencing important administration appointments. First, of course, Farley deferred to the president when Roosevelt let his preferences be known.[35] Second, Farley's interpretations of the president's partisan debts were at times challenged by other party heavyweights.[36] Finally, Farley was at times constrained by the need to negotiate about midlevel appointments with some of the more liberal and antipatronage of the president's top appointees.[37]

Farley thought that the only alternatives to a partisan appointments process were nepotism and cronyism. Thus he averred that "men like Dr. Morgan [Arthur E. Morgan, chairman of the TVA board], who think they are pursuing the only pure course by refusing to accept recommendations from Senators and Congressmen, usually wind up by appointing only their own friends and confidantes [in] a far worse kind of spoilsmanship than any other kind."[38] In retrospect, it is clear that Farley was mistaken. For there was a *fourth* way, an ideologically driven alternative to patronage, nepotism, and cronyism. This alternative was pursued, in fact, in a number of niches within Roosevelt's executive branch.

To begin with, the planners, though for the most part independent operators, were not entirely innocent of attempting to influence personnel decisions. Although Adolf Berle accepted only a limited role in the new administration and did not become embroiled in personnel conflicts, Rexford Tugwell and Jerome Frank together presented a contrasting example of intellect engaged in public life. Frank and Tugwell, who shared a house in Washington, were assiduous "networkers" and were fairly successful in finding like-minded individuals with whom to work in the Department of Agriculture.

Frank filled his office with men from the top law schools, including Abe Fortas from Yale, Adlai Stevenson from the University of Chicago, and Lee Pressman, Alger Hiss, John Abt, and Nathan Witt from Harvard. In their home, Frank and Tugwell would often meet after hours with Frank's aides from the department. The AAA's ideologists found compatriots and dinner companions, furthermore, in the Office of the Consumers' Counsel of the DOA, directed by Frederic C. Howe, and in the office of the secretary of agriculture, where they worked closely with Paul Appleby, C. B. Baldwin, Louis Bean, and Mordecai Ezekial. Ezekial was a true find, a civil servant with a planning philosophy and innovative ideas about agriculture. What these men had in common was an intention to reorganize agricultural production and distribution in harmony with changes in the industrial sector and with just attention to the interests of consumers.[39]

In light of the planners' success at influencing personnel decisions, it is understandable why George Peek targeted both the Tugwellians and the Brandeisians for this famous barb: "A plague of young lawyers settled on Washington. They all claimed to be friends of someone or other and mostly of Felix Frankfurter and Jerome Frank. They floated airily into offices, took desks, asked for papers and found no end of things to be busy about. I never found out why they came, what they did, or why they left."[40]

But it was especially the Brandeisians, the friends of Felix Frankfurter, who became adept in the New Deal at boring from within to influence the executive establishment. There are two main reasons for this. First, insider status was difficult to gain and easy to lose at the start of the institutionalized presidency. The brain trusters were not locked into their positions, and Brandeis and Frankfurter were quick to take advantage of the opportunities that became apparent with the withdrawal from favored status or employment of the likes of Tugwell and Berle. In fact, none of the New Deal's early leaders even had an office at the White House, and among Roosevelt's top aides, only Louis Howe, James Farley, and James McIntyre —all up to their chins in party affairs—had job descriptions that included daily communication with the president. The Brandeisians, perhaps because they had not shared equal status with the planners during the campaign and the interregnum, were keenly aware of how important it was to struggle for access and proximity to the chief executive. They knew, that is, that they were engaged in a battle for the president's mind. By contrast, Tugwell and Berle "had not realized," Tugwell later wrote, "that other voices were being heard, and that our arguments were far from conclusive."[41]

Second, Brandeis and Frankfurter had vast prior experience in placing their protégés in high places. Frankfurter especially, as Justice Brandeis explained in 1913, had "a faculty, rarely equalled, of hearing about 'possible opportunities' for men capable of doing good work."[42] Indeed, before the New Deal opened up even vaster job opportunities for his protégés, Professor Frankfurter had routinely placed his former students not only as Supreme Court clerks but in lower courts and on Wall Street as well.

Because Brandeis and Frankfurter were determined to exert as much influence as they could over the shape of New Deal policy, they sought to extend as broadly as possible their expertise in what Frankfurter termed "personalia."[43] The highest-level men and women who ended up owing their appointments to Brandeis and Frankfurter (called by the press "Felix's Happy Hot Dogs") worked in the Departments of Labor, Interior, and Agriculture. If not for the sudden death of Senator Thomas Walsh and his replacement in the president-elect's plans for the cabinet by Homer Cummings, the Brandeisian personnel network would also likely have penetrated the Justice Department. The Brandeisians' top men in the Labor and Interior departments were the solicitors Charles E. Wyzanski and Nathan Margold, respectively. In the TVA, the Brandeisian network's success was even greater, as David Lilienthal not only handled the legal work of the agency but served on its board of directors as well. These men in turn helped place others recommended by Brandeis and Frankfurter.[44]

Sometimes the men steered into government by this team fell short of their patrons' expectations. In part, this was because Brandeis and Frankfurter were not litmus-testers; they extended their help to some individuals who disagreed with them on important points of policy in the belief that these persons, being reasonable and intelligent, would eventually awaken to the truth. The most notable individual in this category was Jerome Frank, who became a vociferous enemy of the Brandeisian cadre in the New Deal. At other times, Brandeis, Frankfurter, and their well-placed friends simply failed to get their candidates suitably placed; this was the case with Dean Acheson and Learned Hand.[45] They did not give up efforts to influence a particular agency's personnel once they lost battles such as these, however. Instead, they turned their attention to the conversion of those men who had received appointments. Their most persistent efforts in this regard were aimed at gaining insider status with the president comparable to that enjoyed by the brain trusters during the campaign.

Berle proved impervious to Frankfurter's incessant efforts to bring him around to the justice's point of view. Moley was a more attentive student, and although he was never fully persuaded by Brandeis or Frankfurter, he did help to ensure a hearing within the White House for their ideas. The effort to convert someone of Moley's or Berle's status came to an end after Thomas Corcoran and Benjamin Cohen achieved insider status at the White House. These two, best known as legislative draftsmen for the tax, finance, and social security bills passed during the so-called Second New Deal, were faithful students of the justice's philosophy. Recent research into their partnership demonstrates how they served the interests of their cadre. Corcoran and Cohen would initiate the process by visiting Brandeis at his apartment and

> discussing the activities as well as the problems of the administration. Their purpose was not to receive policy ideas, but only to inform him

37

of the situation in the executive branch. Brandeis would . . . make no effort to instruct his visitors regarding the possible alternative solutions to the problems facing the Roosevelt Administration. Then, after these conferences, the Justice would send his specific policy ideas to Frankfurter in a detailed letter that on occasion even suggested areas of needed study by his "boys" at Harvard Law School. The professor would then gather the necessary material and send it to FDR. . . . The president then completed the circle by suggesting some of these ideas to Corcoran and Cohen for drafting.[46]

Corcoran and Cohen were quite conscious of being Brandeis's instruments. Brandeis's desire to maintain judicial appearances made Corcoran's frankness on this point bold. In correspondence with Frankfurter while the professor was overseas for an extended stay during the New Deal, Corcoran and Cohen characteristically assured Frankfurter that they were not neglecting their duties. They went regularly, they wrote, to "Isaiah" for enlightenment. They knew, finally, the value of their positions, for "the government," as Corcoran announced on one occasion, is "not just the top man. . . . A government is the top one hundred or two hundred men. What really makes the difference is what happens down the line before . . . and after . . . the big decisions are taken."[47]

In practice, of course, these power centers—the president himself, Farley, and various people of ideas—did not operate separately. In choosing Roosevelt's initial entourage of top-level appointees, representatives from all of these camps were involved, with Roosevelt and Farley taking the lead. The appointment process got under way formally when Roosevelt told Farley, Howe, McIntyre, and Early in November of the rewards they were to receive in the new administration. In the remaining months before assuming office, Roosevelt, in conferences with Farley and a few others at Warm Springs, Georgia, chose candidates for many of the remaining top appointive posts in his government.

It was in this way that Roosevelt's initial cabinet members were selected. The cabinet that emerged was balanced along traditional lines. Cabinet members, almost needless to say, were largely non- or even antiideological. Those who came closest to being people of ideas were Harold Ickes, Frances Perkins, and Henry Wallace. All proved helpful to the people of ideas who served under them. Ickes and Perkins were most compatible with the Brandeisian philosophy. Wallace, a mystic with an idiosyncratic ideological profile, worked sometimes alongside the planners in his department. None of these individuals, however, was selected for cabinet membership on the basis of ideological considerations. Perkins was the cabinet member who had known the president-elect for the longest period of time. She had served Roosevelt effectively when he was governor and was noted for her skill as a mediator, an important qualification for the head of the Department of Labor. Ickes represented the Bull Moosers in the president's coalition. Wallace was chosen for his expertise in agriculture, for his experience as an agricultural spokesman, and for reasons of geographical balance.

In early February, in further meetings at Warm Springs, Roosevelt decided upon additional appointments. His discussants were his partisan lieutenants, James Farley, Ed Flynn (the boss of the Bronx, who had been Governor Roosevelt's secretary of state), and Louis Howe. It was this group, aided by a series of confidential reports Farley had commissioned detailing the behind-the-scenes maneuvering of each state's delegates at the national convention, that made sure that Roosevelt paid his debts. In the words of Flynn, "We were primarily interested in taking care of the original group of people who had started out with us in the campaign prior to the convention." Of this small group of thirty-four, whom Flynn refers to as the original "investors" in Roosevelt's campaign (they had, in fact, each contributed two thousand dollars or more), there was not a single individual who wanted a post that did not receive one.[48]

The fates of Roosevelt's ideological advisers were also decided upon during these conferences of party professionals. Frankfurter was offered the solicitor generalship, which he declined, and jobs for the brain trusters were decided upon.[49] Berle wished to stay full-time at Columbia but accepted a post at the Reconstruction Finance Corporation. He was also, of course, to be available to the president for private counsel. Tugwell was confirmed, though not without difficulty, as the assistant secretary in the Department of Agriculture. Moley, finally, went to the State Department to keep an eye on the secretary of state, Cordell Hull, and to perform numerous ad hoc tasks for the president, with whom he had daily contact.

As for lower-level jobs, their distribution involved "a complicated series of consultations, negotiations, and trades between the department heads, the White House staff (particularly Howe), National Chairman Farley, key Senators, and others who had access for various reasons."[50] This complex process was weighted institutionally in Farley's advantage. Thus, it was common practice for Farley to recommend, and for department and bureau chiefs to accept, the placement in department and bureau personnel offices of a man to serve as Farley's eyes and ears. And to prevent any mistakes or circumventions of the patronage system, Roosevelt instructed his small White House staff never to send forward an appointment to the Senate unless it had at least been seen by Farley.[51]

Over time, the least influential of the power centers involved in this administration's personnel affairs overall, the people of ideas, improved their lot. Secretaries Perkins and Ickes, Harry Hopkins, and Hugh Johnson, in particular, learned that Farley was sincere when he lectured on the fundamental importance of reciprocity in politics. Specifically, after Perkins and Ickes acceded to Farley's pressure for particular high-level appointments for party loyalists, the patronage chief left them a freer hand to steer their young lawyers, professors, social workers, and other committed individuals into government through low-level positions in their rapidly expanding domains.[52]

Personnel Politics in the Great Society

If the only image Lyndon Johnson wished to convey in his one successful campaign for the presidency had been that of a middle-of-the-roader, he would not have needed input from people of ideas at all. But Johnson also sought in 1964 a mandate for a distinctly liberal policy agenda: to build the "Great Society."[53] Polls taken at the time indicate, however, that he failed in 1964 to gain any such mandate. Johnson, in fact, stands out among presidents elected from 1960 to 1980 as second (significantly) only to Reagan in the low number of detailed pledges made on the campaign trail.[54] But Johnson's objective failure to mobilize the people in support of a grand departure in domestic policy did not affect his perception of the election results nor his attendant relations with people of ideas.[55]

The men who wrote the Johnson domestic agenda wanted to move beyond the principle of distributive and, less clearly, redistributive justice to something bolder. They wished, most simply, to enrich culture through political means. In the buzzwords of their own making, they were "quality of life" (Stevenson) proponents who took for granted an "affluent society" (Galbraith) in which "excellence" could be pursued through "tough-mindedness" (Schlesinger), "vigor" (Kennedy), and an "end to ideology" (Bell).[56] And in all aspects of their domestic agenda, the mainstream liberals involved in presidential politics in the 1960s demonstrated a tremendous desire for action, a desire to *do something now.*

What most needed to be done was to solve the "problems" of modernity, now that economic-based conflicts were giving way to other issues. The solutions favored by liberals were putatively scientific and therefore not fit subjects for shrill debate. Indeed, they believed that social cleavages as a whole, and especially those centered about principles, or ideology, were obsolete.[57] Those who dared to present themselves as defenders of a world-view that provided transcendental, absolute knowledge about social relations, such as southern segregationists and Vietnamese communists, were consequently dismissed as either liars or sleepwalkers. When the liberals themselves defined some problem as "spiritual" or "moral," they characteristically took pains to avoid the appearance of absolutism. Values, presumably even those of the mid-sixties liberal community, were historically determined, not supernaturally revealed. "Enrichment," "fulfillment," "expression," the ultimate values of the liberals, were but vessels to be filled at a later date.

Buoyed by their certainty in the scientific basis of their beliefs, the technocratic liberals of this era went to great lengths to deny their enemies a decent fight (as would their descendant, Michael Dukakis, in his 1988 bid for the presidency). Those who were against them were certain in any event to be buried by the "velocity of history," to use one of Arthur Schlesinger, Jr.'s favorite phrases.[58] In the meantime, liberals sought to educate, not eradicate, those who would choose the "past" over the "future." Eric Goldman, Johnson's replacement for Schlesinger ("court historian" for President Kennedy), even thought he perceived in 1969 the movement of conservatives toward the liberal "consensus." "Over time," he observed, "the conservatives are wising up to the need for government intervention." President Johnson, unfortunately from this perspective, had misused his opportunity to help such people deepen their wisdom.[59] But it hardly mattered in the long run, according to Goldman, for those who already had the firmest grasp on the future were the "metro-Americans," whose numbers would grow exponentially in the future: "the junior executive, the lawyer, the accountant and his wife in the suburbs of New York, Chicago, or San Francisco. . . reading Saul Bellow's *Herzog,* John Kenneth Galbraith's *Affluent Society* and David Riesman's *Lonely Crowd* [and] caring about political leaders who cared about men like Bellow, Galbraith and Riesman." These were the people, Goldman believed, who sought knowledge, not in myths or traditions, but through experimentation, experience, "hard" facts, and analysis.[60]

Drawing from this brief summary, as well as from Johnson's main speech on the Great Society, delivered to graduating students at the University of Michigan on May 22, 1964, we can examine the ideological attributes of the mainstream liberal world-view. To begin with, the liberals definitely claimed logical certitude for their beliefs. On this point, the Johnson administration picked up where Kennedy's left off. Both preached the ethos of logical analysis; in fact, according to one of his aides, Johnson himself was "mesmerized" by the planning, programming, and budgeting system (PPBS), the public administration marvel of the day.[61] Johnson, furthermore, in his quest for unanimity in decisions, and with his contempt for "extremism," was comfortable with the language, if not the person, of Arthur Schlesinger, Jr., who worshipped at the altar of logic in his speechwriting for Kennedy. In President Kennedy's "Reason at Yale" speech, Schlesinger, along with John Kenneth Galbraith, Theodore Sorenson, and a few others, had written of the demise of philosophical and ideological conflicts and their replacement by "problems" amenable to "logic." In Johnson's Great Society speech, he announced in complementary fashion the three great "problem" areas in American life: cities, ugliness, and education.[62] Johnson promised to assemble "the best thought and the broadest knowledge from all over the world" in order to solve the problems associated with these aspects of national life. The idea that there might be some other way to arrive at publicly useful knowledge would appear absurd from this point of view. The liberals, if nothing else, were certain of their *method.*

The question whether the mainstream liberals of this period claimed to possess absolute truth demands a cautious answer. On the one hand, they held absolute knowledge in contempt when others sought to claim it in public discourse. It was associated with the "myths" and "ideologies" that they considered to be the chief causes of turmoil in the world. On the other hand, mainstream liberals would occasionally refer to certain issues as moral or spiritual in substance. This was especially true in the case of civil rights but also in the case of Great Society programs. Thus, in the Great Society speech, after describing to his audience the "challenges" involved in "elevating" the "quality of our American civilization," Johnson said: "You can help build a society where the demands of morality, and the needs of the spirit, can be realized in the life of the nation." The referents of the terms "moral" and "spirit," however, were not typically clarified in liberal oratory, and they were not revealed in Ann Arbor. Thus, "community with neighbors" and "communion with nature" were mentioned later in this speech as values with a spiritual or moral basis, but the authority for that determination was left unspoken.

Despite the ambiguity in their claims about morality, the weight of evidence leans toward a qualified yes to the question whether the liberals claimed to possess absolute truth. For the Great Society experiment as a whole rested on a notion of man's inherent nature as ultimately good, if not perfectible. Thus, helping to "elevate our national life" as Johnson said in Ann Arbor, or to enhance the "quality of life," as Democratic liberals had been saying since 1956, when Adlai Stevenson first used the term in political debate, could be interpreted as a transcendent obligation based on the possession of absolute truth as to the nature of man and the purpose of his existence.[63]

With regard to the third claim ideologists make for their beliefs, in his Great Society speech, Johnson signaled the wide embrace of his and his speechwriters' vision clearly. The goal, he said, is "abundance and liberty for all. . . . But that is just the beginning." The "city of man," he continued, should serve not only the goals of liberty and affluence but the "desire for beauty and the hunger for community."

Moving to the ascriptive component of the ideal type, we observe a significant deviation from the ideological: the Great Society architects did not impute value ascriptively. Even on the periphery of Great Society thought, leftist liberals (such as Richard Goodwin, Frank Manciewicz,

Michael Harrington, and Paul Jacobs, all of whom were on President Johnson's payroll or served on one of his task forces at one time or another) found fault not so much with persons as with the "system" of America's capitalist political economy.[64]

Apparently, as a consequence of such reasoning and of the certainty, examined above, that the sheer "velocity of history" would make dissent obsolete, the mainstream liberals who designed and tried to implement the Great Society never realized what they were up against.[65] In offering a detailed transfer culture, by contrast, the liberals followed the ideal type closely. The Great Society meant to do something *now* and, in so doing, to remake American society. In a review of presidential rhetoric, Theodore Windt found, in fact, that Johnson's speeches as president represented a "rhetoric of action." The president, that is, "saw problems and sought to solve them immediately."[66] The very point of intellectual activity was presumed to be to solve society's problems. The approved style of thinking, Christopher Lasch has observed, managed thereby to provide "unequivocal answers to questions which might otherwise have prevented the kind of total political commitment that American intellectuals seemed so eager to make."[67] Or as John P. Roche, one of Johnson's most trusted people of ideas, observed: "We [liberals] are not absolutists in the metaphysical sense, but we believe that one has to make an absolute, total commitment on behalf of the truth but dimly seen." Such intellectual risk-taking was an attitudinal pillar of the Great Society.[68]

Finally, the northeastern seaboard provided the setting for the key institutions associated with mainstream liberalism. These institutions included Ivy League and a handful of other selective colleges and universities, the *New York Times* (especially the editorial pages), the Urban League, Americans for Democratic Action, the *New Republic,* the *Washington Post,* the Democratic Advisory Committee, and the Kennedy compounds in Massachusetts and the suburbs of Washington, D.C.

In terms of cognitive structure, then, the people of ideas associated with Johnson's presidency were close cousins to the people of ideas in the Roosevelt and Reagan presidencies. The largest departure from the ideal type, the liberals' difficulty in understanding that what was common knowledge in their task force meetings or academic seminars was not common knowledge in America—that even the smartest liberals, that is, have enemies who must be taken seriously—proved to be a significant constraint upon their impact on politics in the 1960s. This peculiarity of mainstream liberal thought continues to this day, in fact, to influence the prospects for liberal success in American politics. It was widely reported in 1988, for example, that Michael Dukakis failed to comprehend the seriousness of George Bush's attacks on his moral sensibility. After all, Dukakis announced in a speech partly drafted by a one-time scribe of John Kennedy's,

Theodore Sorenson, the election was about "competence, not ideology." In later chapters, I will return to this chink in the liberals' ideological armor. The question to be taken up now, however, is to what extent the personnel and advisory practices of the early Johnson administration provided input for people of ideas, chinks and all.

Lyndon Johnson was drawn to mainstream liberals and their ideas for both personal and political reasons. With respect to the former, President Johnson's desire to win the admiration of the entire American population extended beyond what might be explained in purely political terms. As John Roche recalled: "In October of 1964, Johnson decided that the original scenario for the election, which was that he, Johnson, was going to go to Mount Sinai and communicate with God while Humphrey ran against Goldwater, was not going to get more than 90 percent of the votes, so he threw himself into the campaign."[69] And, describing the victory to Doris Kearns, Johnson said of his election: "It was a night I shall never forget. Millions upon millions of people, each one marking my name on their ballot, each one wanting me as their President. . . . For the first time in my life I truly felt loved by the American people."[70] To keep this "love" alive, Johnson wanted, as Roche puts it, "to do good, to be loved as the guy who did good."[71] And to Johnson, doing good meant doing things for people, giving them things. In the president's words: "Some men want power simply to strut around the world and to hear 'Hail to the Chief.' Others . . . to build prestige, collect antiques, and to buy pretty things. Well, I wanted power to give things to people . . . all sorts of things to all sorts of people, especially the poor and the blacks."[72]

Johnson's intensely personal presidential goals led him to seek a close association with the leaders of liberal opinion. They may not have liked each other much—the animosities and suspicions between Johnson and the "Harvards," as he called all educated northeastern seaboard elites, were famous even before the Vietnam War tore the two apart—but both had an absolute passion for action. And the "Harvards" had a transfer culture sufficient to make Johnson look like, if not become, an ideological prophet.

Political circumstances surrounding the 1964 campaign also inclined Johnson to reach out for the assistance of people of ideas. Johnson recognized that if he were to hold together and expand the growing coalition of public and private elites assembled by his predecessor, he would have to win over to his cause at least some of the academics and authors with whom the Kennedys were so famously associated. Thus, immediately after Kennedy was assassinated, Johnson made a series of personal pleas to Kennedy loyalists asking them to stand by him. And when Johnson's sys-

44

tematic personnel operation for his caretaker term cautiously got under way a month and five days after Kennedy's death, Johnson gave his close aide Jack Valenti his personal OK to begin the task by working through Kennedy relation Sargent Shriver.[73] Johnson became convinced over the course of his elective term, furthermore, that the people of ideas associated with Kennedy and, more generally, the presidential wing of the Democratic party controlled his success as president (as well as his place in the history books). (In retirement, a bitter Johnson was convinced that he would "have been the greatest President in his country's history had it not been for the intellectuals and the columnists.")[74]

In response to both personal and political incentives to seek the collaboration of people of ideas, Johnson took a number of steps. Symbolic honors were bestowed upon leaders of the liberal intellectual community until they could no longer be counted upon to accept them graciously. Combining symbolism with substance, furthermore, the Johnson White House went on an annual search for new ideas (more fully described in chapter 4). In the process, during his elected term Johnson commissioned nearly two hundred task forces, some of the most notable of which were characterized by a strong ideological presence. In the War on Poverty task force, for example, mainstream liberals made up the core membership, while Michael Harrington, Frank Manciewicz, and Paul Jacobs constituted a vocal radical-left minority. Eric Goldman's original informal brain trust for Johnson, organized in March 1964, furthermore, also relied upon notable members of the liberal intellectual community. The domestic affairs branch of this brain trust consisted of, in its entirety: Paul Freund (Harvard Law School), John Kenneth Galbraith (Harvard), Richard Hofstadter (Columbia), Edwin Land (Polaroid, and Cambridge intellectual circles), Margaret Mead (American Museum of Natural History and Columbia University), David Riesman (Harvard), Robert Wood (MIT), and Paul Ylvisaker (director of public affairs programs at the Ford Foundation), all luminaries in the liberal intellectual firmament of the time.[75]

Looking beyond the solicitation of advice, the president's team placed a high priority on youth, brains, and dedication to public service in selecting full-time executive branch appointees. According to John Macy, the long-time advocate of professional public administration who was placed in charge of Johnson's personnel operation (as well as made director of the Civil Service Commission, a combination that was prohibited by Congress in 1978),[76] the criteria that guided the Johnson administration's appointments comprised the following:

1. intelligence
2. youth
3. professional reputation, preferably in the public sector

4. commitment to the program the appointee would be administering

Additionally, women and racial minorities were to be given preference in recruitment and hiring.[77] The affinity between these criteria and the substance of liberal ideological thought is strong. The "ideal" candidate according to this list would likely be an exemplar of "tough-minded" youthful intellect and commitment to public sector innovations. More clues as to the ideological character of these criteria are available in the way that they were weighted, interpreted, and implemented.

Macy believes that intelligence was the most highly sought-after factor. Johnson, according to Macy, was very interested in whether a candidate had been elected to Phi Beta Kappa, how quickly he had earned his Ph.D. degree, and whether he had been employed by or had graduated from an Ivy League institution. Because the concrete referents for this criterion were for the most part institutional, it operated as a mechanism to bring into the executive branch's directive positions men and women with ties to northeastern academic circles. And it was in these circles that one could find John Kenneth Galbraith, Arthur Schlesinger, Jr., Eric Goldman, Richard Goodwin, John P. Roche, Robert Wood, Charles Haar, and McGeorge Bundy, all of whom were eminent liberals and all of whom were employed by the Johnson administration. Because, however, Johnson and Macy did not distinguish between a technical graduate degree from MIT and a Ph.D. in sociology from Harvard, this was still, especially at middle levels, a decidedly indirect substitute for an ideological criterion.[78]

As to age, Macy recalls that Johnson "was constantly looking for people who were in the bracket below 40." There were even separate files established in Macy's office to hold the folders of "BYM," or "Bright Young Men."[79] These were, for the most part, young Ivy League graduates with a commitment to progressive social legislation. And every member of the White House Fellows, a group chartered by Johnson at the advice of Eric Goldman, had a separate folder in the BYM file. One White House Fellow, Doris Kearns, sent a memorandum to the president near the end of his term in which she extolled the president's record in regard to age. "Not only has the Johnson White House opened its general ranks to an extraordinary number of young people, but amidst the very highest ranks, it boasts the lowest *average* age in recent history."[80] Sometimes, possibly drawing from his BYM files, Johnson would talk up the youthful vigor of his presidency, as when he gave the press a list of the "17 young men who make the White House tick."[81] But these documents were not kept just for use in public relations. In the legislative development process under Joseph Califano, ideas solicited from these men were used in putting together the annual legislative wish list, which suggests the importance Johnson attached to the first two criteria in his personnel policy.[82]

The affinity between the third and fourth factors in Macy's list—professional reputation and commitment to the program one would be administering—and the interests of people of ideas is ambiguous. These criteria at times favored the appointment of career civil servants.[83] But in staffing new programs, such as those designed to wage the president's War on Poverty and build his Great Society, the application of these criteria could, and sometimes did, propel into government service the very people who as advisers or task force leaders had urged the creation of a particular new agency or the assumption by an old agency of a new responsibility.

With regard to the final formal criterion, minority status, this was, at least in theory, just as important as finding BYM willing to devote themselves to public life. Thus, in the citation on John Macy's Medal of Freedom, awarded to him on Johnson's final day in office, he is praised for both "setting a standard of excellence that will serve as a benchmark for many years to come" and making the government "fairer."[84]

In addition to the formal criteria, there was one final aspect to the selection of personnel, especially of those men and women who would report at least occasionally to President Johnson in their jobs. In the restrained words of G. Calvin Mackenzie, "What was important was loyalty to the President and his programs." In Johnson's more colorful language: "I want *loyalty*. I want him [any appointee] to kiss my ass in Macy's window at high noon and tell me it smells like roses."[85] Even Macy, though he downplays loyalty in his discussion of the selection criteria, recalls that "loyalty was an important word that showed up," and that it included a "commitment . . . to him personally."[86] The application of this standard often worked against the interests of people of ideas, as will be observed below in my analysis of the Model Cities program.

In practice, Macy's operation can be seen to have built upon Kennedy's beginning in professionalizing this aspect of the presidency. Kennedy's personnel operation, under the direction of two Harvard Business School professors, Ralph Dungan and Dan Fenn, had, among other innovations, compiled a talent bank of potential appointees. Macy's improvements upon the Kennedy administration's procedures began with the enlargement of this talent bank. The number of individual candidates in the talent bank grew from two thousand in January 1965 to sixteen thousand in January 1969, and the files on these candidates, along with information on term expirations, incumbents, and the like, were computerized. Macy also tripled (to six hundred) the Kennedy staff's list of "contacts" who could be called upon for help in evaluating candidates.[87]

The selection process that Macy developed typically worked as follows: The procedure began with the development, if one did not already exist, of a detailed job description. Next came "a listing of the best of the candidates with comments from the evaluators of talent, the national political committee, and the state and local committeemen and women, as well as congressional sources affected."[88] The candidates themselves were culled from all available sources, with an emphasis on using the talent bank and the contacts list. Next, the executive selection staff (Macy and his top aides) ranked the candidates. After the FBI cleared each name on the final list, the results of the search were presented in a terse memorandum for the president.

Things did not, of course, always proceed according to plan. As late as August 20, 1965, Marvin Watson, Johnson's political expert, was in fact sending memos to Cliff Cater, of Macy's staff, with requests that probably would not have been necessary if the procedure described above had been running smoothly. "Please set up," Watson asked in one memorandum, "a procedure immediately so that before a nomination is made, the proposed nominee sends a letter stating his desire for the job. . . . Also set up a procedure . . . whereby those Governors and state chairmen who should be notified about a nomination are so notified before an announcement is made."[89]

Another departure from the theory of personnel policy involved the influence of party on selections. As Macy recalls, political considerations were to be "injected" by Johnson at the final stage of selection.[90] Actually, there was in the Johnson White House something of a shadow personnel operation, operating purely on the basis of political pull, that mitigated but did not destroy the impact of its competitor. Of course, some candidates for office were recommended by political friends of the president. These candidates were most often screened and evaluated separately from Macy's operation. There is no written record of the operations of Johnson's informal personnel operation; consequently, there is no way to determine the frequency with which Johnson ignored the recommendations of Macy's staff in order to make a patronage appointment. Still, two factors suggest that Johnson did not often compromise the meritocratic (and incidentally ideological) for the political approach. First, the testimonies of Macy and Coffey suggest that Johnson took a strong interest in personnel operations and that he was considerably more willing than at least his immediate predecessor had been to rely upon his professional personnel staff to select candidates for even the most important subcabinet positions.[91] Second, especially once he became president, Johnson's idea of party-building had little to do with the formal institutions of the Democratic party, except insofar as they might be useful in advancing his personal control over Congress and contributing to the reelection bid everyone expected him to make in 1968. Thus, a "party" appointment in Johnson's administration was as likely to involve awarding a commission charter to a member of the "President's Club" (a supposedly secret fundraising organization headed by New York businessman Arthur Krim) as appointing the law partner of a Democratic congressman to the Federal Trade Commission.

The practice of personnel selection in the Johnson administration, then, did not fundamentally diverge from Johnson's personnel "philosophy." While the administration's theory of personnel selection gave considerable indirect weight to ideology, the practice seems to have erred only slightly in the direction of increasing the influence of party politics. Thus, though factors *directly* relating to neither ideology nor party were most important in both practice and theory, personnel selection in the Johnson administration was structured to provide significant opportunities for ideological input into this administration. Support for this interpretation is provided by a memorandum from Macy to Johnson, written near the conclusion of Johnson's presidency. This document is an important survey of the results of Johnson's personnel strategy. Macy wrote that

> of the total number of executive positions, 261, or 44.8 percent, spent the majority of their professional careers in federal service. 130, or 22.3 percent, came from the career Civil Service. 98, or 16.8 percent came from the career Foreign Service. 20 appointees had their principal experience in the Legislative Branch, and 13 in the career military service. Appointees from either business or legal backgrounds account for another 35 percent of the major presidential appointments in the Executive Branch. . . . University backgrounds have characterized 72, or 12.4 percent, of the appointees. . . . 25 of the full-time appointees have been 35 years of age or under at the time of their appointment by the President.
>
> A total of 50 Negroes have been appointed to major executive and judicial posts, including the first Negro in the Cabinet and the Supreme Court. . . . In addition, 58 Negroes were appointed to part-time assignments on boards and commissions.
>
> The President has appointed 25 women to full-time executive and judicial positions, and 201 women to part-time assignments.
>
> 97 of the executive appointees are Phi Beta Kappa, including 5 cabinet members—Rusk, Wirtz, Freeman, McNamara, and Connor.
>
> Of the appointees, 69, or 9 percent, possess Ph.D.s. The total number of earned degrees represents 936.

Finally, Macy noted, "Each state in the union has at least one appointee, with the leading states being the District of Columbia, New York, Maryland, and California, Virginia and Texas."[92] True to theory, then, the ideal Johnson appointee would seem to have been a young person (preferably also a member of a minority and a woman) with a graduate degree and experience in public service.

49

Within the White House itself, finally, the number of BYM about the president was impressive. When Johnson named seventeen "young men who make the White House tick" in early 1968, *U.S. News & World Report* noted approvingly that "their common background turns out to be more Ivy League than Texas, more academic than political . . . the group has earned five Harvard degrees, three from Yale, three from Columbia and two from Princeton. Academic honors include one Rhodes Scholarship, four Phi Beta Kappa memberships," and fifteen of the seventeen had graduated with honors, high honors, or highest honors from their undergraduate institutions. Included in this group were dedicated liberals such as Frederick M. Bohen, James Gaither, Ervin Duggan, Ben Wattenberg (now a leading neoconservative), Lawrence Levinson, and Matthew Coffey, four of whom worked with Joseph Califano in preparing legislative initiatives each year.[93]

The overall indications, then, are that the potential existed in the Johnson administration at least to pursue ideological strategies for the management of policy. But this potential was only partially realized: those ideological appointees who answered the president's invitation to join his cause, and who made their way beyond task force operations and the White House and into the executive branch agencies, found themselves constrained by LBJ's management style. Johnson was not ignorant of the importance of management and administration. In his memoirs, for instance, the president wrote that the 207 laws that were the "landmark achievements" of his administration were but "the building blocks of a better America," not "ends in themselves." With particular reference to his urban policies, he wrote that laws passed under his guidance merely helped put in place a bureaucratic organization that then had to be put to good use: "Before we could deal with the problems of the cities," he wrote, "we needed to develop the organizational machinery. . . . Our urban programs had grown into a network of separate fiefdoms. We pulled them all together."[94] Indeed, Harry McPherson recalled that Johnson's concern for management on occasion reached a feverish pitch. "On two or three occasions," McPherson wrote, "he's sent out a memorandum saying everybody is to put down exactly what he does, and we're really going to put this thing in boxes, just the way General Eisenhower had it." Despite these good intentions, the president's managerial skills were notoriously uneven and inconsistently applied. "That either never lasts or never gets done," McPherson continued. "I was told to do it one time and I never even did it."[95] As a personnel manager, then, Johnson was often guilty of inattention. Especially as his term progressed, the president became preoccupied to the point of distraction with America's involvement in the war in Vietnam.

Even before Vietnam became an obsessive interest within the

White House, the attention paid to appointees suffered as a consequence of the tremendous priority Johnson assigned to legislation. There was simply not enough time or energy left over to oversee any particular program's implementation, since many more new ones had yet to be created. A comment by one of his White House staffers expresses well the observations of many of Johnson's aides: "To get things started, to keep a full legislative plate before the Congress" was the president's bedrock "philosophy."[96]

Sometimes Johnson seemed to try to compensate for his inattention to day-to-day management problems with a short-lived bout of suffocating scrutiny of the most minute details of an aide's work. According to R. Tanner Johnson, although "Johnson gravitated toward a more-or-less orderly formalistic type managerial system, his personal style frequently disrupted his staff and the system that he sought to institute."[97] Johnson's occasional hectoring of his appointees about such minutiae as the cleanliness of their desks was, furthermore, often combined with bouts of extreme anger, diminishing the morale of his administration and hindering the rationality of program administration.[98]

Johnson typically did nothing beyond speech-making to inspire or direct those appointees below the level of deputy or, in some cases, assistant secretary. Johnson disdained, in particular, Kennedy's imitation of Roosevelt's practice of seeking information from the middle ranks of his appointees. "I don't call some sixth desk man in the State Department," he is reported to have said, "I talk to Dean Rusk."[99] In this way, as with the pattern of suffocation alternating with inattention, the president diminished the prospects for an inner-directed cohesiveness resulting from having ideological appointees in his service.

An indication of how this worked at ground level can be gained from data collected in a survey of appointees from the Johnson presidency through the Reagan presidency undertaken by the National Academy of Public Administration (NAPA). In the NAPA survey, Johnson appointees, although they were exceptional in the degree to which they, in contrast to the appointees of Nixon, Ford, Carter, and even Reagan, rated "participating in history" as a major source of job satisfaction, did not link this with service to Lyndon Johnson. "Serving an admired President" was cited by only 15.7 percent of Johnson appointees in the survey as a "major job satisfaction," below the average of 26.9 percent and significantly below the 54.3 percent of Johnson appointees who cited "participating in history." Johnson may have articulated a prophetic, historically significant message, but he did not thereby become a prophet himself.

President Johnson entered office in 1963 with the potential to be a great partisan leader. He proved himself equal to that task when he gained passage of stalled party initiatives in the Democratic-controlled House and Senate. He also entered office with at least the hope of becoming something more: a visionary president who started the nation on the road to a Great Society. In the pursuit of this goal, the president relied extensively on people of ideas. They drew up the blueprints that he presented to the Congress. They also agreed to serve, in many instances, in full-time capacities in his administration. Johnson's personnel policy was well-suited to their enrollment in the crusade to build a Great Society.

Yet a tremendous gulf separated this president from the people of ideas who formulated and then answered his call. While Johnson's background was almost purely political and partisan, the mainstream liberals thought the time had come to put politics aside and advance the liberal consensus. Their methods demanded, in fact, that political, partisan conditions not be applied to the implementation of their innovative policies. President Johnson could not help them in this respect. The party system and the president's lifelong entanglement with its rules and traditions could not be swept away after they were no longer needed.

Personnel Politics in the Reagan Presidency

Ronald Reagan got his start in electoral politics before a national television audience on October 27, 1964, when he gave a rendition of "the Speech," a no-holds-barred attack against Democrats, liberals, high taxes, and big government. Reagan was fifty-three at the time, had been a registered Republican for only two years, and had never before taken an active part in electoral politics. Nevertheless, Holmes Tuttle, a conservative Los Angeles businessman, along with some like-minded industrialists and entrepreneurs who had bought the airtime for Reagan's speech as part of the Goldwater campaign, decided after this performance to sponsor Reagan for the governorship of California.[100] When Reagan assented, the millionaires, Reagan's proto–kitchen cabinet, sent their man to audition, not with party leaders, but with a political management firm, Spencer-Roberts, which in turn solicited help from the Behavior Science Corporation, which provided the candidate with index-card-sized bits of information he might assimilate within the framework of his "political philosophy."[101]

Reagan's first, successful bid for elective office established a pattern that was repeated in subsequent campaigns. In 1980 the kitchen cabinet was still around, raising funds and providing advice on appointments. William Casey, a man of the old school of Buckley-led conservatism, along with Edwin Meese, directed the campaign, while supply-siders and think-tank fellow Martin Anderson provided Reagan with his index-card-sized bits of information. For their part, the New Right helped by raising funds to defeat liberal senators and congressmen who would stand in the way of a conservative redirection of policy, and encouraged nominally Democratic southern evangelicals to cross party lines to cast their ballots for Reagan. The institutions of the nonreligiously based New Right, including the Heritage Foundation and the Lehrman Institute, meanwhile worked diligently to draft the blueprints implicit in the conservative world-view. The neoconservatives, finally, operated through their magazines and advisory organizations to challenge liberal assumptions on foreign and domestic policy.

The ideological character of the schools of thought associated with Reagan's rise to power can best be understood through an examination of some of the leading figures who helped put the "movement" in conservatism: William F. Buckley, Jr., the undisputed leader of the Old Guard; Lewis Lehrman, on the New Right; Irving Kristol, a neoconservative; and Reagan himself.

William F. Buckley, Jr., and the National Review

It is an irony of postwar history that while the threat of communism drove Arthur Schlesinger, Jr., Peter Vierick, and the American parties to a so-called vital center, it drove traditionalists, libertarians, and anti-Soviets to coalesce *against* that center and everything to its left. The conservatives responded in this way because they saw the world through the polarities of an ascriptive ideology, which led them to perceive liberals as well as communists as their enemy. (The liberals could more comfortably hold to a centrist stance because, as shown above, they lacked the ascriptive component of a purely ideological world-view.)

William Buckley's role in forging this coalition was vital. Buckley brought these groups together under the umbrella of the *National Review* and kept magazine and movement together through social as well as intellectual stewardship. By sponsoring fortnightly dinners for *Review* editors at the Buckleys' Manhattan mansion, sailing trips about Long Island Sound on the Buckleys' yacht, and black-tie dinners for hundreds of guests at the Plaza Hotel in New York City every five years, Buckley has, in the somewhat hyperbolic words of William Rusher, the *Review's* former longtime publisher, "done for conservatives what is done for liberal intellectuals through Guggenheim fellowships, receptions at the Ford Foundation, sabbaticals at the Kennedy School, and Pulitzer prizes."[102] In addition to his efforts on behalf of the *Review*, Buckley has had a central role in establishing numerous other conservative organizations, including the International Society of Individualists (ISI), Young Americans for Freedom (YAF), the American Conservative Union (ACU), and the Conservative party of New York state.

Reagan traces his conservatism in part to his readership of the *National Review*;[103] when he entered the White House, he paid homage to

Buckley by offering him the post of U.S. Ambassador to the United Nations. Believing, however, that if he had to work through channels to reach Reagan, he would not have the same quality of access to the president as he hoped to maintain in his informal roles as adviser, friend, and editor of one of the "party presses," Buckley turned down the offer. "It's one of those funny situations," Buckley explained, "where the person I am closest to in the government is the President."[104]

With respect to the ideal type, Buckley rates generally "high" marks, though with interesting exceptions. To begin with the issues of logical certitude and absolutism, Buckley combines the two as he once combined strands of thought in the *National Review*. (Buckley recently retired from active editorship of the journal.) In proposing, that is, that revealed truths yield political imperatives, Buckley means to stake out a perfectly logical position: To Buckley, revealed truths relate clearly to political positions. Simply put, God meant man to be free, and suffering is part of the bargain. To go beyond ameliorative social policy is, consequently, to be ignorant of God's will.[105] When fully qualified, there is nothing illogical about such a position.

As for the putative comprehensiveness of his thought, the answer here must be more qualified. Buckley's positions on political and social issues are comprehensive, but it is not always clear what standards he means to apply in staking out his positions. There is no master key to the universe in Buckley's thought. The further one gets from the first-order proscriptive implications of revealed truth in Buckley's thought, the less unwavering he appears to be. Although Buckley believes homosexuality to be a sin, for instance, he caused a furor in the Reagan years by arguing that a homosexual congressman should be professionally ostracized, not for his homosexuality, but for the "unruliness" with which he expressed his sexual preference. And with regard to the ascription of value to various persons, Buckley is too devout a Catholic to make ultimate judgments on the basis of temporal distinctions, though his rhetoric does at times make use of polarizing inference rules.

Finally, while Buckley expresses enthusiasm in his writings for the policy agenda of the Right, he draws a sharper line than do most conservatives between those conservative ambitions that are acceptable and those that must be passed over in silence. It is notable in this regard that at a dinner celebrating the thirtieth anniversary of the founding of the *National Review*, at which President Reagan, Congressman Jack Kemp, and columnist George Will spoke with hope and triumph, Buckley took the occasion to remonstrate that in the end, we may not win our battle against the "suicide of the West."

Buckley helped make the country safe for Reaganism. He did this mainly through the dissemination of ideas. In his words, "It cannot be disputed that the general direction in which conservative politics has traveled in the past three decades has been mapped out by *National Review*." But also, Buckley has himself entered political debate and built institutions for the transmission of ideas into politics. As he says, "I have always felt what was needed was a combination of the two—institution-building and intellectual debate."[106]

Lewis Lehrman and the Lehrman Institute

Unlike Buckley, who typically takes the long view on political affairs, some members of the Old Guard, including the *National Review*'s longtime publisher, William Rusher, had heard enough debate as early as 1964, when they drafted Barry Goldwater into the race for the presidency. After the Republican insurgents' humiliating defeat that year, a new group of conservatives emerged who were less confident than Rusher and his colleagues had been that victory was imminent for the movement. Maybe, New Right leaders such as Lewis Lehrman reasoned, there was more groundwork to be completed first.

Lewis Lehrman was disappointed with Harvard and Yale when he was a student at those elite schools. The faculty seemed to be more interested in theories and abstractions than in policy and politics, and the graduate students were "immature." Lehrman therefore decided not to pursue an academic career after obtaining his master's degree at Yale and instead entered the family business, which grew under his direction into a highly profitable chain of drugstores. Lehrman conjoined his wealth with his ambitions when, in 1972, he converted his townhouse on Manhattan's Upper East Side for use as the site of the Lehrman Institute.[107]

Lehrman's idea in founding his institute was to "bring together serious men and women of every point of view and cause them to study . . . policy." "The social democrats and the liberal elites would thus be exposed," he reasoned, "to conservative ideas." This would lead to the triumph of conservatism, Lehrman was certain, because the "psychology of leadership" is such that people naturally will give up their obsolete modes of thought when "they see a better set of individuals and ideas."[108]

Judging from what the Lehrman Institute actually accomplished in its nearly two decades of operation, Lehrman indeed created a forum for wide-ranging intellectual competition. The institute was in the 1980s the most academic of the major conservative think tanks. The board of trustees included not only conservative luminaries such as Edwin Feulner (president of the Heritage Foundation), Irving Kristol, and Michael Joyce (director of the Bradley Foundation) but also two highly esteemed professors at Johns Hopkins University, Robert Tucker and David Calleo. And fellows of the Institute included such respected scholars, some of them quite liberal politically, as Paul Kennedy, Doris Kearns, Theodore Draper, and John Lukacs.[109] By 1980 the Lehrman Institute and its founder were a recognized part of the conservative movement. The institute provided one of the forums in which the ideas of the supply-side movement were debated, and its founder raised funds for Reagan's reelection as director of Citizens for America.

The attributes of ideological thought that Lehrman exhibits are numerous. With regard to the certainty with which Lehrman holds his views, David Stockman's remark that Lehrman's "type was much in evidence in St. Petersburg in 1917" is suggestive.[110] Indeed, Lehrman's economic arguments in favor of a return to an international gold standard, as well as his more "mainstream" propositions, are presented as logically coherent and logically related to his core libertarian economic and traditionalist, New Right social beliefs. Just in the past several years Lehrman has, furthermore, come to base his economic and other propositions upon absolute values. He began his political career devoted almost entirely to questions of economic policy. When, for instance, he first ran for elective office—against Mario Cuomo for the governorship of New York—he ran on a narrow economic platform. Some time afterwards, Lehrman converted from Judaism to Catholicism and began to take a greater interest than before in social issues, particularly abortion.

The comprehensiveness of Lehrman's ideas is exhibited in his attempt to establish a logical parallel between the civil freedoms of slaves and those of fetuses. "Abortion, like slavery," Lehrman argues, "allows equals to rule over equals without their consent, depriving the child in the womb not only of the right to liberty, but of the right to life as well." The "usual arguments about viability, intelligence, pain, quickening, meaningful life, or unwanted children," Lehrman continues, "are as irrelevant as earlier arguments that the poor, black slaves were better off under the rule of a benevolent master."[111] Lehrman's point here rests clearly upon moral convictions (Lehrman even takes minor offense at the term *social issue*, preferring *moral issue*) and putatively comprehends all of American history as a moral contract. Lehrman generally shies, however, from ascribing value to persons on the basis of their antagonism to his ideas or their failure to live up to his ideals. Yet it is undeniable that according to his beliefs, there are but two polar categories of persons when the issue is abortion. Finally, though Lehrman is not as triumphalist as the Old Guard was when plotting for Goldwater, he does express a belief in the imminence of conservative rejuvenation. His "blueprint" is specific, detailed, and, he believes, practical.

Lewis Lehrman, with his emphasis on economics and social issues and his credentials as an institution builder, candidate for elective office, and fundraiser, exemplifies the attributes not only of ideological thought but of what has come to be known as the New Right, whose other leaders

56

include Paul Weyrich, Richard Viguerie, Edwin Feulner, and the evangelists Pat Robertson and Jerry Falwell.

Irving Kristol and The Public Interest

Despite his association with William Bennett, Jack Kemp, Elliott Abrams, William Kristol (his son, who served under Reagan as Bennett's chief of staff and now performs the same job for Vice President Dan Quayle), and other Reagan-era public figures, Irving Kristol's most extensive connections and influence have been within the conservative movement itself. Editor of *The Public Interest,* his staff is generally composed of interns fresh out of undergraduate or master's programs who will go on to editorial, writing, think-tank, and foundation jobs. Kristol is also a close associate of William E. Simon, profiled in an earlier chapter, and has long been the patron of Leslie Lenkowsky, the former director of the Institute for Educational Affairs.[112]

Kristol has moved away somewhat from his opening editorial in *The Public Interest,* in which he proclaimed the magazine to be reaching beyond ideology for a sort of technocratic truth.[113] Kristol's central theme in the articulation of his contemporary beliefs is, not scientific certainty, but maturity. "While Americans are by now habituated to utopian rhetoric, they are still quite sensible, because of the basic sociological facts of life," he explains. "Americans go to a lot of morbid movies, but I think most of them are quite cheerful."[114] The people of this country, being mature, have learned to take chances. Here Kristol mixes his maturity theme with one of his favorite topics, opportunity: "You have to take chances, to risk things, in democratic politics. You risk a deficit for achievement of transformations of the economy and society via a restructuring of marginal tax rates. If the Congress won't let you control spending at the same time as you cut taxes, you do it anyway . . . don't let them set the agenda."[115] As for the experts and technicians he once had such high hopes for: "Your first priority is to shape the future of the society. And you don't listen to bankers, and you don't listen to economists. If you have a crisis, you just hope they're in office and not you."[116]

Kristol's prescriptive and proscriptive ideas are carefully ordered and are taken to be logically indisputable. He does not oppose social entitlements as a whole, but he does oppose Aid to Families with Dependent Children, Head Start, and certain other welfare programs, because he believes that their implementation has been socially divisive.[117]

To the question whether absolute values are a basis for Kristol's political positions, the answer is a yes. On the one hand, in arguing against the "adversary culture" of America's professorial elite, Kristol makes clear that his ultimate concern is with "the *spiritual* base of bourgeois society." On the other hand, and unlike many other conservatives, Kristol does not claim to know just what absolute values might be articulated to save our bourgeois culture: "All we can say with some certainty, at this time, is that the future of liberal capitalism may be more significantly shaped by the ideas now germinating in the mind of some young, unknown philosopher or theologian than by any vagaries in annual GNP statistics."[118] Reflecting this "compromise," Kristol refers to the absolute values of neoconservatism as "rabbinic" rather than "prophetic."

Kristol's views are, in addition, broadly comprehensive, though in a less rigorous way than is true for many other conservatives. Neoconservatives, Kristol has written, believe in many things. In economics, they believe in economic expansion, "not out of any enthusiasm for the material goods of this world, but because they see growth as indispensable for social and political stability." In foreign affairs, they see (even in the 1990s) a clear danger of military confrontation. In social policy, finally, Kristol and his peers are unforgiving of what they see as the utopian fallacies of planners and social helpers.

With regard to ascription, one cannot deduce from Kristol's ideas the value of any individual on the basis of such categories as social or economic status or heritage. Nor does he see liberals and political opponents as inherently flawed persons. Kristol is perfectly capable, however, of taking a tongue-in-cheek swipe at "them." "It is *they*, not us," he has written, who are excited. "It is even they (specifically, it was Michael Harrington) who gave us our name in the first place."[119]

On the issue of imminence, Kristol would side with William Buckley. In Kristol's succinct statement: "Human history is not the march of enlightenment. It is as much a history of *re*gression as of *pro*gression."[120]

Ronald Reagan and "Reaganism"

Ronald Reagan was probably the most ideological president of the first eight decades of the century. His views are logically consistent within the framework of his overall philosophy. His actual policy conduct at times contradicted his beliefs, but that is another matter. Furthermore, in conversation he reportedly routinely attributes his principles to his day-to-day experiences as a boy, an actor, and a politician. He builds his ideas, that is, from the ground up.

About particular items within his world-view Reagan's logical certitude is unshakable. As a consequence, what appears as disingenuous rationalization to the casual observer of Reagan's political career (for instance, Reagan's refusal as president to concede that "revenue enhancement" equaled "tax increase") can perhaps best be explained in terms of his ideological certitude (in this case, about the evils of big government and the virtues of tax reductions). The ideologue's fundamental beliefs simply *must* be right, and he must be righteous in acting upon them. Thus, as Fred

Greenstein has observed, President Reagan's White House advisers quickly learned that to get their boss to accept a change in policy that threatened one of his core principles, they had first to package their idea in an ideologically neutral or appealing guise.[121] Reagan's close-mindedness is also apparent in his notorious looseness with facts. The details simply do not matter so much when your ideas are inherently unfalsifiable.

As to the absolutism of his beliefs, over more than two decades Reagan has consistently claimed to derive his principles from a religious interpretation of the founding of the United States. On the occasion of his first inaugural, for instance, Reagan said: "We are a nation under God, and I believe God intended for us to be free. It would be fitting and good, I think, if on each Inaugural Day in future years, there should be declared a day of prayer." In a commencement address at Notre Dame University in 1981, Reagan spoke of the Founding Fathers, who "gave us more than a nation. They brought to all mankind for the first time the concept that man was born free, that each of us has inalienable rights, ours by the grace of God."[122] Reagan did not, furthermore, adopt this manner of speech for its appeal to the New Right of the 1980s. As early as 1964, in "the Speech," Reagan had sought to base his support for a flat tax on the inalienable rights of man. Equating Lyndon Johnson's tax policies with Marxism, Reagan asked his audience: "Have we the courage and the will to face up to the immorality and discrimination of the progressive surtax, and demand a return to traditional proportionate taxation?"[123] Progressive taxes, to Reagan, are not merely bad policy; they are quite simply bad.

The comprehensiveness of Reagan's beliefs flows from his dual focus upon America's strength (its antistatist traditions) and promise (to spread this strength around the world).[124] Before a group of evangelicals in 1983, Reagan addressed himself to America's strength:

> Explaining the inalienable rights of men, Jefferson said, "The God who gave us life, gave us liberty at the same time." . . . Well, I'm pleased to be here today with you who are keeping America great by keeping her good. Only through your work and prayers and those of millions of others can we hope to survive this perilous century and keep alive this experiment in liberty, this last, best hope of man.[125]

Yet one more illustration of Reagan's comprehensiveness is that unlike in the case of President Nixon especially, it is impossible to say whether President Reagan valued foreign or domestic affairs more highly. This ambiguity suggests that because his ideas are ideologically grounded, they are close to being seamless.

Even as president, Reagan reportedly favored stories about "welfare cheats" in the Cadillacs they buy with relief money,[126] but to say that as president he ascribed value on the basis of income levels is not true in and

59

of itself. It is fair to say, however, that Reagan assigned negative values (immorality) to able-bodied persons who go on relief for longer than a short time. It is the fact of being dependent upon the impersonal state that Reagan still sees as necessarily demeaning.[127] But Reagan never loathed the poor. The real "morality play" in his world-view has always been based on principles, not income. In Reagan's words, from his 1964 speech:

> For almost two centuries we have proved man's capacity for self-government, but today we are told we must choose between a left and a right or, as others suggest, a third alternative, a kind of safe middle ground. I suggest to you that there is not left or right, only an up or down. Up to the maximum of individual freedom consistent with law and order, or down to the ant-heap of totalitarianism; and regardless of their humanitarian purpose those who would sacrifice freedom for security have, whether they know it or not, chosen this downward path.

The liberal, not the welfare cheat, plays the devil in this scene.[128]

Finally, despite the timeless nature of some aspects of Reagan's vision of America as the "shining city upon a hill" and his clear mythologizing of the American founding, it would be perverse to deny to Reagan's beliefs a "transfer culture" component. After all, helping to put Reagan in the White House was the most concrete, linear, historical success of the modern American conservative movement.

The fit between Reagan's views and the ideal type of ideological thought, in conclusion, is extraordinary. When Reagan came to office, furthermore, he harbored goals that dovetailed with the character of his thought and propelled him and his ideological compatriots into a close association.

From the New Deal to 1980, presidents tended to see the executive branch as an arena for problem solving. Ronald Reagan, by contrast, looked at the executive branch as an arena in which to implement a preconceived agenda. As the president himself said two years into his first term:

> I was on the trail long before I thought I would be actually engaged in public life. . . . There's going to be no change on my part. . . . What am I doing here putting up with all this at my stage in life if I weren't here to further all the things I've been talking about. . . . I came here to do this one thing, to accomplish as much of what I've been talking about over the years as was possible to accomplish.[129]

What needed to be done, more concretely, was to overturn the Great Society. "I'm here," the president noted to himself in his diary in 1982, "to undo the Great Society." "It was," Reagan continued, "LBJ's War on Poverty that led us to our present mess."[130] The Reagan team knew that to implement their agenda would require, among other things, careful selection of executive appointees. Only right-thinking persons would be able, it was thought, to withstand capture by the bureaucrats. In the president's words, "I think one of the characteristics of many, many years of the New Deal is that there is a permanent structure of government in place with a New Deal flavor [which] is a powerful force within the bureaucracy."[131] In addition, through the control of appointments it might be possible, as the president once put it, to "institutionalize the revolution that we launched when we came here."[132]

The systematic effort to make strategic use of personnel policy in the Reagan presidency flowed from this confluence of ideological motivations and associations.[133] The driving force behind the subsequent effort to appoint and appropriately manage ideological appointees was Edwin Meese, who, after all, had majored in public administration as an undergraduate at Yale and had sought the advice of the NAPA during the transition.[134] One of the most important decisions made by Meese, along with the transition's personnel chief, E. Pendleton ("Pen") James, was that the following criteria would be used in selecting Reagan's personnel:

1. philosophical commitment to Reagan's agenda
2. integrity
3. competence
4. toughness (ability to resist capture by the bureaucrats and to withstand criticism by the press)
5. team play[135]

The first item is unique. Indeed, except for it, a group of public administration experts might have come up with the same criteria. James's own account of the implementation of these standards suggests as much. James, an executive recruiter who had worked in Nixon's personnel office and who had ties to Reagan's kitchen cabinet, apparently thought of the criteria as a two-pronged test: "He [Reagan] wants good people around him," James explained in an interview with this author, "but we also want to make sure that ideology is there too. You know, the five criteria." The official, fivefold version of the criteria was not forgotten, however, after this list was made up. James, in fact, had the criteria printed on business cards and instructed his staff to keep these with them at all times. The criteria made such a mark in the White House, furthermore, that when James left office, the president, in his letter of thanks, which hangs on a wall in James's office, spelled out the criteria point by point.

After the election, the transition team task force finished writing job descriptions, established a set of priorities among positions, listed candidates by substantive area, and coordinated policy proposals. The transition leadership, along with the president-elect and the kitchen cabinet, also decided who would sit in Reagan's cabinet. Though ideology was never forgotten in this process, collegiality was a priority in the selection of the cabinet, and this somewhat dampened that group's ideological character.

In the selection of a treasury secretary, for example, concerns about team play led to William E. Simon's withdrawal from consideration. Simon, a certifiable man of ideas very much in line philosophically with the president-elect who also clearly met all the other criteria, was the kitchen cabinet's consensus choice for treasury secretary. He reportedly made it known through Justin Dart, a kitchen cabinet charter member, however, that he would not come on board "just" to be secretary of the treasury, a position he had held under the two previous Republican presidents. Though Simon denies this, he is reported by persons involved in the search to have wanted to direct both the Council of Economic Advisers (CEA) and the Office of Management and Budget (OMB) from the Treasury Department. When discussions through intermediaries reached an impasse, Simon called Reagan to withdraw from consideration. Recovering from Simon's decision, which Reagan termed a "bombshell," Reagan's advisers came up with another "Simon-pure" person of ideas, Lewis Lehrman, as a substitute candidate. The original feeling within the group about Lehrman was positive, but his stature, unlike Simon's, was not such that he could be offered the position without others being considered. James thus brought up the name of Donald Regan, whom he knew professionally. William Casey seconded James's mention of Regan, and it was decided that both men would be interviewed. Thus, on consecutive days, James and Meese met with the candidates in a private dining room at the University Club in Washington, D.C.[136]

Lehrman, who was tested on the first day, flunked. He reportedly spent the entire interview lecturing these two economic laymen about the significance of fixing international exchange rates—the gold standard. In Lehrman's sophisticated understanding of neoclassical economics, gold is related to all other aspects of domestic and international economic policy and can therefore be a pedagogical wedge into a general discussion of economic policy. But if this is how he spoke of gold in that private session, it did not come across clearly to his interviewers. Again, there were concerns about the willingness of an ideological candidate to be a team player. Regan, by contrast, is not burdened by ideological passions. Perhaps as a consequence, he seemed to James to "have a much more complete view of what the president wanted done in economic policy." Also, Regan was not a Reagan man, which, ironically, might have helped him, because he made it clear that he was ready to "reach out to the *various* ideologues and groups associated with Reagan's economic policy." In the Treasury Department and the White House, Regan would prove true to the impression he gave at his interview, being intent on doing whatever the president wanted done (though it was left to him to divine what that was).

Despite the "loss" of the Treasury job to a nonmovement member, the Reagan cabinet was broadly representative of the schools of conservative thought associated with Reagan's quest for the White House in 1980. William French Smith (attorney general), Edwin Meese (counselor to the president), and Caspar Weinberger (secretary of defense) were California Reaganites, though Weinberger operated independently of the kitchen cabinet circle and Meese (along with the infamous James Watt, secretary of the interior) had ties to the New Right. The neoconservatives' ambassador to the cabinet was Professor Jeanne Kirkpatrick, who served as the U.S. ambassador to the United Nations. The Old Guardists, for their part, felt close to William Casey (director of the Central Intelligence Agency) and comfortable with most of his cabinet peers (especially Malcolm Baldridge, secretary of commerce, and John Block, secretary of agriculture). The supply-siders, finally, who were aligned with the New Right, and who are considered further in chapter 5, claimed David Stockman as one of their own. Finally, the director of the Environmental Protection Agency (EPA), Anne Gorsuch, was a New Right ideologue. Under President Carter her position was of cabinet rank.

The White House itself had an even more distinctly ideological cast than did the cabinet. Of Reagan's initial top White House aides, only two were nonideological Republican stalwarts, Vice President George Bush and Chief of Staff James Baker. Reagan's two policy directors, Martin Anderson (domestic) and Richard Allen (foreign) were linked closely to the New Right (and to conservative think tanks—the Hoover Institution and the Heritage Foundation, respectively). Anderson, furthermore, doubled as a California Reaganite. Michael Deaver (deputy chief of staff) and Pen James were also California Reaganites, and Murray Wiedenbaum (chairman of the CEA) for a short time helped the supply-siders.

As to subcabinet appointees, it is significant that the Reagan team even *had* a strategy for their selection. Prior administrations had delegated much of the responsibility for subcabinet appointments to members of the cabinet. By contrast, in the Reagan administration, the White House sought control of *all* appointments, including not only second- and third-tier departmental positions but federal judgeships and schedule C appointments (primarily personal and special assistants to subcabinet appointees).

True to their plans, the Reagan team employed an exceptionally structured system for vetting candidates. After the cabinet secretary and the White House personnel office agreed upon one or more candidates for a subcabinet post, a folder of information was sent to Anderson and Allen, as well as to Lyn Nofziger (the White House political affairs director) and Fred Fielding (who handled conflicts of interest). At this stage Fielding would have the Federal Bureau of Investigation (FBI) conduct a twenty-four-hour name check on the candidate. Nofziger spent his days, not dealing with the Republican National Committee or congressmen, but trying to ensure that only those with a clear Reaganite record were admitted to government. In fact, Nofziger, the person in charge of "politics" in this process, was the most vociferous and consistent detractor of applicants with Republican party experience, "Nixon-Ford retreads" in the vocabulary of the Reaganites.[137] Allen and Anderson, finally, were expected to use their independent sources of information to evaluate a candidate's reputation and to check his or her views for conformity with the conservative agenda.

The next stage was the daily 5:00 P.M. meeting of James, Baker, Meese, and Deaver. It was another first in the annals of personnel policy for the president's top aides to spend this much time alone, much less together, discussing appointments. Deaver's role was, surprisingly, the most interesting. "If there had to be a patronage man at these meetings," James recounts, "it would be Michael Deaver." He "attended all the meetings, but his eyes tended to glaze over a lot. . . . He was more concerned than the rest of us with rewarding certain individuals." Deaver was, of course, the man who took care of the president's and his wife's special friends, such as Charles Wick, who is said to have been chosen over neoconservative Norman Podhoretz to head the United States Information Agency. What is interesting is that James interprets this as patronage. To Ronald Reagan's first director of personnel, and the first presidential personnel assistant to hold the rank immediately below cabinet level, as well as to have his offices in the White House's West Wing,[138] patronage had nothing in particular to do with parties, but was simply the practice of giving government jobs to persons who did not deserve them.

The result was, according to G. Calvin Mackenzie, an authority on presidential personnel practices, that in the important "second round" of appointments in the first year, Reagan's foreign policy appointees "shared a world view founded on deep skepticism of the motives of the Soviet Union."[139] In the regulatory agencies, former industry executives were placed in charge of regulating the industries they had spent their lives developing.[140] In social and health policy, strategic positions were occupied by "pro-life" and "pro-family" men and women. In economic policy, supply-siders were a dominant presence at the Treasury Department. Throughout the administration, the impact of ideological staffing could be felt. Twenty-three of the authors of the Heritage Foundation's famous *Mandate I* volume had found their way into the new administration by the beginning of the Reagan presidency's second year.[141] Mackenzie goes so far, in fact, as to call Reagan's subcabinet appointees a "new class of federal administrators."[142]

The NAPA survey of political appointees, mentioned above, provides evidence of the effectiveness of the Reagan approach in achieving a high level of ideological conformity in appointments, especially at the sub-cabinet level. Reagan's officeholders were exceptional in the degree to which they "would like to see more political appointees" in the government. This was, in fact, the only question dealing with appointees' attitudes toward career bureaucrats that elicited highly divergent answers from the respondents from different administrations. In a symbolic coincidence, the 50 percent or so of "very conservative" respondents from the entire sample who favored more appointees was virtually identical with the percentage of *all* Reagan appointees who wanted more political control of the government. Fewer than 10 percent of the moderate and very liberal respondents and fewer than one-third of the Johnson, Nixon, Ford, and Carter appointees felt similarly. The significance of this is that a desire to see more appointees, especially in the American context, translates easily into a desire to increase presidential power over the direction of public policy.[143]

The NAPA study also suggests that Reagan's appointees—the so-called trained seals–worked as they were intended to: as implementers of a preconceived agenda, not as problem solvers. Specifically, Reagan's appointees were the most critical group in the poll in terms of how they rated the responsiveness of their civil service employees. Furthermore, Reagan officeholders reported that they had an unusually easy time dealing with the White House and special difficulty mastering the informal networks of politics in Washington. These findings suggest that the men and women sought out by James and his associates to do battle with Leviathan continued once in office to be oriented toward Ronald Reagan and his anti-statist philosophy. In addition, Reagan's appointees took exceptional satisfaction in serving their president. This single datum about Reagan's appointees is, in fact, *the* item in the NAPA survey that most clearly distinguishes the Reagan administration from all others.[144] This too lends credence to the idea of Reagan as a movement leader and his appointees as movement followers. In the language of the anthropologists discussed in chapter 1, ideological transfer cultures involve prophetic leadership and intense commitment from followers.

Further evidence of the extent to which personnel selection practices were in accord with theory in the early Reagan administration is provided by that administration's record of judicial appointments. Court appointments in fact took on special significance under Reagan, because split party control of the government made it clear that victory on some fronts would not likely be forthcoming from the legislature. In the early 1990s, there is already some evidence that Reagan's appointments to the Supreme Court have changed the direction of federal law on issues of abortion and affirmative action. As with the selection of cabinet versus subcabinet appointees to the executive branch, furthermore, there is evidence that some of Reagan's lower-court appointees were even more intensely ideological than those he appointed to the highest court. In particular, the Reagan administration's appointees to the twelve circuit courts of appeal deserve scrutiny. At the lower, district court level, the Reagan administration respected senatorial courtesy in appointments, and at the level of the Supreme Court, the Senate's scrutiny of nominees was fairly intense, even while the Republicans held the majority of Senate seats. The appellate courts occupy the strategic middle ground between the Supreme Court and the district courts.

By the time that he left office, Reagan had appointed the majority of judges on seven of the eleven numbered circuit courts of appeal plus the majority on the prestigious Appeals Court for the District of Columbia Circuit. Overall, over 48 percent of the full-time judges sitting on the circuit and district court levels at the end of his two terms were Reagan appointees.[145] And according to the classification scheme of the *Almanac of the Federal Judiciary*, these judges were far more conservative than their fellow judges who had been appointed by previous presidents. According to David McKay's analysis, based on the *Almanac*'s classifications, none of Reagan's appellate court appointees sitting at the end of his second term were liberal, 9.6 percent were middle-of-the-roaders, and 90.4 percent were conservative; the figures for Nixon's appointees (the next most conservative) were 16.1 percent, 35.5 percent, and 48.4 percent, respectively.[146]

The most significant strides toward the conservative ideologization of the courts came in the first term when an extremely centralized and ideologically self-conscious selection process was employed to name over thirty new judges to the appellate bench.[147] The results were impressive, as the Reagan administration showed a distinct preference for two types of appointees: conservative academics, looked to by the White House as future leaders of their courts,[148] and sitting district court judges. While 23 percent of Reagan's first-term appellate court appointees were academic advocates of conservative judicial interpretation, only 14 percent of President Carter's appellate court appointees were law professors at the time of their appointment, while the comparable figures for Ford, Nixon, and Johnson appellate court appointees were 2.5 percent or below.[149] And whereas approximately one-half of the appellate appointees of Presidents Nixon, Ford, and Johnson were serving at a lower level in the judiciary at the time of their appointment, three-fifths of the appellate court judges appointed in Reagan's first term belonged in that category.[150] The Reagan administration's preference for both groups can be explained with reference to Reagan's overriding ideological concerns. In the case of the former group, the ideological rationale for selection is obvious. And in the latter case, it is presumably easier to evaluate the likelihood of a candidate's judicial "restraint" on the basis of previous judicial decisions than on the basis of prosecutorial or private law experience (not uncommon backgrounds for any recent president's judicial appointees).

The professors-turned-jurists appointed during Reagan's first term leaned ideologically in the direction of one or the other of the two major conservative schools of jurisprudence: *interpretivism* and *law and economics*. The interpretivists (Robert Bork, Antonin Scalia, Ralph Winter, Patrick Higginbotham, and, less clearly, Paco Bowman and J. Harvie Wilkinson III) believe, in the words of Bork, that in the United States, "the sole task" of the judge "is to translate the framer's or the legislator's morality into a rule to govern unforeseen circumstances."[151] One who believes otherwise, who "insists upon the rightness of the Warren Court's performance," seems ready to Bork to "claim for the Supreme Court an institutionalized role as perpetuator of limited coups d'etat." The upshot for the interpretivists is that "of course . . . broad areas of constitutional law ought to be reformulated."[152]

The law and economics professors-turned-jurists (Richard Posner, Frank Easterbrook, Kenneth Starr, and, to a lesser extent, Bork also) show their conservative stripes, not in an abhorrence of judicial activism, which they are willing to tolerate and even embrace so long as that activism's guiding principles can be plainly stated, but in their belief that economic principles and, in particular, cost-benefit analysis should be applied to the interpretation of statutory law.[153] According to Frank Easterbrook, when judges become more cognizant of economics, they will be less susceptible to calls for a "'fair' division of the spoils in a zero-sum-game" and more prone to "pay less attention to today's unfortunates and more attention to the effects of the rules" they make for future players in what might then emerge as a "positive-sum-game," one in which all players may win.[154]

In Donald Regan's memoirs, he revealed some of the "secrets" of the Reagan administration. The most important, though not the most celebrated, was that President Reagan essentially never told anyone what to do. He would either accept decisions as *faits accomplis* (even the fateful decision that led Regan to the White House and Baker to the Treasury Department) or, occasionally, set boundaries for decision making by saying no to an idea brought to him by one of his aides.[155] The only time Larry Speakes, Reagan's press secretary, heard the president forcefully deny his aides control of a decision, in fact, was in the case of reversing the personal income tax reductions of 1981.[156] Reagan's ideology instructed him that the supply-side reduction in marginal rates of personal taxation was a historic accomplishment, not a negotiable starting point in economic problem solving. But when the subject was not supply-side economics or the military budget —when, that is, an issue could not be fitted into Reagan's ideological template—he left its resolution to others.

Even if Ronald Reagan was not always in charge, however, he returned frequently enough to his conservative convictions to make those in government ever mindful that he was a president with a difference. Thus, even the non-ideologues in this presidency knew that they had to take ideology seriously if they wanted to last long in Reagan's Washington. Being an ideologue, in fact, could even be an asset in the bureaucratic infighting within this administration. Perhaps this is what Joseph Sobran, a *National Review* senior editor, had in mind when he wrote in 1986 that

> Reagan has done something to political dynamics. Like Franklin Roosevelt, he has established a momentum that will probably survive his tenure in office. This is not entirely due to him personally, because, like Roosevelt, he is most important as a symbolic presence around which other forces . . . can operate. Conservative activists and policy analysts are achieving countless little victories in Washington because Reagan is there.[157]

Conclusion

This chapter has charted some preliminary aspects of the convergence of ideologists and the three presidencies in question. Franklin Roosevelt came to office heavily indebted to party leaders and possessing a personal antagonism toward systematic abstract thought. Understandably, Roosevelt as president proved to be more heavily wedded to the older system of partisan advisory structures and personnel selection strategies than to the emerging ideological approach to his office. The ideologists of the 1960s reaped the benefits of the professionalization of the White House that was just getting under way in the New Deal. They also gained on account of the intense personal stake that Lyndon Johnson felt in winning over to his side the liberal opinion makers who had been affiliated so famously with his predecessor. But only in the Reagan administration did the ideologization of the presidency achieve systematic proportions in *all* aspects of campaign advising, personnel selection, and policy implementation.

And with each movement toward the ideologization of these aspects of the presidency, the presidents under study turned toward persons with impressively similar ideological pedigrees, despite their different interests and beliefs. This is worth stressing because of the implication that as a consequence, evaluating the role that ideologues have played in our recent politics necessarily takes us beyond choosing sides among the various schools of thought represented in the ideological conflicts over federal policies in the United States since the thirties. Indeed, if, as is argued throughout this work, ideological responses to modern problems are virtually inescapable for an increasingly influential segment of our polity —given ideology's societal function and the increasing structural incentives for the integration of ideological proponents within presidencies of achievement—then it is of considerable importance that the sectarian debates of present and past ideologists be studied collectively, so as to achieve as realistic and comprehensive a perspective as possible on an emerging model of American presidential politics.

Chapter Three
Defining a Mission for the TVA: The Roosevelt Administration

Franklin Roosevelt's New Deal, of which the Tennessee Valley Authority was an original and principal part, was a triumph for neither socialism nor fascism, bolshevism nor monarchicalism. In discussing Roosevelt's programs today, in fact, these terms are useless except as epithets. Modern American ideologies arose under peculiarly American circumstances: the absence of an old feudal order against which to hurl the power (and barbs) of the masses; the vertical and horizontal dispersion of the government's power through the institutions of federalism and the separation of powers; and national traditions celebrating individual initiative and distrusting military might. Under such conditions, it is not surprising that the classical ideologies of neither the Left nor the Right took root. Ironically, however, by virtue of the same tenuous relationship between these famous isms and American circumstances, to associate the program of an American president with one of these foreign ideologies has always been a favorite ploy of those who would unconditionally damn an administration's efforts. The critics of Roosevelt thus made common appeal to the demons of socialism, Bolshevism, and other heresies.[1] But Roosevelt's critics largely missed their mark, for within the New Deal, the adherents of "foreign" ideologies were largely irrelevant.

Because of the extraordinarily weak echo of European ideologies in the United States, some politicians at the time, most notably Franklin Roosevelt, and many writers to this day, such as the historian Arthur M. Schlesinger, Jr., have denied that the New Deal had any philosophical or ideological basis: it was all a matter of pragmatic experimentation. This is not so.[2] The content of ideological thought within a polity, like the phenotypic expression of the underlying genetic pattern of an organism, depends upon a variety of circumstances. Ideologies, like other evolving

70

"organisms," must be studied in their appropriate contexts.

In the United States in the 1930s, ideological warfare within the government pitted adherents of planning against advocates of corporatism and what I earlier labeled Brandeisianism. The principal division, between advocates of the first and third options, dominated the TVA in its early years, as the original board members and the president who appointed them struggled to define the mission of the new agency. The board's chairman, Arthur E. Morgan, was an advocate of planning and an administration ally of Rexford G. Tugwell. His co-director, David E. Lilienthal, was a protégé of Felix Frankfurter and an advocate of the trust-busting philosophy of Justice Brandeis. The third member of the board was Harcourt Morgan, a member of the southern agricultural establishment with an idiosyncratic world-view, who was opposed on principle to the leadership of Chairman Morgan. The struggle among these men highlights both the reality of and the constraints upon the impact of people of ideas in this early presidency of achievement.

The Inception and Development of the TVA Proposal

The central figure in shaping the law that established the Tennessee Valley Authority was the president himself. The proposal to establish the TVA represented an amalgam of subjects with which Roosevelt had an acquaintance as governor and about which he cared deeply, such as land-use planning, hydroelectric power generation, and reforestation.[3] In conjoining such items, the president did not, however, begin from scratch. The catalyst for FDR's thought about the Tennessee Valley was a prior set of bills calling for the governmental development of an idle hydroelectric plant on the Tennessee River at Muscle Shoals, Alabama. And in thinking about the planning aspects of the TVA bill, Roosevelt may have been influenced by the ideas of city planners such as his uncle, Frederic Delano. To understand the development of this legislation, then, requires analysis of several factors, culminating in the president's own vision of a new sort of government agency but beginning with the older Muscle Shoals bills and their congressional champion, Senator George Norris.

Senator Norris

In the 1920s, George Norris, the self-proclaimed "Fighting Liberal" from the Midwest, led two unsuccessful efforts to transform the idle hydroelectric plant at Muscle Shoals, Alabama, into a publicly owned and operated facility.[4] The plant had been built to manufacture explosives for World War I. After the war, debates over its proper use became a staple of national politics. Senator Hugo Black wanted the facility to be put to use in the manufacture of fertilizer for local farmers. Industrialist Henry Ford offered to develop the plant and the surrounding region to demonstrate the effectiveness of planning-for-profit. Senator Norris, in an analysis that was to prove important in the battle to define the TVA's priorities, saw the issue as a contest between the "power trust" and the broad diffusion of electricity. The "power trust," Norris was certain, represented the "greatest monopolistic corporation that has been organized for private greed." In its efforts to "perpetuate its control of the natural resources of the nation," this avaricious combination engaged in "disgraceful, distasteful, and disreputable means."[5]

The underlying principle of Norris's evaluation of Muscle Shoals's potential, and the principle pervading his interest in the TVA, was that electric power should not be developed for profit. "This natural resource," Norris wrote in regard to the flow of electrons through a wire, "was given by an all-wise Creator to his people and not to organizations of greed. No man and no organization of men ought to be allowed to make a financial profit out of it."[6] Electric power generation, Norris wrote, "ought always to be under public control, public ownership, and public operation." Under Norris's leadership, two bills that would have permitted public development of the Muscle Shoals plant passed the Congress but were vetoed by Republican presidents. Looking toward a Democratic victory in 1932, Norris was hopeful that his legislation would triumph at last. He was not, however, carried away with enthusiasm for the particular Democrat who would win the election.

Franklin Roosevelt

Early in the 1932 campaign, Norris and fellow battlers against the power trust were cautiously optimistic about Governor Roosevelt. Senator Norris felt "certain," according to his associate Judson King that Roosevelt would sign Norris's languishing bill, but not until his speech of September 21, at Portland, Oregon, did Roosevelt specifically endorse the public development of the Muscle Shoals facility. The reason for Roosevelt's apparent hesitation can be inferred from the opening lines of this speech. "I don't hold with those," Roosevelt stressed, "who advocate government ownership or government operation of all utilities."[7] Despite any fear that Roosevelt might have had about being tagged a socialist for his ideas about watershed development, he went ahead on this occasion to state firmly his support for public development at Muscle Shoals and similar areas. The government, he stated, should own all hydroelectric sites, and furthermore, communities had "the undeniable basic right" to set up their own service if they did not find the service rendered them by private utilities satisfactory. And in either sort of public power project, the government should have the authority to "transmit and distribute [electricity] where reasonable and good service is refused by private capital." This, he stated, would give the people an "essential birch rod in the cupboard." Public competition against utilities was desirable even in the absence of private company failure, that is, because it would keep the private companies honest. Public electric projects could be thought of as "yardsticks," Roosevelt told the Portland audience, and should be established in the four regions of the nation. He identified the site at Muscle Shoals by name. "Judge me," he said in a rhetorical flourish at the close of his address, "by the enemies I have made. Judge me by the selfish purposes of the utility leaders who have talked of radicalism while they are selling watered stock to the people."[8]

Those who knew the governor had cause for at least mild surprise on the occasion of his Portland speech. In New York, Governor Roosevelt had launched a high-profile campaign for the public development of power generation along the St. Lawrence River. In part because the river is an international boundary, however, Roosevelt was unable to accomplish his objective. The U.S. Department of State under President Hoover was not inclined to assist the Democratic governor of New York in this venture. Roosevelt did maneuver the New York assembly into creating a St. Lawrence Commission, which recommended, as Roosevelt had intended, the creation of a New York Power Authority, to which he appointed Frank Walsh, Morris Cooke, James Bonbright, and Leland Olds, all well-known opponents of the utility magnates.[9] Yet Roosevelt had never before explicitly and fully endorsed the Muscle Shoals plan, nor had he proposed, as Norris had, a broad program of public ownership. Thus, the Portland speech was an important milestone along Roosevelt's path toward proposal of a Tennessee Valley authority. From the point of view of those who wished to see a truly dramatic program in the Tennessee Valley, however, the best was yet to come.

As president-elect, Roosevelt vastly broadened his pledge with respect to the public development of the Tennessee River. On a circuitous trip to Warm Springs, Georgia, during the interregnum, Roosevelt stopped to tour a part of the Tennessee River Valley with Senator Norris and a large entourage of public officials, private advisers, and reporters. The night of this excursion, Roosevelt spoke at Montgomery, Alabama, and indicated that he did not see in Muscle Shoals merely an opportunity finally to give life to an aging proposal. Rather, Muscle Shoals represented a chance "to accomplish a great purpose for the people of many States and, indeed, for the whole Union. Because there we have an opportunity of setting an example of planning, not just for ourselves but for the generations to come, tying in industry and agriculture and forestry and flood prevention, tying them all into a unified whole over a distance of a thousand miles."[10] And days later, on February 2, in a casual conversation with reporters at Warm Springs, Roosevelt expanded his vision of the project so as to encompass some of his favorite ideas for dealing with the Depression, such as industrial decentralization, the movement of urban populations to rural areas, and the application of the principles of city planning to larger areas.[11]

Roosevelt himself was apparently responsible for this dramatic enlargement of his agenda for the Tennessee River Valley.[12] Senator Norris, Judson King, Felix Frankfurter, and the New York Power Authority commissioners—those men, in other words, with whom Roosevelt had communicated over the preceding months with respect to his agenda in this area of policy—as a rule did not interpret watershed development in terms of an experiment in planning for the general social and economic welfare of a region. Indeed, Senator Norris was reportedly dazed by the sweep of Roosevelt's ideas.[13] Tugwell certainly became a booster of the authority and saw its value precisely in terms of its potential to demonstrate the usefulness of planning, but there is no evidence that Tugwell took part in formulating Roosevelt's early plans for the TVA. Similarly, those who would give Arthur Morgan credit for the planning aspects of the president's proposal have slim evidence to support their claim.[14]

Roosevelt needed neither tutoring nor prodding to articulate a grand conception of the promise of the public development of the Tennessee River Valley. In the judgment of Arthur Schlesinger, Jr., by 1932 Roosevelt's interests in the land, forests, and water were "an old absorption." Also, Roosevelt had since the 1920s been convinced that America was losing its soul to urban living. Thus, in that decade "he had discussed the possibility of keeping people on the land by combining farming with part-time local industry."[15] As governor, Roosevelt continued to elaborate his ideas on the theme of a "balanced civilization," and by 1932 he had become enamored of planning as the means to accomplish his humanitarian goals. In fact, in the careful judgment of Michael J. McDonald and John Muldowny, Roosevelt probably provided the inspiration for the actual language of the TVA's planning sections through his keynote address at a 1931 conference on regionalism held at the University of Virginia.[16] In any event, Roosevelt was well versed in the topic of planning, and as Schlesinger aptly notes of the legislation establishing the TVA, "Perhaps no law passed during the Hundred Days expressed more passionately a central presidential concern."[17]

Legislating the TVA

Roosevelt's trip to Muscle Shoals and subsequent public statements were more than enough of a hint for Senator Norris and his staff to begin work on another "Muscle Shoals bill." In the House, John McSwain of South Carolina, chairman of the Military Affairs Committee, also began work before the inaugural on potential legislation. The earliest versions of these House and Senate bills, in fact, were submitted to the respective chambers of Congress on March 9, a month before President Roosevelt formally requested legislation from Congress to create the TVA.

Norris's earliest version of the act creating the TVA contained clear references to Roosevelt's intention that the authority to be created be charged with broad planning responsibilities. The earliest versions of this bill's planning sections appear, therefore, to have been prepared by Norris's staff as part of their general effort to bring the old Muscle Shoals proposal "up to date," to conform with the new president's bold ideas about regional development. As for Arthur Morgan, his contribution at this stage was to draft a clause—which was added to the end of section 22 of the Norris bill—authorizing TVA planners to work with local governments and other agencies, and not solely with state governments, when pursuing whatever planning goals the president might articulate.[18]

After his inaugural, Roosevelt conferred with Norris, McSwain, and a few other members of Congress about Tennessee Valley legislation. This conference did not settle differences between Norris's bill (which was closest to the president's ideas) and the more conservative proposals being entertained in the House, but it did indicate that there was ample goodwill and that compromise was possible. Thus, it was with "the outlines of a bill already in place" that Roosevelt, a month after his inauguration, sent to Congress a special message setting forth his legislative aims with respect to the TVA.[19] This message, delivered on April 10, forcefully laid out Roosevelt's ambitious plans. The occasion for the proposal, Roosevelt made clear, was "the continued idleness of a great national investment." But restarting the power plant at Muscle Shoals was, Roosevelt continued, "but a small part of the potential public usefulness of the entire Tennessee River." "Such use," Roosevelt proclaimed,

> if envisioned in its entirety, transcends mere power development; it enters the wide fields of flood control, soil erosion, afforestation, elimination from agricultural use of marginal lands, and distribution and diversification of industry. In short, this power development of war days leads logically to national planning for a complete watershed involving many states and the future lives of millions. It touches and gives life to all forms of human concerns.[20]

Therefore, Roosevelt recommended to Congress the Tennessee Valley Authority, whose duty would be to plan and carry out conservation and development work in the region "for the general social and economic welfare of the Union." Finally, in the same speech, Roosevelt added a personal plea for the recognition of planning as an imperative of modern living:

Many hard lessons have taught us the human waste that results from lack of planning. Here and there a few wise cities and counties have looked ahead and planned. But our nation has "just grown." It is time to extend planning to a wider field, in this instance comprehending in one great project many states directly concerned with the basin of one of our greatest rivers.

The day after Roosevelt's message was delivered, new versions of the bills originally introduced in March were brought before the Senate and the House. In the wrangling that ensued, Senator Norris remained steadfast in his support for a bill that reflected the president's expansive conception of the TVA. Norris's bill (S. 1272) was recommended by the Senate Agriculture Committee without hearings. In the House, the Military Affairs Committee held the only congressional hearings on the legislation, from April 11 to April 15.

In these hearings, as well as in floor debate, the president's proposal was deemed "socialistic," a "soviet experiment," "an attempt to graft onto our American system the Russian idea," "socialism and Russianism on a gigantic scale," and even part of an apparent plot by "the professors" to "deflate the structures of the country."[21] These criticisms were sharp, but they hit only a portion of their potential target. For the ideological "problem" that inspired such invective was the already dated one of the government's entry into the utility business, not the government's novel intention to begin a wide-scale experiment in social engineering.[22] In fact, the most "radical" homegrown ideological aspect of Roosevelt's proposal, its planning potential, was virtually ignored by critics at this time.

During the hearings before the House Military Affairs Committee, the innovative planning sections of the proposed legislation (sections 22 and 23 of the act as passed by the Congress) were brought up only once, on April 12, by John Taber of New York, who opposed the bill. Taber's complaint was that these sections seemed to authorize future appropriations for "anything that is hinted at in this bill." Chairman McSwain attempted to refute Taber's charge by insisting that "the section . . . is nothing more than a pathway making a suggestion for future action." In any event, McSwain assured Taber that "we will tighten that up so that you and all other members of the House would have no doubt about it."[23]

In subsequent debate on the floor of the Senate as well as the House, only slightly more attention was devoted to these sections of the bill. The vagueness of section 22, which authorized the president to make surveys and plans for the area to promote the "general welfare" of its citizens and to foster the "orderly and proper" physical, economic, and social development of the region, provoked a New England critic of the proposed legislation to ask, quite sensibly:

What does this mean? We took no testimony [on this section]. No testimony was offered as to what the staggering, gigantic propositions may mean in dollars and cents to the American people. It provides for the general welfare of the citizens of said area. I ask the Membership of the House what the general welfare of the citizens of this whole territory means.[24]

Picking up the same theme later in the bill's consideration, another House critic asked again of section 22: "What can this language mean?" It was, he concluded, the "most sinister" and "insidious" of all aspects of the proposed act.[25]

These few remarks, plus a stray mention in the Senate on May 1,[26] constitute the full extent of congressional deliberations on the planning sections of the TVA bill. In part, this was a consequence of the haste with which the bill was debated. Also, it was a tribute to the intelligent handling of the legislation by the supporters of the president, who in defense of their bill spoke in down-to-earth terms, refusing the ideological bait of their opponents. In this, John McSwain and other representatives followed the lead of Roosevelt, who, when asked by Senator Norris how he would explain the philosophy behind the TVA, said he would tell the nation that it "was neither fish nor fowl" but that whatever it was, it "would taste awfully good" to the people of the valley.[27] Indeed, according to Donald Davidson, a historian of the Tennessee River, "In general, to Southern congressmen at least, the TVA bill was simply another Muscle Shoals bill in a somewhat altered form."[28] The legislative results of this strategy were impressive. In the Senate, the Norris-dominated conference bill was approved on May 16 without a roll call. The House gave its concurrence the next day in a disciplined party vote: while only 28 Democrats voted against the bill, 18 Republicans voted in favor of it, and 88 against.[29]

The act that the president signed into law the following day (48 Stat. 63) was a significant presidential victory. On the power and fertilizer fronts, the efforts of House members to constrain the president's leeway had been rebuffed. The TVA, under the president's ultimate control, was to have the capacity, if it so desired, to transmit as well as to generate electric power and was to exercise its own judgment with respect to the production of fertilizers. The controversial "yardstick" (Roosevelt's "birch rod in the cupboard") was not mentioned at all, yet the potential for its creation and use was implicit in the law.

The sections on planning, furthermore, though the subject of little interest in the legislative history of the TVA, seemed to hold out some promise of great authority should the president desire to interpret the relevant provisions broadly. Section 22 authorized the president, in vague and expansive language:

to make such surveys of and general plans for said Tennessee basin and adjoining territory as may be useful to the Congress and to the several States in guiding and controlling the extent, sequence, and nature of development that may be equitably and economically advanced through the expenditure of public funds, or through the guidance or control of public authority, all for the general purpose of fostering an orderly and proper physical, economic, and social development of said areas.[30]

In carrying out such surveys and plans, this section continues, the "President is further authorized . . . to cooperate with the states affected thereby, or subdivisions or agencies of such states, or with cooperative or other organizations, and to make such studies, experiments, or demonstrations as may be necessary and suitable to that end."[31] Three weeks after passage of this legislation, the president issued an Executive Order (no. 6161) directing the board of the TVA, in language as vague and open-ended as in the TVA Act itself, to implement this section of the statute.[32] Section 23 of the law further stipulated that in accordance with section 22, "the President shall, from time to time . . . recommend to Congress such legislation as he deems proper to carry out the general purposes stated in said section, and for the especial purpose of bringing about [among other things] the economic and social well-being of the people" living in the territory.

To return to the theme of this chapter: The circumstances under which Roosevelt came to the presidency, and the manner in which he confidently assumed the burdens of leadership, provided an occasion more than sufficient to unblock old Democratic bills such as the Muscle Shoals legislation. Roosevelt, however (like Johnson thirty years later), was not content with merely passing old legislative proposals. Thus, he took old Muscle Shoals bills and added to them some of his own ideas about land-use planning, industrial decentralization, and other topics. Consequently, the TVA was not only to innovate in public power development and fertilizer production —the subjects of the old Muscle Shoals proposals—but to serve as a social "laboratory" as well.

If the president had realized at the time that the discretion he had won in the passage of the TVA bill would lead to an embarrassing controversy over the very meaning of this program, perhaps he might have sought to think through the potential for conflict in this law. If interpreted and implemented in a way that gave great weight to its planning provisions, this law might be read as a mandate for self-help cooperatives, the redrawing of municipal boundaries, the restructuring of local economies, and perhaps even the restriction of free enterprise in small towns and the replacement of competition with cooperation among religious organizations. All of these, in fact, were items on the agenda of the TVA's original chairman. If, however, the act was interpreted and implemented, as it was by the board's other two original members, so as to stress the production and distribution of electric power and the manufacture of fertilizer, an entirely different set of priorities might emerge. But it was not in the president's nature to seek to resolve contradictions and ambiguities, especially not in the abstract. As a consequence, it was left to the board itself to wrestle with this law's self-destructive potential.

Implementing the TVA

The president, who had been given great discretion by the TVA Act to determine the administrative setup of the authority,[33] selected Arthur E. Morgan to be chairman of the TVA board in March 1933. As I observed above, Dr. Morgan began influencing the TVA during its legislative passage. His involvement was of marginal impact on the letter of the law, but the fact that he was brought into the process so early led him to believe that what the president *really* wanted from the new authority was the same thing Morgan wanted, namely, a visionary agency given not only to generating electricity and making fertilizer but to planning for the total betterment of the South.

Before proceeding to the consequences for the TVA of this understandable but, for the president, regrettable assumption, it is necessary to discuss Dr. Morgan and his co-directors and to analyze the differing ideological views they brought with them to the TVA board. For this ideologically contradictory piece of legislation happens to have been implemented by three men representing among them two of the distinct ideological streams woven into the New Deal.

The Chairman of the Board, Arthur E. Morgan

Roosevelt had been reading Arthur Morgan's newsletter, *Antioch Notes,* for several years before he became president. Thus, Morgan recalls that when Roosevelt interviewed him on April 13 (three days after Roosevelt sent his message to Congress calling for the establishment of the TVA), the president "seemed to be talking in the spirit that I associated with Eleanor Roosevelt," that is, in terms of social uplift and collective action. And when Morgan questioned why the president would want him for such a responsible position in his government when the two men did not know each other, the president responded, "Haven't I been reading *Antioch Notes* all these years? I like your vision."[34]

Whether Morgan's vision represented the president's primary interest in Morgan cannot be known. Morgan was a prominent American dam builder in his day. And while Roosevelt needed a hydraulic engineer for the top slot on the board, he did not necessarily require a social visionary. Roosevelt was adept, furthermore, at speaking in the idioms of diverse men. Still, Roosevelt himself had put planning into the TVA legislation, and he and Morgan cared deeply about many of the same things. So it is fully understandable, even if inconclusive, that Morgan came away from his initial private meeting with the president, as well as from subsequent meetings, believing that Roosevelt backed his vision of the TVA 100 percent.

Morgan's vision bears analysis. It was, to begin with, peculiarly comprehensive and idealistic, and Morgan was determined to apply his vision to the job at hand in the TVA. In fact, Morgan, who would later devote years of his life to a biography of Edward Bellamy and found a consulting company for the propagation of plans for rational community organization, judged the TVA job at the time he accepted it as the "sort of thing I have been wanting all my life to do."[35] What Morgan meant by this is suggested in the following passage, written late in his life in defense of his leadership of the authority:

> The evolutionary process after three billion years of gradual development had produced patterns of value that resulted in humanity, with perhaps unlimited time to continue and perhaps unlimited possibilities of future development. . . . We cannot, therefore, fulfill our lives as individual beings. . . . The meaning of my life [is] what will be achieved through me for humanity as a whole. In keeping with this view, I have tried to make my life a positive force in the struggling emergence of a new human purpose.[36]

Morgan located a principal obstacle to the emergence of this new human purpose in "the deeply embedded heritage from mankind's animal ancestors." This was the preeminent barrier to an "evolutionary breakthrough to a new and better order of living" comparable to the advances of the early Christians, Buddhists, and Zoroastrians over their pagan predecessors.[37]

In the early 1930s, Morgan saw this obstacle weaken. He was inspired by what he thought of as "emerging traits of excellence" in modern man. These traits included respect for human unity, honesty, goodwill, and sound physical as well as moral living. Morgan was intent in the TVA to take advantage of the consequent opportunity for mankind to achieve a world-historical transformation in its capacities and purpose of life. For each individual, this would bring the benefits of a "full personhood." Thus, Morgan was convinced that the TVA should "be concerned with *every* aspect of the region's well-being."[38]

At the base of Morgan's pyramid of interests was personal character. Using an analogy from civil engineering, Morgan explained that

> personal character in a social order is like the quality of the metal used in bridge building. If personal character is on a low level, then there

comes a time when no refinement of social planning and no expenditure of public wealth, however great, will create a good social order. . . . In my opinion, life in America is approaching that point. . . . [Thus] for perhaps the next half-century or more, the burden of our attention and our loyalties and the full drive of our aspirations should be given to bringing about a revolution in the personal character of the American people.[39]

Toward this end, Morgan promoted, contrary to his remarks in the above passage regarding social planning and government expenditures, just those two items in the TVA.

Morgan's thought was highly ideological. Being a radicalized American liberal, Morgan claimed logical certitude, absolute truth, and comprehensive explanation implicitly on the basis of what scientific reason, goodwill, and hard work could accomplish. Morgan was so certain of his ideas that he assumed they would be logically compelling and accessible to any thinking individual. (As a consequence, in his interactions with other board members, Morgan would routinely overestimate his persuasive powers.)[40] The absolute truth that Morgan purported to possess was indefinite, but only because human nature and the purpose of humanity as a whole were seen to be evolving. The future, in any event, promised to be transcendently superior to the present. This was not a contingent possibility but an irrefragable extrapolation into the future of Morgan's interpretation of human history. Similarly, the comprehensiveness of Morgan's thought comprised a promise of things to come. For, though there are no canonical texts containing the comprehensive, absolute truths of a planner, his method of analysis and social organization putatively can improve all aspects of life. Indeed, all aspects of life must be encompassed in a planner's programs, for what he offers is a systemic model of existence in which each variable is attuned to all others. This is what Morgan offered his fellow board members and the people of the Tennessee Valley.

Morgan did not shy, furthermore, from ascribing value to people on the basis of certain of their characteristics. Morgan believed that the masses lacked certain virtues necessary for human betterment but that they could be lifted out of their impoverishment through moral education. Morgan himself once contrasted this attribute of his thought to what he saw as one of the weaknesses in Lilienthal's world-view: "Lilienthal assumed that the motives of people in general tended to be sound and that their primary need was for information and the opportunity . . . to give expression to their motives. In contrast, I believed that information and resources were not sufficient for human well-being because the mass of people, with selfish motives and purposes, are likely to put information and power to poor use."[41] Another category of people to whom Morgan ascribed negative value was politicians. Thus, Morgan characterized FDR as a split personality. The president's good side Morgan associated with moralism, educational initiatives, social uplift, rational planning, and the First Lady, Eleanor Roosevelt. The dark side Morgan attributed to politics.

Finally, Morgan's imminent historical consciousness was highly developed. In an extension of the theory of evolution to human society, Morgan predicted evolutionary breakthroughs in the capacities and purposes of human existence. Morgan was determined, in the TVA as at Antioch College, to act as a catalyst for mankind's anticipated leap to the next stage of historical realization.[42]

Dr. Morgan's Co-directors

In an exchange of letters immediately following FDR's selection of Arthur Morgan to chair the proposed TVA board, the two men reminded each other of the crucial significance of personnel. In Morgan's letter, he stated his belief that "the success of this project will depend very largely on the key personnel." In his reply, FDR concurred word for word.[43] Morgan thereafter set out to find candidates to recommend to the president for the remaining board positions. FDR wanted one of these slots to be filled by a public utilities expert, the other by an agricultural expert, preferably from the South. The president suggested several men to Morgan but left the search to him.

Harcourt Morgan

For the agricultural spot, Morgan first recommended George Crawford, whom the president rejected for political reasons. It was indicative of Morgan's cooperative attitude and self-confidence that he would recommend Crawford, who was best known as a former president of the Tennessee Coal, Iron and Railroad Company. Crawford, who was salaried at the then extraordinary figure of five hundred thousand dollars per year, was known among progressives as a humanitarian who had introduced advanced labor practices in his companies against the opposition of senior board members. Morgan was pleased by this enlightened use of power, but he was also impressed by the man's standing in the world of big business. Thus he endorsed Crawford on the ground that the "businessmen of the South and of the iron and steel industry have great confidence in and admiration for him. His presence on [the] board would greatly strengthen it against public attack by [the] utilities."[44]

Roosevelt was not persuaded. Judson King, Norris's associate and, as director of the National Popular Government League, a leading critic of the "power trust," opposed the appointment. King believed that Morgan's recommendation of Crawford indicated a dangerous naiveté on Morgan's part, and he communicated his reservations to Marvin McIntyre. McIntyre, who handled the president's schedule and performed other services for the overtaxed White House staff, penned in the margin of Morgan's telegram praising and recommending Crawford, "King wants it held up." Morgan was asked to find someone else.[45]

Dr. Harcourt A. Morgan, president of the University of Tennessee and no relation to the chairman, was Arthur Morgan's substitute candidate. He had been recommended to Morgan by officials in the Department of Agriculture, in the land grant colleges, and at the Russell Sage Foundation. Dr. Morgan, though raised in rural Canada, had spent his professional life in the southern United States. In his various positions as an agricultural expert and public servant, he had stayed at the leading edge of agricultural production technology.

Morgan's professional life had given him practical experience in politics as well as technology. In efforts to prevent crop damage from pests in Louisiana, Morgan learned the art of gentle persuasion. This, he came to believe, was the only method truly available to a government bureaucrat dealing with suspicious farmers. Morgan's political education had extended even to engineering logrolling agreements with New England congressmen to gain appropriations for fighting pests that were infesting southern crops.[46]

In 1905, Morgan moved to the University of Tennessee, where he continued in the patterns he had established in Louisiana. He worked, that is, through traditional institutions in a nonpartisan, nonrousing manner. He aligned himself, in particular, with the land grant college system. He did not attempt, therefore, to extend the benefits of his work to the poorest farmers, who were generally not included in such colleges' experiments. He did not, however, have any aversion to the common life of the agricultural farming family. Indeed, he spent considerable time visiting such families and their communities. Characteristically, when Harcourt Morgan wished to enroll students in his university's new agricultural college, he traveled on horseback through the hills of Tennessee to line up prospects. Morgan was named president of the University of Tennessee in 1919 and president of the Association of Land Grant Colleges and Universities in 1927.

Over the years prior to his appointment to the TVA board, Harcourt Morgan had developed a world-view of some detail and breadth which he called the "common mooring." The product of years spent teaching farmers the purpose of conservation and related measures, his vision was homegrown. It was based on his belief that "we have sinned against the soil, the crop, and the animal. Our punishment consists of wasted soil, low production, burdensome pests, high-priced feeds, poorly fed animals, congested markets, and worse than all else, the turning of the best manhood from the farm."[47] Morgan continued to elaborate and teach this worldview as a TVA board member. In his pedagogy, he used charts to display the oxygen cycle, the rainfall and evaporation cycle, and even the role of industry in the common mooring. Decentralized industrial production, he believed, had a role to play in restoring the earth to health and returning "the best manhood" close to the farm. Like Roosevelt, H.A. Morgan sought a balance between the rural and the urban dimensions of modern life.

The problems with which Harcourt Morgan was concerned were the foundation, he thought, of the most significant challenges facing the American nation. In a 1939 commencement address, Harcourt confidently stated his belief "that democracy will survive. However, if it does not, it will be because we have failed to reconcile the demands of individual initiative with the public interest in the conservation of our basic natural resources."[48] The big question according to Morgan was how to adapt agriculture and industry to fundamental natural laws such as the interrelatedness of irrigation and transport in a river basin.

Harcourt Morgan's ideas were similar in some respects to those entertained by the agricultural planners M. L. Wilson and Rexford Tugwell. Like the planners, Morgan aspired to a systemic understanding of the problems of agriculture. These men all believed, furthermore, that the New Deal offered an opportunity to acquire and apply such an understanding. The South was an obvious place to begin, for the poverty of its farmers was acute and the first steps toward raising their standard of living were fairly obvious. In the rootedness of his vision in the soil, however, H. A. Morgan proved himself to be more a planter than a planner.

Though Harcourt Morgan did claim logical certitude and absolute knowledge, his thought fails the ideological test in its other aspects. Morgan did not dichotomize persons into categories of opposite value to society. Thus, he was committed in the TVA to work with the common people of the region in promoting the public welfare. He was, by contrast with the other Morgan, not intent on planning from above. Nor was he, as were other ideologists in the New Deal, interested in transforming from below the relative status, income, and power of the social, racial, and economic groups of the region. He was true, in this respect, to the post–Civil War ethos of the white South, which distrusted all "carpetbaggers" but reserved special scorn, to borrow the words of Johnathon Daniels, for "the ones who came down here to improve us."[49]

Finally, H. A. Morgan saw no possibility of a great leap forward in human progress. Indeed, if he possessed an image of historical time at all, it was a profoundly conservative one. The widespread acceptance of the common mooring would bring *back* putatively happier and healthier conditions to southern life. Thus, H. A. Morgan distrusted the quick and radical breaks from common practice advocated by A. E. Morgan.

David E. Lilienthal

Arthur Morgan had not noted the philosophic differences between himself and Harcourt Morgan when he recommended the agriculturalist to the president. What he admired was Morgan's personal integrity and dedication to public service. In recommending to the president a man to fill the remaining board position, Arthur Morgan again took no notice of conflicting world-views. He did, however, appreciate at the earliest date that David Lilienthal's personality was in tension with his own.

A. E. Morgan came to believe many years after the fact that Roosevelt had been determined to appoint Lilienthal to the board regardless of Morgan's recommendation. Roosevelt was beholden, Morgan reasoned, to the Progressive senators who backed the young utilities expert. Roosevelt's actions at the time of this appointment suggest, however, that such considerations were not paramount. In fact, Morgan himself brought up Lilienthal's name. Before he did so, Roosevelt suggested two other men to Morgan, both of whom Morgan argued against on the basis of their reputations as vehement opponents of the private utility companies. As Morgan repeatedly stated, his intention was not to fight the utilities but to reason with them. Significantly for the future of the TVA, Morgan took the president's willingness to drop these two candidates as another solemn indication that Roosevelt backed Morgan's conciliatory and cooperative power policy.[50]

In looking for a replacement candidate, Morgan sought the advice of Justice Louis Brandeis, who praised David Lilienthal as an expert on utilities regulation and as a man dedicated to the public good. Brandeis had heard his daughter and her husband, who were active in the battle to establish public service commissions in the states, speak highly of Lilienthal. Brandeis had also a short time before met personally with Lilienthal, at the suggestion of Felix Frankfurter. That meeting had come about when, in the winter of 1932, Lilienthal realized that his tenure with the Wisconsin Public Service Commission (which he had recently helped to establish) was insecure. Thus Lilienthal sought to broaden his contacts by seeking the advice of men such as the Supreme Court justice. Lilienthal reports in his diary that at their meeting, Brandeis gave him an overview of his philosophy of government and his agenda for the next administration. Lilienthal must have been impressed, for at the time of his appointment to the TVA board over half a year later he recorded in his journal that Roosevelt's ideas for the TVA sounded "very much like Brandeis's ideas applied to a particular area."[51]

Acting on Brandeis's recommendation, though convinced that he had suggested Lilienthal's name only by the happenstance that the justice's daughter had once spoken favorably of the man, Morgan interviewed

Lilienthal at the Palmer House in Chicago on May 30. Before the interview, Morgan investigated his subject and reported his findings to the president. In a telegram to Roosevelt, Morgan described his future nemesis as "brilliant, thorough, accurate, aggressive, fair, loyal, and committed to public interests." "His shortcomings," Morgan noted, were "personal ambition and not too dignified methods of satisfying [a] craving for publicity."[52] Morgan's interview confirmed this mixed but generally favorable report.[53]

Morgan knew, to some extent, that he was inviting trouble with this appointment.[54] Morgan even recalled long afterward that a personal friend had warned him that Lilienthal was likely to "steal the show" from him, which he did.[55] But Morgan believed that he could control other men by his acute application of psychology. Thus as the TVA got under way, he purposely entrusted Lilienthal with power that he might use against the chairman, thinking that this would allay the younger man's "natural envy" of the older, more experienced man's position and authority.[56] What Morgan did not know, and refused to recognize later, was that Lilienthal was different from him in ideological terms and was, in fact, a member of a network of like-minded individuals under the tutelage of Brandeis and Frankfurter, whose chosen enemies were planners such as himself.

Morgan was considerably more perceptive about Lilienthal's ambition. Lilienthal was only thirty-three at the time of his appointment to the TVA board. He had been on a fast track since his days as an undergraduate at De Paul University, where he excelled in athletics and public speaking and was elected president of the student body. In his first year at Harvard Law School, after deciding to become a labor lawyer, he courted the friendship of Felix Frankfurter and Frank P. Walsh, a prominent labor lawyer. After graduation, Frankfurter and Walsh helped place Lilienthal with Donald Richberg's small Chicago law firm.

In Chicago, Lilienthal began to seek more auspicious avenues for his ambition. He contributed to popular journals, took part in the La Follette presidential campaign of 1924, and drafted progressive legislation for the Illinois legislature. Soon, he was looking about for a field less well-trodden than labor law in which he could make a bigger name for himself in less time. By his thirtieth birthday, Lilienthal had become an acknowledged leader in his new specialty—public utility law.[57]

Lilienthal's last career step before joining the TVA was his appointment by Governor Philip La Follette to the Wisconsin Railroad Commission, soon transformed under Lilienthal's leadership into the Wisconsin Public Service Commission. His vision of the commission as "an aggressive fact-finding agency armed with administrative powers to seek out the facts and act upon those facts" led him to deal authoritatively with even the holding companies that controlled local power companies. Lilienthal thus dissented from the traditional judicial conception of the work of state regulatory bodies. He was sufficiently daring, in fact, that the legislative confirmation of his reappointment by a lame-duck governor was far from certain.[58]

The facts of Lilienthal's career do not confirm him as a likely member of any particular ideological camp. Progressivism was a diffuse movement, and Lilienthal's involvement in it had been narrowly focused on specific issues. Also, though a student of Felix Frankfurter, he was not chosen by the professor for a clerkship with Justice Brandeis or another top federal judge, honors reserved for Frankfurter's most promising students. Perhaps Frankfurter recognized that beneath the surface, Lilienthal's views on the major issues with which liberals were engaged were only partially formed.

From his college years through his battle with Arthur Morgan, Lilienthal was troubled by his inability to articulate a "philosophy of life." Before entering law school, for instance, Lilienthal recorded in his diary his repugnance toward harsh working conditions and his concern for the quality of life among laborers but fretted because he was unable to give theoretical or philosophical force to these feelings beyond a superficial echoing of socialist polemics. In law school, Lilienthal was still intent on dramatic changes to better the lives of laborers but had, in his words, "fortunately lost the appetite for revolutionary phrases and emotion-arousers—the stock phrases of 'wage-slaves, curse of capitalism,' etc., and so on." "Too much passion," he remarked, "is being lavished on dreaming of the revolution—too little thought expended on how it will be made a sane, happy, orderly revolution."[59] It would be years before Lilienthal worked out for himself the content of this hoped-for revolution.

In the midst of the TVA controversy, Lilienthal was still unsure of himself ideologically. In a diary entry in April 1937, he wrote a highly perceptive "self-appraisal," noting that although he was very bright, he was "not profound." He possessed a "strong rebellious impulse" with respect especially to "economic and social matters," but this was "largely emotional and instinctive." "You have been carried along so far," he wrote, "by an intense and absorbing desire for achievement, the contest spirit; make a place for yourself; get somewhere, etc. . . . In five years in public life you have leaped from relative obscurity to a place near the top. What are you going to do with it now that you have got what you have been driving for?" A final entry of this sort was dated January 10, 1939, after Morgan's humiliation and Lilienthal's ascendancy to the unofficial leadership of the board. Lilienthal, perhaps feeling guilty that he could not rationalize his success in more principled terms—in the language, that is, of Arthur Morgan—confessed: "Last night the puzzle that has been going through my head repeatedly came to a focus somewhat in this question. What is your philosophy? What is the conviction that ties everything together into a life, that integrates all the parts of your life, that keeps you going? I don't know the answer. . . . It has been troubling me a good deal."

Even if Lilienthal did not know his own mind very well, his self-observed "emotions" and "instincts," as well as his relationships with Frankfurter, Brandeis, and Corcoran,[60] predisposed Lilienthal to recognize planners as his ideological enemies when he encountered them in the TVA. Planning, he observed while a TVA director, "has an attraction for persons of a vague and diffuse kind of mind given to grandiose pictures not of this world." As a TVA director, Lilienthal would on many occasions express his distaste for "human engineers," "uplift," and "a patronizing kind of benevolence."[61] He was drawn, consequently, to find inspiration in the Brandeisian creed, a halfway house in his trek toward an independent philosophy of life.

In the years after his dispute with A. E. Morgan, while still serving the TVA, Lilienthal finally developed his emotions, biases, inclinations, and instincts into something approaching a comprehensive world-view. He announced his achievement in the popular volume *TVA: Democracy on the March*, first published in 1944. The philosophy expressed in this book is "grass roots" democratic planning.[62] Quoting Whitman, incorporating H. A. Morgan's conception of a common mooring, and praising the good sense of the people of the Tennessee River Valley, in this volume Lilienthal described himself and his followers as "dreamers with shovels," a phrase the president liked sufficiently well to comment upon its aptness for his entire administration.[63]

In a typical passage, Lilienthal approvingly quotes from Thurman Arnold's *Symbols of Government:* "[Utopian planners] usually bungle their brief opportunities in power because they are too much in love with an ideal society to treat the one actually before them with skill and understanding. Their constant and futile cry is reiterated through the ages: 'Let us educate the people so that they can understand and appreciate us.'" By contrast: "Here is the life principle of democratic planning . . . an awakening in the whole people of a sense of this common moral purpose. Not one plan, once and for all, but the conscious selection by the people of successive plans."[64] In the Tennessee Valley, Lilienthal would later remark, he found "an extraordinary capacity for citizen managerial leadership."[65] It was imperative that this capacity be allowed to flourish, furthermore, because, as Lilienthal noted in a 1949 volume, "big government will get bigger and more highly centralized unless there is a conscious, continuous, creative administrative and legislative effort to reverse the trend." Aiding this effort, Lilienthal wrote, was the central mission of the TVA under his leadership.[66]

Commentators as diverse as Philip Selznick, Edward Banfield, and Rexford Tugwell have cast a critical eye upon grass roots planning. The grass roots approach as applied particularly to the agricultural program of the TVA, Selznick found, did not represent so much a departure from past practices as an adaptation to them. The grass roots theory rationalized the TVA's reliance upon the land grant colleges and extension service and those organizations' hostility to the more unsettling agricultural endeavors of other administrative units in the New Deal. Without such an accommodating theory behind them, however, the TVA's innovators might not have accomplished anything at all, Selznick argued.[67] Banfield and Tugwell have offered similar analyses, though the latter, especially, thought the theory's functional utility was a poor excuse for its promulgation.[68]

The grass roots theory, although very much the personal product of its author, was highly compatible with the ideology of the Brandeis-Frankfurter nexus. Lilienthal, in his elaboration of the ideas he followed during his struggle against Morgan, made claims, as did all Brandeisians, to a logically certain and compelling explanatory framework. Like the justice, furthermore, Lilienthal was hostile if not close-minded about there being a planning path to publicly useful knowledge. The planners were not to be compromised with, but defeated if at all possible, for they possessed no legitimate alternative view of society. Lilienthal's framework, it was also claimed, comprehended the various domestic functions of government, though not of all human life. Absolute knowledge, meanwhile, was claimed in the negative terms of the mainstream twentieth-century American liberal. Lilienthal was also Brandeisian in his failure to ascribe value to people categorically. Lilienthal's institutional links to the Brandeisian cadre, especially through his mentor Frankfurter but also through the Progressive senatorial bloc and the person of Thomas Corcoran, were established early in the TVA feud. Finally, even when he departed from the ideal type of ideological thought, Lilienthal aligned himself with the Brandeisians; that is, like Brandeis, Frankfurter, and their other protégés, Lilienthal articulated an essentially conservative, non-imminent, historical consciousness.

Taking a wide view, then, we may see the TVA board as divided between persons associated with the two principal warring factions of ideologues in the New Deal. In the process of thrashing out a mission for the TVA, it did not take long for the potential for conflict so evident in this arrangement to be realized.

The Feud within the Board

Stage 1: Organizational Matters and Positioning

When they sat down for their first board meeting on June 16, two of the three directors of the TVA were quite certain they knew what the president intended for their agency. David Lilienthal "knew" that Roosevelt had in mind an application of what the director from Wisconsin thought of as Brandeis's ideas. Consequently, Lilienthal put the issue of the "power trust" and what the TVA might do to break it at the top of the TVA's agenda. Arthur Morgan was even more certain that he knew the agency's intended mission: the TVA was "a chance to create a new cultural environment." Roosevelt, he later recorded, "had much the same outlook. . . . To his mind, too, [the TVA] should be concerned with *every aspect of the region's well-being*" (emphasis added).[69] Harcourt Morgan, meanwhile, at first stayed clear of the issues dividing his colleagues, being primarily concerned with the authority's agricultural program. Still, he gradually began to edge toward Lilienthal's side in the confrontation over whose understanding of the president's intentions was to prevail in the TVA.

In their earliest associations, H. A. Morgan was assiduously cultivated by Lilienthal. Lilienthal, following the pattern of his law school years, allegedly flattered and drew close to the older man, becoming his "chauffeur" as well as his confidante. Arthur Morgan later claimed, in fact, that Lilienthal even arranged the office architecture so as to increase his contact with Harcourt Morgan, while limiting the prospects for casual association between the two Morgans.[70] Arthur Morgan, for his part, annoyed the other two directors with his imperious manner. He had begun to make decisions for the board before it was actually convened, and he did not hide his irritation at having to change his ways after the board began its collective work. After only two weeks in operation, Arthur Morgan complained to his wife, "Ours is one of the few agencies in the government that is being run by a debating society instead of by one man, and it takes time when we might be moving with speed."[71] These personal tensions worsened over time.

The ideological cleavages within the board also quickly grew more troublesome. As Lilienthal recorded in his journal, the board members discussed at their first meeting what attitude to take toward the private utilities. "This," he foresaw in an entry from 1933, "will require a good deal of working out." A. E. Morgan, who abhorred competition and possessed a profound faith in the force of reason, insisted that the board approach the private utilities with an open mind. He also spoke grandly on this occasion of the broader vision he held for the TVA's work.

In an attempt to exercise his leadership, Morgan soon afterwards sought by memorandum to establish an understanding on power policy. The authority, he wrote, was intended "to promote the orderly and well proportioned development of the economic and social resources of the Tennessee river area, including the generation and transmission of power, as a beginning and as a laboratory of planned development." "The aim is not," he stated with obvious reference to Lilienthal's contrary view, "to begin a contest for the general substitution throughout the southern states of public for private operation at the present time."[72]

Morgan recommended instead an explicit division of territory with Commonwealth and Southern, the holding company managed by Wendell Willkie, which controlled most of the private utilities in the region. This division would continue for a fixed period of time, during which the authority would promise not to compete directly in areas already served by the private companies. At some later date the TVA might expand its operations beyond the boundaries of this covenant. In fact, if the experiment worked well, the private companies would be asked voluntarily to relinquish additional portions of their service area to the public authority. Morgan urged quick action because without such an agreement,

> the present course, of discussing the sale of power with all inquirers, but with no suggestion of policy to the private utilities, is equal to a declaration of war, and tends to result in attitudes which will lead to competition through duplication. . . . The present course . . . will surely result in an attitude of strife and antagonism.

And this, he assured his associates, was against "President Roosevelt's opinion . . . that the Tennessee Valley Authority should limit the area of its activities in power transmission, and should, if feasible, maintain harmonious relations with private utilities." Morgan added in conclusion that the delay in reaching agreement on a policy was embarrassing him before Willkie.[73]

Lilienthal objected strenuously to Morgan's ideas. Making such an agreement with the private utilities, he thought, would be premature at best. Instead of a grand plan now, Lilienthal recommended "that we proceed carefully from one point to another, feeling our way as we go along acquiring more information about the territory, our other objectives, etc." Overly ambitious planning, Lilienthal reminded Morgan, had the tendency to involve "the making of far-reaching commitments the consequences of which we cannot foresee." Furthermore, Lilienthal wrote, "candor compels me to say that I am most skeptical that we can hope for genuine 'cooperation' with the private utilities." Such a presumption runs "counter to every reasonable expectation." In conclusion, Lilienthal advised (or warned) the chairman that he would seek the advice of some "time-tested public men," including Senator Norris, on this matter.[74]

At a meeting in early August, Harcourt Morgan, per prior agreement with Lilienthal, proposed a formal division of responsibilities that solidified but temporarily prevented the explosion of these cleavages. Lilienthal was to handle utilities and legal affairs, Harcourt Morgan the agricultural program, and A. E. Morgan engineering, construction, social and economic planning, forestry, and the integration of the authority's work. Because they flawlessly utilized the logrolling potential in this arrangement, Harcourt Morgan and Lilienthal became virtually sovereign in their own domains.[75] The board members were able to divide administrative responsibilities among themselves in this way, it should be recalled, because the TVA law was nearly as vague with respect to the actual structure and conduct of the board as it was with respect to the purposes to which its work should be directed.

By attempting occasionally to coordinate the board's work, Arthur Morgan managed, however, to keep alive the board's debate on principles. By not absenting himself from power disputes, that is, Morgan continued to provoke the ire of Lilienthal. And while Lilienthal feared that Arthur Morgan was overly solicitous of the other person's point of view when dealing with Wendell Willkie, he feared that the chairman was too quick to command and dictate to the common people of the valley. In his first major address as a TVA board member, Lilienthal appropriated the pejorative tag made popular by Herbert Hoover to denounce what he saw as the weakness of Chairman Morgan's philosophy. There was a danger in planning, Lilienthal intoned, "of *regimentation*—of pouring human beings into and communities into a mold fashioned from above."[76]

In a more positive vein, Lilienthal stressed in his speeches the issue of public power. This fit well with the common interpretation of the TVA as "an attempt at revolution through electricity." Lilienthal frequently reiterated this theme. In a speech in October 1933, for example, he quoted Stuart Chase, a prolific extoller of the marvels of electricity, the spread of which promised "the oncoming of a new kind of civilization . . . a world replete with more freedom and happiness than mankind has ever known."[77]

In line with this popular interpretation of the TVA's mission, Lilienthal pressed for greatly expanded consumption of electricity as a part of the TVA's power policy. The rapid diffusion of electric appliances would sufficiently increase demand, he argued, to allow the TVA to achieve economies of scale in the generation and distribution of its product. As a consequence, the TVA might promulgate a low yardstick value for the private utilities to match. As for the broader purposes of the TVA, Lilienthal observed, characteristically: "This long-range program calls for hard-headed idealism. It must be idealistic, so that the President's objectives will not be lost in a mass of detail. . . . But it must be hard-headed and practical. . . . We are grappling here not with an academic exercise, but with the most stubborn and ruthless facts of present day life."[78]

Lilienthal's jibes at Morgan would become more direct as the years passed, but it was already evident to whom he referred when he spoke derisively of the overly "idealistic" person who saw the TVA as an "academic" exercise. Rexford Tugwell had tried to dissuade Morgan from publicizing prematurely those aspects of his vision for the TVA that prompted Lilienthal's remarks, but Morgan ignored his supporter's advice. Consequently, as an admiring researcher has somewhat reluctantly observed,

"Some of Morgan's ideas, if interpreted as firm and imminent policy, did sound strange."[79]

Dr. Arthur Morgan proposed a cooperative economic system with its own tokens of credit for parts of the valley. The editor of a local paper who had been cultivated by Lilienthal sarcastically proposed coonskins as the new legal tender. In his public comments and in magazine articles, Morgan habitually referred to the valley as a "laboratory," which led to talk of the people of the region as Morgan's guinea pigs. Morgan proposed state legislation under which land improperly cultivated would be forcibly purchased and resold "to someone who will treat it properly." With an equally heavy hand, the chairman tactlessly observed to businessmen that there were "at least four times as many merchants" as were needed in most American cities, and to local politicians that there were far too many layers and units of government below the state level. And he proposed a code of ethics for TVA employees the enforcement of which would have required the government to probe into the drinking, gambling, and even sexual habits of its employees.[80]

The thrust of the chairman's ideas was interpreted in very positive tones by foreign devotees of centralized planning. Even after Morgan had been forced from the scene, Julian Huxley, for example, was able to see in the TVA the promise of grand government planning. Writing in 1943, he said, "Although the adjustment of the individualist traditions of private enterprise to the needs of central planning is apt to generate friction . . . the friction can be minimized by understanding." Huxley, perhaps with Morgan's experiences in mind, cautioned that understanding was required of the planners as well as the planned-for. "The planner," he wrote in the same work, "placed in charge of the destinies of a region finds himself in a position not unlike that of Jesus when the devil took him up into the high mountain to tempt him with all the kingdoms of the earth and the glory of them. . . . So the planner sees the grandeur and beauty of his plan, and thinks of all the happiness that he will be able to confer. But what really tempts him is the lure of power." Despite the difficulty, the planner "must not fall down and worship the devil of power."[81] A few years earlier, there had been many who worried that Chairman Morgan might not be able to resist the temptations described by Huxley. Morgan gave such worriers little comfort when, for instance, in a speech in Chattanooga in April 1934, he openly implied that the TVA might indeed be undemocratic, as its critics had charged. "In a perfect government," he said on that occasion, "there would be some elements of communism, some of democracy, some of technocracy, and some of dictatorship." What mattered was, not which model best described the situation, but "to achieve sincerity towards oneself and others . . . and to nurture a strong and passionate commitment to serve the common good."[82]

The fullest flowering of Morgan's utopianism came in his plans for the area around the TVA's new dam at Norris, Tennessee. Early efforts were made to make the relocation of tenant farmers from the Norris Dam reservoir to other locales an experiment in cooperative living. Under the plan drawn up by Morgan's aides, families who volunteered to enter the intended "experiment" would, in the words of one of the plan's authors, be "forced into a close-knit community" to determine whether their renowned individualism was really a "condition and not a characteristic." Though this resettlement program was halted before it began by the TVA's legal department, under the direction of James Fly, a Lilienthal ally, a more sustained effort at planning was undertaken for the model town of Norris itself.[83]

Norris, a planned community for the builders and, later, the operators of the Norris Dam, was to be the cooperative commonwealth in microcosm. Its inhabitants were in fact treated like few other employees of a major construction enterprise. They were surrounded with educational and cultural opportunities (including classes in English, government, history, arithmetic, home planning, music, and more) and were given time to make use of them. They were housed in TVA-owned homes and dormitories, situated as if Norris were an English garden city, with rings of small buildings surrounded by woods.[84] Scientific experts were on call to help the villagers with their education, their home life, and even the planting of their gardens. Everything was designed to promote cooperation.[85] There was to be but one store for each category of goods that the authority determined the people should desire. Thus the Norris Cooperative Society, which operated the village's food store and service station, was guided and subsidized by the TVA board. When the venture could not pay rent, its rent payments were waived. When the venture could not meet its debt obligations, the authority picked up the tab.[86] Competition among institutions of religion, communion, and philanthropy was also to be proscribed. A controversy flared up within Norris and among observers nationwide, in fact, when it became apparent that the authority, in its "comprehensive" planning for this Bible Belt community, had made no provisions for religious observances.[87]

Some southerners resented the town of Norris, Tennessee. As one historian from the South has sarcastically written, "Country folks could not live in a park, away from means of subsistence. And anyway, in those rather small houses, just what would you do with a pack of children and a lot of kinfolks?"[88] And to Westbrook Pegler, a contemporary critic from the region, Norris seemed implicitly to insult the communities already in existence in the region. To him, Norris was "Camp Fauntleroy." It seemed to tell the visitor that the natives "on the whole had done rather poorly" with their resources.[89] The community did seem to others, though, as late as the mid 1940s, to be thriving as a home for the TVA's more permanent employees, whatever its value to the natives of the region.

Stage 2: The Reappointment Crisis

Between the spring of 1933 and the spring of 1936, the TVA grew tremendously. The construction program in particular got off to a fast start. Five major dams were under construction in 1936, and there was virtually unanimous praise from the press and expert observers on the competence and public-spiritedness of the TVA's thousands of employees. The agricultural program, under Harcourt Morgan, was productive as well, manufacturing phosphate fertilizers at the Muscle Shoals plant as a fundamental step toward revitalizing the region's common mooring.[90] Although Dr. Morgan's program was considerably more cautious and conservative than either the president or Chairman Morgan would have preferred, he was allowed to proceed. This was largely a matter of priorities. The power program under Lilienthal raised larger and more contentious issues. Furthermore, Arthur Morgan believed that Harcourt Morgan deserved a great deal of latitude because he was a good man. "I know less about [H. A. Morgan's] program than I do about that of Mr. Lilienthal," wrote the chairman in 1936, "but I have such regard for his ability and for his personal integrity of purpose that I have not been worried about the operation of that program."[91]

Lilienthal's work in the first three years of the authority's existence was also at least moderately successful. Lilienthal negotiated in this period a multiyear contract with Commonwealth and Southern that was generous enough to the utility to please Arthur Morgan yet left the TVA sufficiently free to distribute its electricity, which satisfied Lilienthal and his trust-busting friends. The president was also pleased. On a three-day trip through the valley, Roosevelt exulted at Tupelo, Mississippi, to whose residents the TVA had brought electricity: "What you are doing here is going to be copied in every State of the Union before we get through." "This," he continued, in his characteristic effort to synthesize diverse perspectives, "is not regimentation; it is community rugged individualism [in which the individual] is going to be encouraged in every known way from the national capital and the state capital and the county seat to use his individualism in cooperation with his neighbors' individualism so that he and his neighbors together may improve their lot in life."[92] And Tennessee River Basin congressmen also thrilled to Lilienthal's electrification of the region's hitherto neglected areas, as well as to the employment the projects of the authority brought to the valley. These benefits offset the hard feelings some members of Congress harbored because of the lack of patronage in the TVA. (The TVA took seriously the principle of meritocracy in hiring of its personnel.)[93] All of this progress, however, could not mask the disharmony within the TVA when in 1936 Arthur Morgan sought to block Lilienthal's reappointment to the board. In the ensuing controversy, members of the executive and congressional leadership became heavily involved.

By 1936 Morgan had concluded that Lilienthal had to go. To begin with, he had been violating what was to Morgan a central tenet of the TVA's policy, the proscription against political appointments. Morgan believed that his junior colleague had secured two low-level jobs for friends of a couple of Tennessee congressmen. The TVA's personnel director, and a Morgan ally, Floyd Reeves, even refused to sign the appointment papers of one of these men without a request from the board. In addition, Morgan had been informed that Lilienthal was controlling the TVA's Washington office so as to circumvent the chairman. Morgan was further aware of rumors that Lilienthal was criticizing Morgan in conversations with congressional and public power leaders. Finally, Morgan was suspicious that Lilienthal was not being fair with the private utility companies in determining yardstick rates. Morgan interpreted this last transgression as a threat to his professional and personal honor: he had given his word to the president and to Wendell Willkie that he would deal with the private utilities on a gentlemanly and cooperative basis.[94]

Lilienthal's term on the board was scheduled to end on May 18, 1936. In the fall of 1935, Morgan discussed his problems with Roosevelt at Warm Springs. At that meeting, Roosevelt went so far as to discuss with Morgan possible successors for Lilienthal. This left Morgan with the impression that Lilienthal was not to be reappointed. "So far as I could see, he entirely agreed with me."[95] Several months later, Morgan brought up the matter with Harcourt Morgan, who seemed not to be unduly concerned. Arthur Morgan even sought the support at this time of Senator Norris, who said he was committed to Lilienthal so long as President Roosevelt seemed to be, and Harold Ickes, who was more sympathetic. Ickes recorded in his diary that A. E. Morgan had come to him "seeking information" about Lilienthal and threatening to quit if his co-director were reappointed.[96]

Morgan's efforts were unsuccessful, as the president quietly reappointed Lilienthal. In part, Lilienthal had won the right to stay by outmaneuvering Arthur Morgan in the month before the president's decision. Lilienthal had learned just one month before his appointment was to lapse that he was in danger. With his considerable political skills and contacts, Lilienthal mobilized support rapidly. The La Follettes, Felix Frankfurter, and other public power advocates spoke to Roosevelt on Lilienthal's behalf during this crucial period. Furthermore, Lilienthal, with the help of Frankfurter, Benjamin Cohen, and Senator La Follette, wrote to Senator Norris a masterful letter putting forth, in the context most favorable to Lilienthal's position, the issues dividing the board. The real debate, it was asserted in this letter, was over power policy. Would the TVA acquiesce to the private utilities' demands or be tough enough to fight? Roosevelt, the authors of this document surely recognized, was speaking in combative tones in 1936, the year in which he "welcomed the hatred" of the economic royalists who were "unanimous in their hatred" of him. The power trusters had, in any event, long been central figures in Roosevelt's hagiography, and Lilienthal and his friends were quick to take advantage of this.

Roosevelt found himself, consequently, in a dilemma. The feud's ramifications for his plans eventually to pursue the establishment of regional authorities in other parts of the nation could not easily be separated, he thought at this time, from the partisan and personal issues involved. Thus he explained to Lilienthal, in regard to the choice Morgan was trying to force upon him: "We just can't have either thing happen. . . . If I don't reappoint you, it will be heralded all over the country as a power company victory, and if he resigns . . . coming at this time, it will be bad for the project and for the whole idea of planning." In an ominous finale intended perhaps to motivate the impressionable Lilienthal to rally behind his chief, Roosevelt warned: "If we fail . . . we may be faced not only with economic and social revolution, but (here he leaned forward and pointed at me) political revolution."[97]

With Chairman Morgan, Roosevelt also used a range of explanations and persuasions. The government's effort to conserve human resources was at stake, he reminded the conservationist of human resources. If Lilienthal were dropped, it would be seen as "the first victory against your fundamental beliefs and mine." Roosevelt even made an appeal to Morgan's charity, or presumed humility. "I have told you," he wrote to Morgan, "of the somewhat heavy load which is on my shoulders at the present time. I ask your sympathetic consideration."[98] With both men, the president used one last tactic: dissimulation. As Thomas McCraw, the noted business historian, reports, Roosevelt hinted to each man that after the election he might get rid of the other.[99]

Stage 3: The Power Pool and the White House Hearing

Although Morgan was hopeful that the president would transfer Lilienthal out of the TVA after the elections, he sought immediately after Lilienthal's reappointment to increase his influence, as chairman, over the TVA's range of activities. Thus he proposed that a general manager, to be nominated by the chairman, be put in charge of administration. A board of consultants, also to be nominated by Morgan, would develop long-range power and agricultural goals, and all future decisions of the board would have to be unanimous.

After talking privately to the president, Morgan believed him to be in full accord with this plan. At a meeting with all three directors, however, the president rejected the unanimity provision, the chairman's prerogative in making appointments, and the hiring of consultants to watch over the areas of policy previously delegated to Arthur Morgan's co-directors. Rebuffed once again by Roosevelt, Morgan temporarily retreated to his Ohio homestead to contemplate his situation. His feelings of persecution became so intense that at one point during this self-imposed exile he seems to have believed that Lilienthal was in a conspiracy to make the TVA the southern front of a new political alignment, one that would include neither Arthur Morgan nor Franklin Roosevelt. (The La Follettes, Senator Norris, Harcourt Morgan, and James Farley were the other imagined conspirators.)[100]

Arthur Morgan was jolted from his ruminations by a heartening letter from President Roosevelt. FDR, writing to Morgan in July, advised the chairman that his input was necessary to determine the "future of the 'yardstick' in TVA area," as well as the "broader problem in other parts of the country." In conclusion, Roosevelt seemed to suggest, again, that he might be willing to take the chairman's special problems under further consideration if Morgan would consult with him. "The best thing Alfred E. Smith ever said in the old days," the president wrote, "was 'most problems can be resolved by reasonable men if they will sit around a table with a box of cigars and a few long drinks.' I am not certain about the necessity of the cigars and the long drinks but I am very certain about the sitting around the table."[101]

Morgan might not have been so heartened by this note had he known that three days before he wrote it, the president had received a letter from his longtime adviser, Morris L. Cooke. Cooke had written to advise FDR that Arthur Morgan needed some attention, for he was still "quite upset about the TVA situation and especially as to Lilienthal. At the moment, he is in Yellow Springs trying to make up his mind what he ought to do, write a series of letters to the *New York Times*, resign or do something else." This information, Cooke wrote, had come from a friend of Morgan's who had reported that the chairman was "a tired and overwrought man who should have a long rest."[102] Probably most troubling to President Roosevelt was that Morgan might publicize the feud and put him in the embarrassing situation of having to seem to repudiate trust busting or planning, both of which he favored. When Morgan came back to work after two months' rustication, he did so believing that he had the president's personal "assurance" that Lilienthal would be removed at a later date. He thus refrained not only from writing to the papers but from responding to Lilienthal's implicit criticisms in public speeches.

Lilienthal sought at this time to expand even further the framework of perception within which the TVA battle was to be viewed. What separated Arthur Morgan from his co-directors was no longer merely a matter of power policy, much less of petty personality conflicts, but a titanic struggle between contrasting visions of governance. In a speech before TVA employees, Lilienthal proclaimed that he had "no confidence in progress that comes from plans concocted by supermen and imposed upon the rest of the community for its own good" and warned against the "temptation to develop a kind of Alexander-the-Great complex among those of us who are carrying on this project."[103]

Morgan, meanwhile, moved in the opposite direction. He declared privately to some of his allies that his difficulties with Lilienthal did not involve power policy, philosophy, or other substantive issues. It was a matter, he insisted, of personal integrity. Because Lilienthal's character was not popularly seen to be at issue, however, this approach, which Morgan later took public, was a tactical error. This error, in fact, would eventually be used against Morgan not only by Lilienthal but by H. A. Morgan and FDR as well.

Also in Lilienthal's favor going into 1937 was the fact that his ideological allies had been gaining access and power throughout the administration. Lilienthal, furthermore, was not reticent about calling on his friends for help. Thus he rather frequently corresponded with his mentor, Frankfurter, and with Corcoran, as well as with congressional allies, including Senator Norris, and friendly newspaper editors. At Corcoran's suggestion, Harold Ickes was even brought into the action early in 1937. "According to Tom [Corcoran]," Ickes recorded in his diary on September 12, "there is in the making some sort of flood-control set up for the Ohio River Valley and the plan is to take Arthur Morgan from TVA and put him at this new job. I suggested this plan over the telephone to the president some time ago at Tom's instance and the president thought well of it although he doubted whether he could do it administratively."[104] With the president himself, Lilienthal was sympathetic. At one point, Roosevelt remarked to him that Arthur Morgan "is a human engineer . . . he likes the idea of getting people out of the caves and onto a better way of living. You aren't a human engineer."[105] This fit with Lilienthal's seeming plan to broaden the perspective of the dispute. But when Roosevelt took a different approach, Lilienthal moved quickly to agreement. "I'm blessed if I know what policy it is Arthur Morgan wants," the president complained to Lilienthal at one point. "He has talked to me about it, but I haven't the faintest notion what he wants. Have you?" Lilienthal replied, "No, frankly, I haven't. It is too vague for me to follow, and changes so rapidly."[106]

The board became entangled about this time in disputes over policy that led to the president's decisive intervention. A power pooling arrangement was pursued, with the president participating in White House conferences with Wendell Willkie and others. Lilienthal was combative in these conferences, though he seemed at first sincerely to strive for an agreement. Arthur Morgan was upset by Lilienthal's attitude but became caught up in the idea of using the pooling contract to validate his contrasting approach to the issue of the TVA's relations with the private utilities. When, in the middle of the conference, after the November 1936 elections, a federal court, acting on a suit brought against the TVA by a consortium of private utilities, including several affiliated with Willkie's company, issued a sweeping injunction that paralyzed the TVA's expansion, Arthur Morgan made a mistake. As McCraw relates, he "seemed willing to ignore the injunction because he did not believe Willkie to be responsible for it."[107] Lilienthal, by contrast, responded aggressively, accusing Willkie, who might have persuaded the plaintiffs to delay their suit, of a breach of faith. Norris, Cooke, and others were even more outspoken. Roosevelt, perhaps simply not wishing to negotiate from such a weakened position, went along with the combative faction and ended the talks. Morgan thus entrapped himself, appearing to Norris to have gone over to the power trust. To Roosevelt, Morgan appeared naive and "befuddled."[108]

As of the summer of 1936 there had been leaks, planted stories, and personal pleas to President Roosevelt. In the aftermath of the power pooling debacle, more explicit charges and countercharges were aired in the media and in letters to Senator Norris and to Maury Maverick, a congressman from San Antonio whose reputation was the equal of his name. Editorial writers began to take sides or at least to call for decisive presidential action.

While Morgan stuck to his strategy of personal recriminations, Lilienthal continued to rally support from behind the scenes. Thus the La Follettes (father and sons) privately urged Roosevelt to get rid of Morgan, while Senator McKellar of Tennessee urged the same thing publicly. John Rankin, the senator in charge of an important committee overseeing TVA work, reported in a letter to a confederate at the time, "Our friends in the TVA area [i.e., friends of Lilienthal's and Lilienthal himself] are now perfecting their organization, taking in only the ones they know to be absolutely with us."[109]

Meanwhile, Morgan published stories in the *New Republic,* the *New York Times,* and the *Atlantic Monthly* in which he took poorly disguised swipes at the integrity of both his co-directors. (He was by now certain that H. A. Morgan had become the co-conspirator of his nemesis.) He accused them indirectly, but clearly enough given the publicity surrounding the matter by this time, of "incitement to class hatred," the "development of dramatic political issues on which a few men may ride to public prominence," and plain "impropriety" in the conduct of their offices. He also accused the "majority members" of the board of publishing "false and misleading propaganda" about the private utilities.[110]

The press stories and Morgan's articles were too much for the president to overlook. Fortunately for the president, he had dealt with such a situation before. While he was governor, Roosevelt had forced the resignation of the troublesome and embarrassing mayor of New York City by serving personally as the chief interrogator, judge, and jury in an executive hearing on charges of corruption brought against the man. Not only was Jimmy Walker thus forced into early retirement but Roosevelt's reputation for wisdom and justice was enhanced. Roosevelt's patience was great, the hearings suggested, but had been tested beyond endurance by an insolent subordinate. Finally, this method had focused attention on the personal battle between the governor and the accused, and it was the individual, not a class of potential supporters (Tammany Democrats), who was repudiated in the end. Transferred to the TVA, the intended outcome would preserve whatever support the president still enjoyed by that time among Arthur Morgan's supporters, including those excited by his talk of planning. Roosevelt looked forward, after all, to extending the TVA concept throughout the nation. He did not want the planning conception of the authority to be tarnished any more than he wished the Brandeisian conception to suffer harm. At the same time, Roosevelt might satisfy the chairman's enemies with a human sacrifice.

All three directors were thus summoned to the White House on March 11, 1938, to substantiate their charges. Though he probably could not have known that Roosevelt had given advance notice to the other directors, Chairman Morgan, fearing an ambush, had to be summoned twice before agreeing to appear. By the time he did appear, the matter had become a national sensation. Roosevelt, H. A. Morgan, and David Lilienthal were well prepared. The president had had extensive memoranda prepared on each issue likely to be brought up. These documents, which suggested questions for the president, closely followed documents prepared earlier for FDR by the majority members of the board.

Consistent with the Jimmy Walker precedent, however, the "working papers" prepared by the majority members of the board and those used by the president in the hearings did differ in one important respect. The president's memos, unlike those of Lilienthal and Harcourt Morgan, focused on personal issues, denying that policy, much less ideology, was involved. The president's theme was Morgan's alleged "rule or ruin" attitude and his attacks on the character of his colleagues.[111] "I have reluctantly become convinced," the president solemnly announced on March 11, at the first session of these hearings,

> that the work of the TVA Board is now being impeded and that the real issues of public policy which may exist among its members are now being obscured by personal recriminations. It is intolerable to the people of the United States that issues of fundamental public policy should be confused with issues of personal integrity or misconduct. It is intolerable that either majority or minority members of an admin-

istration board should cast doubt upon the honesty, the good faith or the personal integrity of their colleagues, or should charge any of their colleagues with improperly obstructing the carrying out of the Board's decisions unless they are prepared to support such charges by good and sufficient evidence. If there be no such evidence then there should be either a definite end to such personal attacks and aspersions or else resignation from the Board.

I have called this hearing to investigate charges of dishonesty, bad faith and misconduct. I am not concerned at this hearing with the pros and cons of any particular policy.[112]

The president then proceeded to review Arthur Morgan's charges against the other board members, entering into the record numerous lengthy exhibits containing the chairman's allegations, and the president's correspondence with all three board members concerning these charges. The president next attempted to persuade Arthur Morgan to produce "bills of particulars" to support each of these charges. Morgan, however, would not respond beyond reading a short prepared statement.

In his statement, Morgan respectfully declined to answer the president's questions and offered his opinion that the necessary "information and appraisal can best be obtained and made available to the people, to Congress, and to the president by a Congressional Committee which will make an impartial, comprehensive and complete investigation of the Authority's affairs."[113] The hearing continued, without Morgan's participation, so as to establish a full record of charges and denials.

After failing at two more attempts over two weeks' time to elicit responses from Arthur Morgan, the president wrote Morgan on March 22, 1938, to demand his resignation.[114] Roosevelt was careful to substantiate this extraordinary dismissal in a five-thousand-word memorandum "decision," which he read into the record at the last meeting of the tribunal. In this decision, over which he labored personally, the president maintained his narrow focus on Morgan's "grave and libelous charges of dishonesty and want of integrity" against his fellow directors.[115] He also discussed Arthur Morgan's refusal to cooperate with his Chief Executive in a matter pertaining to the president's constitutional responsibility to see that the laws of the land are faithfully executed. Roosevelt wrote that he had been "patient" because of "the debt the public owes Arthur E. Morgan for past services, of his sense of the righteousness of his own convictions, and of the patience with which the public interest demands that a situation of this kind be worked out if possible." In the original draft of this decision, the next line had read: "I have therefore struggled with this problem for nearly two years and in its present acute form for six months." The president, perhaps mindful that this time he might have waited to resolve a bureaucratic conflict even longer than was his norm, struck out "nearly two years" and substituted for it, "over a year."[116]

The president's action did not entirely forestall a public examination of the nation's power and development policies. The Congress began to hold its own hearings into the affair shortly thereafter. Roosevelt was worried that at least two House members of the ten-man committee would use the opportunity to inveigh against the entire project.[117] Nevertheless, these hearings became so mired in complex factual presentations and Arthur Morgan's inability to match the evidence available to the personal recriminations he had indulged in that the matter was not advanced any further in his favor.

The committee was not predisposed, in any event, to favor the appeal of Arthur Morgan. The chairman, Senator Vic Donahey, former governor of Ohio, stated his concern at the outset. "I will resist," he pledged, "with all of the power at my command to keep from putting in the hands of the big utilities of this country any information that will help them wreck TVA." The expectations of the public were high that some wreckage might be done and that the smash-up would be revealing. But on the stand, Chairman Morgan retracted some of his most vitriolic prior assertions, and the press's attention to the matter waned. After several months of hearings, the committee's majority report concluded by commending Chairman Morgan's co-directors for their "forbearance and dignity."[118]

Morgan, to add to his problems, refused to accede graciously to his dismissal. Instead, he insisted that the president lacked the authority to fire him absent the provocations stipulated in the TVA's authorizing statute, being a lack of faith in the statute or indulgence in patronage appointments. His insolence in this matter carried him even to file a civil suit against his president, losing him the residual sympathy of such men as Harold Ickes and Senator Norris.

Neither fish nor fowl, the TVA continued to grow under David Lilienthal. Yet the potential of the authority as conceived by A. E. Morgan and, at times, by the president was not realized. No duplicate TVAs sprung up in the other regions of the nation. The quality of life of the valley's residents was changed by degree, not in kind, through the authority's programs;[119] and the dreams and ambitions of people of ideas were shown to be incidental, not central, to the achievements of President Roosevelt. As a fitting epilogue, in 1948 the town of Norris, Tennessee, was sold to a group of Philadelphia real estate speculators, and its homes were sold at auction.[120]

Conclusion

Democracy may be messy, but it preserves for the people the directive role in politics. Thus, in an era of strong parties and realignments, ideologues entered into the New Deal as bands of competing elites with impact more upon the details of policy than upon the fact of policy redirection itself. The New Deal realignment, that is, gave the nation's elected officials in 1933 a clear mandate for action to relieve economic and social crises and, thereafter, to provide for the security and stability of the population, but it did not give the president and the Congress a clear mandate to support either Brandeisian or Tugwellian action agendas. The strength of the party system thereby served democracy by weakening the impact upon policy that people of ideas might otherwise have enjoyed.

As the party's standard-bearer, Roosevelt personally reflected a profoundly nonideological perspective on this flagship program of his administration. The president never seemed to realize, in fact, the fundamental incommensurability of the two major directions in which his top appointees with ideological identifications were struggling to move the government. Indeed, when early in the first year of the TVA's existence, its board members trooped into Rexford Tugwell's office to ask his help in settling their dispute about the *true* purpose of the TVA, Tugwell was happy to give them his own ideas but said he could not presume to speak for Roosevelt. Furthermore, he did not have the courage, or the cruelty, to tell them, he wrote later, that there might not be a satisfactory answer to their question, that they might be but "the victims of an ill-considered idea" or the "expendable personalities in a presidential experiment."[121]

Roosevelt did not lay out priorities, it seems, because he wanted both planning and trust busting to remain open as options for the future. Roosevelt was free to keep contradictory options open, furthermore, because of the loose way in which the partisan contests of his time structured opinion on the dominant issues of the day. Thus, when Roosevelt spoke with Morgan and Lilienthal privately, he was both willing and able to encourage each in his own language. But when forced finally to resolve the ensuing conflict, the president eschewed the language of either man and spoke instead in the idiom best calculated to preserve his own, and his party's, power.

In conclusion, to Roosevelt, and to the era itself, if it may be personified, the TVA was preeminently a political, not an ideological, matter. Thus, when, at the end of this ordeal, someone sent Roosevelt a copy of the form letter Arthur Morgan was sending to his supporters, Roosevelt wrote over the top of this document his own humorous plea for the return of his most skilled political adviser to help him see this through: "PLEASE COME BACK TO ME LOUIS HOWE AND TELL ME HOW."[122]

Chapter Four
Creating Model Cities:
The Johnson Administration

On January 8, 1964, in his State of the Union address, President Lyndon Johnson declared "unconditional war on poverty in America." The first salvo to come from this administration was an antipoverty law with an innovative Community Action Program (CAP) at its core. CAP was nothing if not daring in intention. The brainchild of liberal sociologists, foundation executives, a can-do Kennedy loyalist who was the model for the hero of John Knowles's prep-school classic, *A Separate Peace,* and an intensely motivated cadre of activists within the government known as "Hackett's guerillas," CAP meant to empower the poor to demand fundamental changes in the distribution of power within their communities.[1] As in the case of the TVA, however, the most innovative aspect of the legislation was hastily included in the bill and largely overlooked in congressional debate. As Allen Matusow, a historian of the era, has written of the War on Poverty legislation, although "it was a highly controversial measure, and many of its proposals were intensely debated . . . Community Action was not one of them." Congressional leaders and the president persisted in thinking of Community Action as an updated National Youth Administration (NYA), a New Deal jobs program that in Texas had been administered by a youthful Lyndon Johnson.[2]

The chaos that followed—the Black Panthers' manipulation of the Oakland program; Saul Alinsky's controversial appointment as a consultant to CAP in Syracuse; and the battle between the Daley machine and the radical Woodlawn Association of Chicago—led to the virtual repudiation of the program by the president and his poverty czar, Sargent Shriver. From the president's perspective, the "kooks" and the "sociologists" had been allowed to run amuck in the War on Poverty.[3] Model Cities was to be different.

The differences were real: the Model Cities program was the product of more extensive planning than there had been for the War On Poverty; it addressed what Johnson saw as the "chief" concern of the "new agenda . . . the problem of the cities";[4] and it pointedly called for "widespread" citizen participation, not, as in CAP, "maximum feasible participation." Furthermore, the Model Cities program was Johnson's *own* program, unlike the War on Poverty, which was part of the Kennedy legacy. The prospects for achievement in Model Cities were correspondingly greater than they had been in the War on Poverty's Community Action Program. The record of achievement under Johnson, however, was slight relative to the expectations that the program engendered.[5] What went "right" and what went "wrong" in the promotion of ideological influence over this central program in the Johnson presidency is the subject of this chapter.

The Demonstration Cities and Metropolitan Development Act of 1966 stipulated that Model Cities, as they came to be called, were to be created out of small towns, medium-sized cities, and the slums of the country's urban centers.[6] The point was to demonstrate what the various branches and levels of government, along with private enterprise and citizens' organizations, could do to improve the quality of life of people living in or near poverty. The act, therefore, empowered the recently created Department of Housing and Urban Development (HUD) to coordinate the activities of executive branch agencies, local and state governments, and citizens' groups for a "total" and "massive" "attack" on the social as well as the physical ills of modern living.[7]

Previous urban policy had been directed primarily at the physical and tangible dimensions of poverty and housing decay.[8] Model Cities, the flagship of the Great Society armada, represented an attempt dramatically to redirect the federal government's policies for dealing with poverty and housing. Attitudes as well as political and economic institutions were targeted by the Model Cities program as among the variables to be adjusted by the government's social engineers.

The intentions of the Model Cities program were very much in line with the tenets of Great Society liberalism as analyzed in chapter 2. Indeed, the plan for Model Cities was developed primarily by mainstream liberal social scientists from elite northeastern universities. Yet even before the program emerged from one of Johnson's task forces, its ideological character had been diluted; consequently, the influence of people of ideas upon the program had been compromised. Basically, Model Cities fell prey in its developmental as well as its legislative stages to the professional politician's preference for distributive as opposed to experimental and redistributive policies. When the time came to implement the Model Cities legislation, furthermore, the counterideological demands of the politicians intensified, and the White House clearly sided with the Congress against the ideologists who had been appointed to run the program from HUD.

From among the hundreds of applications received yearly by HUD, White House and HUD officials chose the ones that would be funded. The ideologically oriented President's Task Force on Urban Problems (hereinafter, the Task Force) had intended this selection process to be competitive and meritocratic. Specific criteria that they had devised to govern selections had been enacted into law with passage of the Demonstration Cities and Metropolitan Development Act. Yet evidence from White House and HUD files, from interviews, and from published sources demonstrates that selections were made more on political and partisan grounds than according to the criteria of the ideologists.

Finally, in addition to fighting a losing battle against the White House and the Congress on these selections, the people of ideas who devised Model Cities and who struggled to control the program's implementation from within HUD had to contend with a small cadre of radical, antitechnocratic people of ideas within HUD, the Office of Economic Opportunity (OEO), the Justice Department, and elsewhere. Whereas the mainstream liberals who developed the Model Cities program emphasized systemic planning and intergovernmental coordination in their work, the radical antipoverty warriors took as their top priority the mobilization of dissent among the poor within Model City neighborhoods. The White House, oblivious to the ideological aspects of personnel management, was of no help in sorting out this confusion. The Johnson administration, it might be said, was locked in a transitional bind. Neither the particularistic politics of the past nor the universalistic politics of the future were strong enough in the mid-1960s to enable the president to guide this attempted policy redirection to fruition.

The Idea for a Model Cities Program

The idea for a Model Cities initiative was developed as part of a process structured by the Johnson White House for the fast translation of ideas into legislative initiatives. This process demands attention because the crazy-for-new-ideas environment of this presidency structured the flow of program initiatives into government in ways that encouraged the recommendation of initiatives with ideological attributes.

The President's Search for Big Ideas: The Johnson Task Force Operation

Looking forward to the beginning of his own presidential term in January 1965, Johnson was searching for ideas that would secure for him a legacy of legislative achievement and domestic policy redirection that he could call his own. In Johnson's own words:

> The old reforms, which had been crying for action since FDR's time, were finally on the books, but in the meantime, other needs, just as critical to life in the 1960s and beyond, were accumulating. . . population growth, . . . city decay . . . separation of man from nature . . . depersonalization of life in the post industrial age. . . . These were not as obvious . . . as poverty and the need for schools and the black man's right to vote, but they were the overwhelming problems of the future.[9]

And "chief among [these overwhelming problems] were the problems of the cities." The Model Cities program was to be the first step toward realizing Johnson's personal legacy of a Great Society. Even in retirement, Johnson persisted in seeing the act that brought the program into being as "one of the major breakthroughs of the 1960s."[10] Thus, it was in the context of building a flagship program for his presidency that Johnson began pushing for a big, bold program to address the much-heralded "crisis of the cities."

In October 1965, Johnson commissioned his Task Force on Urban Problems. It was this group that recommended Model Cities in a December 1965 report to the president. In commissioning this task force, the president did not, of course, call simply for an endorsement of his own ideas or even for their elaboration. Rather, he presented the task force with a broad charter and let its members proceed largely on their own terms to define the problems of the cities as well as to offer programs for their solution. Though the charter provided for this and other task forces was vague, there were pressures in this loosely structured environment that affected what sort of people and what ideas were most influential. To understand these pressures requires a deeper understanding of the Johnson task force operation and, more broadly, Johnson's approach to the legislative cycle.

President Johnson's task forces, which brought intellectuals and interest group leaders together, were but one component of an almost frenzied annual search for new ideas. Even before Joseph Califano took charge from Bill Moyers of the solicitation of ideas for legislative action, the atmosphere within which task forces operated was one of excitement and "blue sky planning."[11] The original Johnson task forces were even described by one participant as "happenings,"[12] and Lawrence E. Levinson, Califano's chief assistant for legislative development, recalls that "a New Deal atmosphere" was present in Califano's office, where aides packaged ideas, including those from task forces, into legislative proposals.[13]

In addition to the task forces, the search for ideas involved the following steps each year: The Bright Young Men (see chapter 2) would be asked to submit legislative proposals. James Gaither, Harry McPherson, and other top aides would visit a select number of the country's elite universities to meet with academicians (assembled on an ad hoc basis by respected scholars and presidential supporters, such as Professor Richard Neustadt at Harvard) to review the progress of the administration, particularly in domestic affairs. Afterwards, Joseph Califano, writing for the president, would ask each participant to send a memorandum to the White House detailing what the federal government might do next to reach towards a Great Society.[14] Every examiner in the Bureau of the Budget was also asked for his or her ideas. As Levinson recalled, "Our job was to try to harness the brain power of the country and to direct that flow of ideas into the problems of the American scene."[15] All of the ideas that came tumbling into the White House in these ways, including those from the task forces, were then assembled and summarized (one page per idea) by Califano and his staff. The point was to maximize the number of new ideas to be presented to the president in thick black books before his State of the Union address was composed. "We did not eliminate any" ideas along the way, recalls James Gaither, who organized the task forces for Califano.[16]

President Johnson's role in this process was inspirational. "I don't recall," Gaither says of the development of the 1967, 1968, and 1969 legislative programs, "any instances where the President [told us] not to study a particular problem and not to come up with a proposal." In fact, he "never rejected a charter [for a new task force] that I'm aware of."[17] And when a task force was impaneled, Johnson (or Califano) would routinely exhort its members to (1) think big; (2) pay no heed to political considerations; and (3) ignore cost. Task force members were also asked to work quickly. Often, results would be demanded in weeks from a task force whose academic members were accustomed to refining ideas over years.[18]

The environment within which the Johnson task forces operated, then, was conducive to thinking up costly, politically contentious, sometimes operationally naive ideas for the expansion of state power to address issues relating to the qualitative aspects of the public good. With respect specifically to the 1965 Task Force on Urban Problems, these factors were not only present but abundant.

The 1965 Task Force on Urban Problems: The Reuther Connection

The 1965 Task Force on Urban Problems was established by the White House for at least two reasons. First, it was part of the frenzied search for new legislative initiatives. Many ideas had come to the attention of Califano's legislative agenda shop over the first year of Johnson's elected term. Califano recommended to President Johnson that some of these—

including the idea for a demonstration project to address the "crisis in the cities"—be considered by task forces.[19] Second, however, the Model Cities Task Force was commissioned as a political favor by the president to an important political backer, Walter Reuther, president of the United Auto Workers (UAW). Reuther had been among Johnson's liberal detractors before Johnson assumed the presidency, and Johnson began cultivating the labor leader immediately after he took office.[20] Ironically, these two motivations dovetailed neatly in the actual composition of the Task Force and its deliberations, for in addition to being George Meany's competitor for the unofficial title of chief labor leader in the country, Reuther was a dedicated liberal, a "red-hot" in the parlance of the new president.[21]

In 1964 the mayor of Detroit, Jerome Cavanagh, served on the first Johnson task force on urban affairs, called the Task Force on Metropolitan Development. That group did not recommend a demonstration cities experiment but noted that some such initiative might be considered at a later date. Cavanagh thought the sooner the better, and he presented the idea to Walter Reuther.[22] Shortly thereafter, Reuther sent a memorandum to the president to press upon him the vision of "an urban TVA." The tenor as well as the substance of this memorandum is indicated in the following excerpts:

> The importance of experiment as a test of meaning and truth—to quote from Herbert Croly's "Promise of American Life" published in 1909, has never been more important than at this moment *when it is suggested by this memorandum,* that President Johnson's *promise of the Great Society* establish a first *physical expression* in 6 of the large urban centers of America, of full and complete and organic neighborhoods for 50,000 people to give meaning to our *ability to* create architecturally beautiful and socially meaningful communities of the twentieth century. . . .
>
> What FDR created for the TVA as a worldwide symbol to combat erosion of the land, President Johnson is asked to initiate to stop erosion of life in urban centers among the lower and middle income population. . . . [These demonstrations would be] the living and inhabited testimony of what the essence of our concern in life really is.[23]

Sometime later in that summer, Reuther made his pitch in a private meeting with the president.[24]

Richard Goodwin, one of the president's chief speechwriters, sent Reuther's memo to his former property law professor at Harvard Law School, Charles Haar. Haar, an urban land use expert, was unpersuaded of the substantive merit of Reuther's proposal, but he was politically astute as to the significance of Reuther's sponsorship. "This proposal," he advised Goodwin, "*in view of its backing,* seems to be one which should be accepted, but with a generous amount of cynical acid" (emphasis added).[25] Califano subsequently added the Reuther idea to those to be taken up by a task force.

It is interesting to follow further the paper trail representing the White House's perspective on the origins of Model Cities. What that trail suggests is that a patronagelike consideration was built into the Task Force's operation from its inception, even though the Task Force's members clearly had their own, apolitical perspective on their work. Specifically, in White House circles the Model Cities idea seems to have been associated overwhelmingly with Reuther's sponsorship. This gave the idea more momentum in the development of the legislative agenda of the Great Society than it could have acquired on its other, including its ideological, merits. Reuther's sponsorship might also help to explain why the White House did not go out of its way in the implementation of this program to aid its ideological administrators, who argued that "politics" was compromising the purity of their idea. From the vantage point of the White House, the program had *never* borne a pure ideological pedigree.

As the 1965 Task Force was officially launched from Califano's office, Califano repeatedly made mention of the Model Cities aspect of its intended agenda with pointed references to the president's obligation to "do something for Reuther" along the lines of Reuther's August 27 memorandum. For example, in a memorandum to Johnson in early October 1965, Califano emphasized repeatedly Reuther's connection to the idea. The first sentence of that two-page note indicates that Califano had met with the budget director, White House aide Harry McPherson, and Professors Robert Wood and Charles Haar (the leaders of the Task Force and, later, high-level HUD appointees). The purpose of the meeting, Califano reported, was "to discuss the ways to go about developing alternatives for your consideration for a cities program next year." The rest of the document focuses squarely on Reuther:

> Walter Reuther discussed with me personally and called me several times about setting up a small group to study the problem of the cities and let you know what, if anything, the Federal government should do about it next year. The possibility in which Reuther is most interested is the so-called "demonstration cities" idea. . . . Reuther has proposed various things for the Task Force and I believe I can work those out with him and with Professors Haar and Wood.[26]

Also in this memorandum, Califano expresses his personal doubts whether the work done by this group should aim toward a "significant legislative program next year" given that "the problem of the cities is so complex." Nevertheless, Califano concludes with the reminder: "As I mentioned above, Walter Reuther said you agreed to set up such a group to study this." In a separate document, Califano presented to Johnson his recommendations for the membership of the Task Force. Of the nine names on Califano's list, six had been recommended previously to the White House by Reuther.[27]

Even after the president gave Califano the go-ahead to set up the Task Force, with a panel roster recommended largely by Reuther, the UAW president's connection was conspicuous in internal White House communications. In another memo to Johnson, for instance, Califano wrote that "this Task Force fulfills your assurance to Walter Reuther that such a group would be set up to consider his idea of demonstration cities."[28] And in a document purporting to explain the issues before the Task Force, Califano outlined for Johnson only two substantive points: A "Marshall Plan for the Cities," which was not pursued, and "The Reuther Plan (Demonstration Cities)."[29]

This perspective, furthermore, was not limited to Califano. In Charles Schultze's lengthy memorandum for one of the Task Force's earliest meetings, he, too, emphasized Reuther's personal connection with the idea of a demonstration program for the cities.[30] And in a recent interview, Lawrence Levinson volunteered at the beginning of a conversation about Model Cities that "Walter Reuther is very important here."[31] In fact, the idea that the White House first took up the Model Cities plan as a favor for Walter Reuther even seemed plausible, in retrospect, to Robert Wood, the professor who headed the Task Force.[32]

Even if the Task Force had been created without Reuther's assistance, however, it is possible that it might have proposed some sort of dramatic, sweeping project for the cities. To understand why, it is necessary to examine the Task Force's perspective, as opposed to the view from the White House, on the genesis of this attempted policy redirection.

The Model Cities Task Force: Membership and Deliberations

Robert Wood and Charles Haar were the leaders of the task force that proposed Model Cities. Wood, the official Task Force chair, was at that time head of the political science department at MIT. The year before, he had chaired Johnson's Task Force on Metropolitan Development. When the new Department of Housing and Urban Development was founded, he was appointed its undersecretary. Haar, in addition to being a young Harvard Law School professor, had also previously chaired a Johnson task force, on Lady Bird's cause, beautification. Haar became an assistant secretary at HUD at the same time that Wood was appointed undersecretary, and in short order Haar became a trusted all-purpose adviser to the president.[33] These academicians, along with Reuther, Whitney Young (head of the Urban League), Edgar Kaiser (industrialist), Kermit Gordon (budget director before becoming president of the Brookings Institution), William

Rafsky (Philadelphia city planner), and Benjamin Heineman (industrialist) made up the original Task Force; Senator Abraham Ribicoff was added before the last meeting. In addition to the official membership, Harry McPherson served as liaison with the White House; Charles Schultze (assistant director and then director of the Bureau of the Budget after Gordon) met with the group on occasion; and Lawrence Levinson took part and made notes of the conversations.

This group, assembled by Califano and Johnson with significant input from Reuther, was given its presidential charter at an October 13 meeting at which Califano represented his boss. The group was charged in the characteristic fashion. They were placed under a gag order, admonished to "leave the driving" of the Congress to the White House, and told to work quickly. Assembled in mid-October, the Task Force was given a December 15 deadline for the submission of an interim report.[34]

On the matters of cost and political considerations, the Task Force was reassured at later dates that those were not its proper concerns. Thus, on one occasion, Task Force members listened to Robert Wood convey the remarkable intensity with which LBJ had a short time before privately expressed to the chairpersons of the 1964 task forces his desire to avoid what he saw as FDR's mistake, namely, letting his domestic achievements be cut short by the economic exigencies of war.[35] Furthermore, Wood personally was told by Califano before the 1965 Task Force first met that "the White House anticipated normal economic growth to generate a 'fiscal dividend' of some $12 billion under existing tax rates during the coming year . . . about $4 billion was likely to go into federal aid programs." Wood, of course, passed this information along to his colleagues.[36]

In addition to these instructions, Robert Wood brought to the Task Force a sense of mission. His job, as he understood it, was not to debate the crisis of the cities but to translate into law the consensus of mainstream liberal thought on the matter. Thus, with the White House's support, Wood froze out of the 1965 Task Force's deliberations any persons who might question the liberal perspective on urban policy.

The year before, as director of the 1964 task force, Wood had had to contend with a diversity of expert opinion on the nature of the urban situation. For although intellectuals who appraised urban policies, as well as a large contingent of professional city planners, were united in the mid-1960s in critically appraising the urban renewal movement of years past, they were divided over what should be done instead. There were plans for "new towns," for the use of social and physical engineering techniques to build futuristic, high-density housing settlements, for an urban extension service, and much more.[37] Many proposals centered about technological breakthroughs or at least their inducement. Others sought social solutions to what many considered to be the root problems in the urban field: poverty and racial discord.[38] There were even those, such as professors Martin Anderson, James Q. Wilson, and Edward Banfield, who argued that the most massive problems of the cities were not likely to be amenable to solution by the federal government.[39]

This last, conservative point of view had been represented on the 1964 task force but was nowhere to be found the next year. Even in 1964 Wood had seen to it that the conservatives, the "Pollyannas and optimists," as he remembers them, were left out of the drafting of that task force's final report. As Wood recalled in an interview, the naysayers had been fogged in at the San Francisco airport on the day of the final task force meeting. Wood and the others took advantage of the weather to approve a "consensus" report for submission to President Johnson, urging that dramatic steps be taken to address the crisis of the urban areas.

On the 1965 Task Force, no conservative voices were heard at either the panel or the staff level. Professor Bernard Frieden, an important member of Wood's staff on the 1965 Task Force, defends this exclusion with the comment that "what Banfield, or one of those others, would have brought to a meeting was a point of view, an ideology."[40] And the mainstream liberal ideology of the time was, of course, vehement in denying the legitimacy of ideological arguments. As to any information that Banfield or the others might have had to offer, Frieden and his colleague Kaplan's comment in their book on Model Cities is instructive and, again, typical of the mainstream liberal thinking of the time. "We shared," they observe about themselves and the other urbanists involved in the development of Model Cities, " . . . a commitment to act in behalf of social goals even on the basis of imperfect knowledge."[41] Questioned about this recently, Lawrence Levinson answered testily that "the range of persons involved in the Task Force represented the range we wanted." "We were trying," he said of the White House's effort radically to redirect the nation's urban policies, "to put the beautiful vase of the American city together again." And that, he implies, was no job for Pollyannas.[42]

At its first meeting, with Wood leading the conversation and with no Pollyannas to slow them down, the Task Force members specified their assumptions. Levinson's notes of the occasion include the following:

> ASSUMPTION
> 1. Unmet urban needs/deficiencies exist on national scale (how to catalogue/characterize deficiencies?)
> 2. Existing program inadequate (how demonstrate—size, time)
> 3. Specialized approaches can remove obstacles and fulfill needs (selective demonstration—block grant—metro response—private sector response)
>
> --
>
> TESTS (1) and (2)—*relatively simple*—i.e. accepted TF/Adm—not

Congress; not significant section of expert community; but previously articulated. *Need*—tough, tight analytical summary—on conditions below acceptable standards, and opportunity costs for affluent society —(Excellence)
Critical test: validity of specialized approaches[43]

Thus, the originators of Model Cities recognized that a "significant portion of the expert community" doubted the validity of the first two assumptions of the Model Cities program. Believing that the doubters had already "articulated" their points of view, however, the Task Force took only the third assumption to be a "critical" issue for substantiation and argument. This document fragment also echoes themes familiar from the analysis of Great Society ideology in chapter 2. The "opportunity costs" of "unmet needs" in the cities, Levinson recorded in the phraseology of Galbraith and Schlesinger, would have to be calculated for the "affluent society." "Excellence" was the ultimate goal of the government's domestic policies.

Moving beyond the Task Force's assumptions, we can observe differences of opinion. But the differences that emerged during deliberations did not compromise the ideological character of the resultant report and program. Thus, although Charles Haar, before the Task Force officially met, was, in the words of note-taker Levinson, "worried about Schultze and Kermit [Gordon]—do they want change?" there was little need to worry. At the first full meeting of the Task Force, Kermit Gordon did not argue against the assumptions of the Task Force's work. "Progress and reforms" were needed, and federal funds would have to be spent to "cajole communities" toward these goals. And the only note that remains to indicate Schultze's contribution at this meeting reads: "Schultze: more than housing."[44]

The other Task Force members were not only in accord; they were full of enthusiasm. Thus, at an early meeting, Reuther spoke of a "bold concept—Doing things better and doing new things," of the need to "Get [the] Country Excited," and stated that "new total communities [were] needed, [with] racial [and] economic integration." Whitney Young, meanwhile, expressed the belief during the same meeting that a successful Model Cities program might even make "diversity" in housing "fashionable." Living in the projects, he hoped, would become a "status symbol." Several Task Force members stressed the sense of urgency to which they were responding. The need, as Haar put it, was for a "dramatic program." Finally, the two professors lectured their colleagues at their first and subsequent meetings on the need for a "planning" approach to the problems of the cities.[45]

The only significant division was over the degree of citizen participation to be required in Model City neighborhoods. This division was a reflection of the split between the more extreme leftist liberal perspective, which urged maximum participation, as in CAP, and the mainstream liberal view, which stressed the technical, as opposed to the political, prerequisites of effective planning. In its report, the Task Force did not entirely break from the participatory ideal central to the War on Poverty. In fact, in the staff report on the Model Cities, which Wood credits as being an important document, Chester Rapkin and one of his associates, Grace Milgram, went so far as to recommend that the Task Force propose "direct action or protest" to citizens in Model City neighborhoods who are struggling to achieve "the competent neighborhood," which Rapkin and Milgram identified as "one of the chief aims of the center city demonstration." And Young and Reuther were reluctant at first to make the Task Force report unanimous because it did not endorse this perspective in strong language.[46] The language finally chosen for the report and incorporated into the legislation authorizing the Model Cities program established a standard of "widespread citizen participation," which represented a compromise between the dominant liberal and the minority radical perspectives represented within the Task Force.

Overall, however, the Task Force's deliberations were a family affair ideologically, and those differences that did emerge confused but did not diminish the ideological character of the work. In fact, Wood's biggest challenge in forging a consensus report was not bargaining with Reuther and Young but keeping out the naysayers and those who might urge some different, more technical direction for the program. Wood had, that is, to fend off attempts by individual urbanists, professional organizations, and the White House's Office of Science and Technology Policy (OSTP) to become involved in the supposedly secret Task Force even after its membership had been decided and its meetings had commenced.[47] The resulting isolation of the Task Force was in full accord with the White House's directions to keep the deliberations secret, even from HUD and its secretary, Robert Weaver, who had a reputation as an overly cautious administrator. Caution, it should be clear by now, was not in demand in this process.

The Model Cities Task Force Report: An Ideological Document

The Task Force report, which was supported by hundreds of pages of staff papers prepared by University of Pennsylvania Professor Rapkin and his small staff of social scientists and social workers, began with a summary of the errors of previous federal urban policies.[48] These past programs, the report argued, had been wrong about both goals and procedures. Previous policy had focused on physical goals—so many new houses built, with particular financing mechanisms and construction technologies, and so on—while Model Cities would be aimed at social as well as "brick and mortar" concerns. This criticism was not intended to suggest the need for a choice between the two goals. A planning approach, recognizing the "systemic" nature of the urban environment, would encompass social, physical, technical, financial, and whatever other goals and procedures might be thought of. Thus, the Task Force report urged a "total" approach. Indeed, "total," "massive," "coordinated," "total environment," "entirely new communities," "no slums in ten years," and similarly grand phrases are extraordinarily common in the record of the Task Force's deliberations. As Bernard Frieden recently recalled, "A lot of people thought that way then." "There was," he said, "a feeling we could do anything we put our mind to," including totally eradicating poverty and racially and economically integrating the nation's cities.

So that the urban crisis might be solved, at once and for all time, the Task Force promoted, as the guiding principles of Model Cities:

1. *Concentration* of resources to demonstrate swiftly what urban communities might become
2. *Coordination* of all available talent and aid
3. *Mobilization* of local leadership
4. *Experimentation* with new technologies and new procedures[49]

Underpinning these principles was the fundamental belief that the Model Cities program could be used as a tool for social engineering, to change prejudice into compassion and economic antagonism into mutual respect.[50] The Task Force came easily to agreement on these principles and much else in the report, finally, because its members thought the program whose creation they were urging was to be entered into only by those cities that had won the go-ahead of a special committee of people such as themselves, who would oversee the demonstrations. Tough choices, therefore, could be finessed until the implementation phase. "We didn't think," Wood stated in retrospect, "of priorities."[51]

In its final form, as drafted by Wood and Haar, what the Task Force report actually proposed was a national competition in which all cities would be invited to submit grant proposals to a "Special Presidential Commission," which would select the most promising entrants for an influx of funds and guidance. Although the Task Force demurred from prescribing program content, its report did enumerate, as did the act itself, performance guidelines for the planning stage. The criteria of the act, in fact, were almost identical to the criteria assembled by Rapkin for the Task Force report (under directions from Wood to "try to take a little bit of something from everyone").[52] Specifically, the demonstration area would have to: be sufficiently concentrated so that an entire neighborhood could be improved; be important enough to the city as a whole that the program would make a clear impact on the total city; help close the gap between the living conditions of the poor and minorities and those of the rest of the community; foster local leadership and widespread citizen participation; bring together public and private assistance; have a visible, physical impact; be financially competent; show results in at least two years and establish a plan for five years.[53] The emphasis throughout was on innovation and experimentation, to find approaches that might be applied elsewhere. The funding was to be generous. First, the winners would receive a grant to develop detailed plans. Then the participating cities would receive "on a priority basis" the full array of funds available from existing grant sources under all relevant federal programs. Under Title II of the act, a federal coordinator was to be assigned to each Model City area to coordinate and speed the receipt of these funds, which were to be merged into a common account. Finally, the federal government was to pay 80 percent of whatever costs could not be covered through existing funds.

The responsibility of the cities, then, was to initiate action through the composition and submission of rational, comprehensive, technically competent plans to achieve such goals as desegregation, better housing stock for the poor and minorities, competent neighborhoods, and, generally, an end to the crisis of the cities.[54] The federal administrators, for their part, would have to "monitor and assure meaningful resident participation; earmark existing grants-in-aid for participating cities; provide technical assistance to hard-pressed city halls; develop performance criteria that would give cities maximum freedom in the use of Model Cities funds but that would still guarantee their use for the benefit of the poor; and evaluate overall program results."[55]

The Task Force did not simply assume that the sheer reasonableness of its planning approach would assure the cooperation of the federal government's many agencies and departments. It instead pinned great hopes, according to Frieden, Kaplan, and Wood, on President Johnson's ability to "knock heads together" and make the government work. Only Kermit Gordon expressed reservations about this aspect of the plan. Even if more Task Force members had shared Gordon's concern, however, it is doubtful that the report would have placed a lighter burden on the federal government. The Task Force members' reliance upon a coordinated, rational planning scenario was an inescapable component of their thinking, regardless of what role the president was expected to play. For as Charles Haar observed in retrospect, it was an "article of faith" that "coordination and concentration . . . would bring significant improvements in the cities."[56] It was, most broadly, a part of the larger liberal faith in the movement of history toward a more rationalized and efficient organization of social and governmental institutions.

As to the number of cities to be awarded money through this program, the Task Force's final report, under pressure from Senator Abraham Ribicoff, compromised the competitive idealism of the original vision of Reuther, Wood, and Haar. Whereas originally, Task Force members had discussed funding five or six demonstrations, by the time they finished drafting the final report, Wood and Haar had raised the total number of cities for the first round of planning grants to sixty-six.[57]

That these ideas were ideological can be demonstrated through the application of the ideal type. With respect, first, to logical certitude, although only in retrospect did one of the architects of the Model Cities program acknowledge that the Task Force took certain ideas to be true as a matter of close-minded "faith" instead of open-minded reasoning, the Task Force's members were dogmatic in their claim to know *the* path to knowledge. They were certain, furthermore, that the knowledge they could obtain through the prescribed technocratic exercises would be sufficient to solve the problems of the urban spirit as well as of the urban housing stock. Those who disagreed were simply left out of deliberations. Still, Task Force members only weakly claimed to possess absolute truth. Although what mainstream liberal social scientists still like to call "values" were acknowledged in Model Cities staff papers, for instance, to have something to do with the crisis of the cities, this acknowledgment was made only in declarative phrases that assumed the self-evident nature of the "moral and spiritual" responsibilities of the federal government. Doing *something* was, apparently, a moral imperative. But as to how exactly to define and approach problems, the Task Force's emphasis on experimentation suggests the limited nature of its members' claims to possess absolute truth. Nevertheless, it is possible to see in the Model Cities program a belief in the possibility of creating a New Man, free of prejudice, myth, and irrational antagonisms. Insofar as this represents a claim to truth based on a reading of the transcendent nature of man, it reveals an unintentional absolutism. The final claim that the ideologue makes for his knowledge— to comprehensive explanation—was definitely present in the thinking of Task Force members. The Model Cities Task Force did not itself claim to possess a comprehensive explanation of urban decay but did claim to know how to acquire a comprehensive explanation for any given locale. Through systems analysis, comprehensive problem identification, and the like, the Task Force expected each Model City to achieve a total understanding of its problems.

Ascription, as emphasized already, is shunned by mainstream liberals. It is not surprising, then, that as with its parent ideology, the view of the world endorsed in the Model Cities report rested upon consensus thinking. Instead of dividing persons into worthy and unworthy groups on the basis of inherent or acquired traits, a characteristic of the pure ideologue, these innovators sought to unite and, indeed, integrate all classes and groups of persons within, first, model neighborhoods and, then, of course, the Great Society itself. Even the "Pollyannas" for whom Wood had so little time were castigated, not as persons of no value, but rather as nuisances: speedbumps on the superhighway of the liberal consensus.

That the liberal "consensus" was advancing and would, if given proper leadership, surge into the future was of course a central article of liberal faith and showed up clearly in the deliberations of the Task Force. The Model Cities program, in fact, attained a position at the very core of a transfer culture, the central tenet of which was that cultural failings might be treated as problems amenable to political solutions and that the consequence of sound treatment would be "forward" progress for American society. The institutional credentials of the Task Force's leaders, finally, were in good mainstream liberal order, bearing the stamps of MIT and Harvard.

To clarify further the ideological character of the Model Cities Task Force, its report can be contrasted briefly with that produced by a contemporaneous intergovernmental task force on urban problems. Ideology, it is worth emphasizing, is not the same as expertise or intellect; not every task force report issued by "experts" or "intellectuals" associated with a modern presidency will be an ideological document.

In 1965 President Johnson, reacting to criticism that he was not being sufficiently respectful of the capability of government employees to think creatively about the country's problems, commissioned a series of interagency task forces. One of these, headed by Robert Weaver, the newly appointed head of HUD, was asked to address a set of specific issues in the field of urban affairs. The highest-priority issue this group had to address was the use of "broad purpose grants to metropolitan areas, for urban and social services."[58] In response, Weaver and his colleagues from the Department of Health, Education and Welfare (HEW), the Departments of Transportation and Labor, the Bureau of the Budget, and other agencies of government recommended incremental changes in administrative policy and an amendment to the law governing the Housing and Home Finance Administration's program of urban planning assistance grants. The amendment would "permit assistance for planning of broad programs of public and social services in conjunction with physical development planning." The chief priority would be to meet, within the first several years of a program, the need for expanded "early childhood, childhood, and youth opportunities." The amount of planning required of locales receiving such grants would not represent a significant departure from standard practice, nor would the federal government be required to coordinate its activities. The subdued nature of these proposals was complemented by the qualified, almost apologetic tone of Weaver's letter of transmittal to Califano upon completion of this task force's deliberations. "These are staff papers," Weaver wrote. "In many instances proposals have not been fully developed and the papers should be viewed as discussion draft papers." Weaver was "hopeful" that "a number of the ideas and proposals" in the papers he was forwarding would be helpful to the president.[59]

This document falls short of the Model Cities Task Force's approximation of the ideological ideal type in several ways. Whereas the Model Cities Task Force report prescribes a "textbook planning" process, as Frieden recalls it, which implies a firm belief in the capacity of local governments to arrive at comprehensive explanations of the flaws in their community "systems," the Weaver Task Force papers project no such claim. The Weaver Task Force was also considerably less close-minded with respect to ways of arriving at knowledge, accepting tradition as a guide to knowledge in policy deliberations. Its authors, that is, were not so certain as were Wood and his peers that the answers to the nation's problems could be unlocked through the rational deliberations of presidential task forces. The members of Weaver's task force came, finally, not from institutions associated with mainstream liberalism, but, rather, from the government's career ranks.

Legislating Model Cities

The push to turn the Task Force's report into a Model Cities bill began on the occasion of the president's message to Congress on the problems of the cities, January 26, 1966. In that message, Johnson wrote in grandiloquent style about his proposal, which followed in detail the recommendations of the Task Force. "Today," President Johnson proclaimed:

> I have placed before the Congress and before you, the people of America, a new way of answering an ancient dream. That dream is of cities of promise, cities of hope, where it could truly be said, to every man his chance, to every man, regardless of his birth, his shining golden opportunity, to every man the right to live and to work and to be himself and to become whatever thing his manhood and his vision can combine to make him.
> The new way of answering that ancient dream is this:
> —to rebuild where there is hopeless blight;
> —to renew where there is decay and ugliness;
> —to refresh the spirit of men and women that are growing weary with jobless anxiety;
> —to restore old communities and to bring forth new ones where children will be proud to say, "This is my home."
> What I have offered is a massive program, involving everything that we know about building homes and schools and parks and streets that are safe from fear.[60]

In the ensuing lobbying of Congress, Robert Weaver, acting as a loyal administrator after being purposefully ignored in the program's development, joined with his newly appointed undersecretary, Robert Wood, to organize interest groups to pressure legislators to pass the program. These two also prepared a special memorandum on the program to be sent to mayors throughout the country; personally talked with a score of mayors; and privately briefed Vice President Hubert Humphrey. Harry McPherson, meanwhile, lobbied newspaper editorial page editors, while Walter Reuther arranged for the American Federation of Labor and Congress of Industrial Organizations (AFL-CIO) to issue a statement of support. And Professor Haar, according to a memo Califano sent to Johnson, was "talking to people like Ed Logue of Boston and other distinguished city planners (who tend to capture the Sunday supplement sections) to explain the program to them."[61] As part of this effort, HUD even maintained a calendar indicating the speaking engagements of private sector friends so that they might be contacted with a request to promote the program in upcoming speeches.

These lobbying efforts and those originating from the White House intensified in May, after a *New York Times* article all but wrote off Model Cities as dead in Congress. At a White House meeting to discuss the situation after this story was printed, it became apparent that while the White House suspected Weaver's commitment, Weaver and his congressional liaison officer blamed the situation on the lack of vigorous presidential involvement in the lobbying effort.[62] After this meeting, Weaver, Wood, and HUD's congressional liaison office accelerated their orchestration of interest group lobbying.

Eventually, with the key assistance of Senator Edmund Muskie, the White House managed to gain passage of a bill that closely followed its original proposal. Haar and Levinson actually drafted the final version of this bill in a back room in the White House. The price of Muskie's help included softening some of the language of the White House proposal; giving greater emphasis to the geographically distributive as opposed to the economically redistributive aspects of the bill; and giving even greater emphasis to the requirement that participating cities engage in comprehensive, systematic planning.[63]

The bill's final passage was also aided by the support of liberal elites who testified on its behalf in hearings chaired by Senator Ribicoff. At those hearings, Senators Ribicoff and Kennedy from Massachusetts blasted Robert Weaver and the administration for offering, in Kennedy's words, "a drop in the bucket."[64] A parade of dramatic testimony from notables of the liberal community helped overcome these senators' impulse to risk passage of the bill before them by demanding an even more daring and contentious substitute. Civil rights leader Bayard Rustin, Walter

Reuther, Claude Brown (author of *Manchild in the Promised Land*), and Attorney General Nicholas Katzenbach spoke at these hearings in favor of the Model Cities legislation. Katzenbach contributed to the record a statement that called Model Cities the "keystone" of the Johnson administration's efforts to overturn the "product of generations of indifference by all the American people to rot and rust and mold which we have allowed to eat into the core of our cities."[65] The testimony of these men helped define Model Cities as a cause that liberals within and without the Congress should care about.

To secure passage of their proposal, the White House and HUD further engineered the addition of $600 million to the general urban renewal authorization for the coming year. This allayed congressional worries that Model Cities, because they were to receive priority in the awarding of such grants, might thereby deprive other communities of their full share of federal funds. The White House also acquiesced to the Senate's addition of an amendment from the floor limiting any state's share of Model Cities funds to 15 percent of the national total. Finally, according to Edward Banfield, by the end of the summer White House officials had promised more than one hundred legislators "that a place would not be overlooked [for them] when the time came to select the 'winning' cities."[66]

In the Senate and in the House, these efforts finally resulted in a winning coalition of northern Democrats and liberal Republicans from primarily northeastern metropolitan districts behind the bill. Overall, northern Democrats in the House voted for the program 114–11; most southern Democrats were opposed (21–49); while Republicans were opposed by better than a four-to-one ratio (81–16). The battle on the floor of the House before final passage was intensely partisan and, according to *Congressional Quarterly*, one of the most heated and contentious of the legislative session. The bill at last was sent to President Johnson for his signature on November 3, 1966.[67]

Overall, the law greatly resembled the bill as envisioned by the Task Force. As to the relaxation of the competitive premise of the program, the Task Force itself was partly responsible, having recommended that over sixty cities be selected for funding. And much of the vagueness of the final law's criteria for selection did not have to be added by Senator Muskie. Since the Task Force was represented in HUD in the persons of Haar and Wood, in any event, leaving such questions to administrative discretion might be interpreted as a victory for the Task Force and its people of ideas. The single area in which the law did fall short of Task Force expectations was in allowing for a less than all-powerful "metropolitan expediter" instead of a federal coordinator. The next year, the relevant appropriations committee even failed to fund the expediter. But there is no ground for supposing that even with the full-force coordinator the Task Force had envisioned, the Model Cities program would not have been overwhelmed by coordination problems. Such problems plagued the program at levels antecedent to the niche to be occupied by the coordinator.

Implementing the Model Cities Program

The implementation of the Model Cities program was beset with political and ideological problems. It was at this stage that the influence of people of ideas suffered serious setbacks. First, it was a problem for the ideologues that the White House selected winners in the Model Cities competition largely on the basis of political criteria. Second, the split between the advocates of heightened participation among the poor and the mainstream liberals created some difficulties. Finally, mainstream liberal ideology itself proved less than effective in this bureaucratic setting. The mainstream liberals had taken on faith too many items in their plan, such as their ability, and that of the president, to coordinate the activities of diverse agencies within the executive branch. To demonstrate the significance of both the political and the ideological constraints that people of ideas encountered at this stage, it is necessary first to demonstrate that the ideologists were not simply written out of the picture after the Task Force's work was done and the law was enacted.

Keeping the Faith

As noted above, the president appointed the two leaders of the Task Force to HUD. Also, while the bill was being debated, HUD established an Advisory Committee on Demonstration Program Development. A Task Force member, William Rafsky, was appointed to chair this committee. And the man appointed to be the assistant secretary in charge of Model Cities, H. Ralph Taylor, met with the enthusiastic approval of both Wood and Haar. The speeches he made in his official capacity make clear, furthermore, that he was indeed within their camp in his view of the federal role in urban affairs. In a representative effort, Taylor explained the essence of a model cities program as being

> a total attack by the city upon a neighborhood—a single area of hard-core slum with a heavy concentration of low-income families, and high concentration of such deficiencies as ill health, joblessness, bad housing, lack of recreational facilities, and poor schools.
> In such attacks we are placing a great emphasis on innovation. . . . We expect cities to look upon the demonstration program as an opportunity to experiment, to attempt the new and different, to become a laboratory for . . . improving the quality of urban living.[68]

And in specifying the prerequisites to success in a Model Cities neighborhood, Taylor listed, first and foremost, "a change in people."

The official interpretation of Model Cities did not differ, in other words, from the Task Force's original interpretation of the program. Indeed, it was Task Force member Rafsky's committee that prepared an influential implementation document, the "Report to the Secretary on the Demonstration Cities Program," presented to Weaver on October 20, 1966. This document provided the basis for the first official interpretation of the Model Cities program, a booklet published by HUD in December 1966 entitled "Improving the Quality of Urban Life: A Program Guide to Model Neighborhoods in Demonstration Cities."[69] These documents closely followed the Task Force Report and its underlying staff papers in all the particulars. Thus, for example, in a section on program highlights in the Advisory Committee's report, the first item listed is a "Total Attack Approach." "This means," the authors clarified in familiar language, "a comprehensive, coordinated, and concentrated effort to mobilize all available resources to rebuild and revitalize the physical environment of blighted neighborhoods and improve significantly the lives of the people living in them." "Innovation" was, characteristically, the next item to be highlighted. The program, it was promised, would provide "an opportunity to cities for experimentation, imagination, and innovation in every aspect." Also, human resource development was highlighted before physical resource improvement, and the development of citizens' participatory "skills" was given special attention.[70] The program guide itself was very much in step with these priorities and this style of presentation.

Even Robert Weaver toed the ideological line laid down in the report, the law, and these program guides. In a 1967 article, Weaver wrote:

> The Model Cities program . . . which may turn out to be the most important single program in urban history . . . provides the nation's first coordinated and comprehensive effort to rebuild entire slum neighborhoods by concentrating on both human and physical problems. It is a revolutionary mechanism to show us how to mobilize vast federal, state, and local forces and direct them to the economic, social, and physical recovery of the neglected areas in our cities.[71]

People of ideas had great influence, then, in establishing the goals and language that were intended to guide the implementation of Model Cities. But there is more to implementation than rhetoric.

Selecting Model Cities: People of Ideas versus Lyndon Johnson

In the implementation of the Model Cities program, the ideologists—Wood, Haar, Rafsky, Taylor, and their peers—suffered a significant defeat. Awards of Model Cities planning grants were made largely on the basis of political considerations. Evidence from the Lyndon Baines Johnson

Library demonstrates that Model Cities were selected in the White House on the basis of partisanship, political support for the president's legislative agenda on the part of congressmen from Model Cities districts, and geographical representation. Even granted that Wood and Weaver never envisaged, as Wood recently wrote to this author, "a tree of wise owls to make the choices," the dominance of political, partisan considerations in the process went far beyond what the record of Task Force deliberations indicates was anticipated by most of its members.[72] Indeed, technical merit seems to have become a minimum threshold requirement, fungible under the right political conditions. (These priorities were exhibited, for instance, by HUD's congressional liaison officer when, in late 1968, he informed H. Barefoot Sanders, his White House counterpart, that "Poteet or Crystal City [both in Texas] would be likely to fail if funded, but could be started if necessary.")[73]

During the Johnson administration, there were two rounds of competition for planning grants, leading to the announcement just before the transition to Nixon's administration of the first nine operational grants. The first round took place over the course of 1967, the second in 1968. Throughout both rounds, factors in selections were *supposed* to be (according to the enabling legislation and HUD's program guide): (1) the commitment of the city to a program for dramatic change; (2) the city demonstration agency's administrative capability; (3) the application's problem analysis; (4) the application's statement of goals and program approaches; (5) the overall innovativeness of the application. In fact, however, President Johnson, in this transitional period in the history of the party system, looked to the party structures of Congress more than to his ideologically charged bureaucracy when it came time to follow through with his most ambitious attempt to redirect the nation's domestic policy.

In July 1967, the Model Cities Administration, working as the staff of the interagency review group, completed its evaluation of first-round applications. On the basis of this evaluation, Weaver recommended to Joseph Califano and the president that the White House move quickly to announce the winners. Recognizing that Johnson had the final say in this matter, Weaver presented to Califano, who passed on to Johnson, a memorandum listing all Model Cities applications. In this memorandum, applications were coded according to (*a*) how the congressional representatives from the applicants' districts had voted on the Model Cities legislation and (*b*) whether HUD recommended them for selection or said that they "could or could not be selected as a model city." Cities that were neither recommended nor marked "could or could not" were presumably below the minimum threshold for technical competence and administrative promise. Those marked "could or could not" were apparently marginally qualified.[74]

As of July 10, 1967, fifty-eight cities were in the "recommended" category and nine were marked possible. Of the nine marked possible, only one originated from a district whose congressman either had voted "wrong" on Model Cities or was a Republican; that one application came, in the code of the memo, from a "R(W)" district. The other eight were coded "D(R)," for Democrats who had voted "right," or "D(NV)," for Democrats who had abstained or missed the vote. Of the fifty-eight recommended applications, only five, or 9 percent, originated from districts whose representatives had voted "wrong." Altogether, 39 percent of the votes cast by congressmen whose districts sent in Model Cities applications were "wrong." The partisanship of the "recommended" and "possible" categories was, by contrast, fairly proportional to the entire set. President Johnson, of course, did not care so much about building up *the* party as he did about building up *his* party, which would give him continued legislative success.

Seventy-five first-round winners eventually were announced from the White House. Of these, fourteen had been judged technically incompetent or marginal by HUD's standards. All fourteen, however, were represented by congressmen who had cast their votes "right" on Model Cities. Furthermore, of the nine that had been marked "could or could not" back in July, only two did not receive funds. These two were the only ones of that set that had diverged from D(R) status: one had been marked D(NV), the other R(W).

Of the first-round winners, sixty-three were announced in November, after that year's elections and after a Model Cities appropriations bill had made its way through the Congress. The remaining twelve were not announced until March of the following year.[75] The March winners were even more overwhelmingly political choices. Six, according to a Califano memo to the president, were "clearly qualified and also will fulfill commitments to our friends." Four were recorded as being those which "Weaver would like to announce" and "which qualify as well." About the final two cities selected, Califano said: "Finally, if you would like to announce cities with two Congressmen who have helped us the following two could be included in the current list."[76] Califano's memo goes on to inform the president, incorrectly, that all of these cities "are those from the first round of planning which did not make it, but which needed additional work" before being found technically competent. In fact, of those in Califano's first category, only two had been deemed adequately prepared. All six, however, were from districts represented by right-voting Democrats. Of those that had Weaver's backing in March, three of four had been recommended on merit by HUD in the summer evaluations; only one had been found in need of further work. There were, finally, no wrong votes among any of these districts, all of whose applications were eventually funded, according to Johnson's wishes.[77]

In the second round, of those Model Cities applicants that received money for planning, six flunked HUD's technical merit test. These were, characteristically, cities in Democratic districts represented by the president's legislative supporters.[78] As in the first round, furthermore, timing was politically determined, although not so blatantly. The White House was eager in the second round, as Sanders explained in a memo to the president, to "avoid the criticism which we encountered last year that we were delaying these announcements until after the appropriations bill was voted on."[79] As Sanders recommended, Johnson held out on announcements in the second round more selectively than in the first.

Finally, committee representation was important to the White House in these selections. In the House, membership on the Appropriations Committee and especially on the Banking and Currency Committee was highly valued. In fact, with respect to the House, R. Douglas Arnold has found that over these two rounds of selections, "support of funding combined with proper committee representation practically guaranteed selection." Fully 99 percent of the members of the relevant subcommittee of the Appropriations Committee ended up with "winners" in their districts. The corresponding figure for the Banking and Currency Committee was 97 percent. By contrast, "non-freshmen who opposed funding in 1967 and who were not members of those committees had an acceptance rate of only 17%."[80]

Coordination: Mainstream People of Ideas versus Turf Fighters and Radical Ideologists

The downplaying of technical criteria in the selection of Model Cities was not, of course, the only problem encountered by HUD officials. An equally vexing problem was the difficulty mainstream people of ideas in HUD encountered in attempting to make their favorite concept, planning, come to life in the bureaucracy. Coordination for the purpose of effective planning was a top priority of the HUD administrators. In trying to achieve it, Wood, Haar, Taylor, and the fellow-traveling Weaver ran into problems with two types of persons within the executive branch, in civil service as well as appointive positions: the bureaucratic turf fighter and the nonmainstream person of ideas.

The Model Cities Act contained a broad directive to "insure maximum coordination of Federal assistance" in directing funds and assistance to demonstration city administrations in each Model City. But the act was silent on the specific objectives of coordination and on how they were to be achieved. The language provided, instead of instructions to the government, a "hunting license" to HUD and its Model Cities Administration. There was, Haar has observed, "much room to maneuver, if little authority."[81] A strategy was therefore devised that rested upon negotiation, persuasion, and cooptation, as opposed to command. The president's personal intervention was not initially a part of HUD's plans to gain coordination. Instead, HUD's appointive leaders took it upon themselves to solicit help from other agencies in the federal establishment early and often, such as when they were compiling a program guide. And in the technical evaluation of Model Cities applications, an informally structured interagency review group was utilized. The help, in particular, of the staffs of OEO, Labor, and HEW, the agencies whose assistance would be especially required in the coordination of revenue flows to Model Cities, was assiduously solicited.

The response, as Haar recalls, was "disappointing to anyone who believed there would be common agreement on general needs and policies and that, once such agreement was reached, all federal departments would link arms and march together into the sunset."[82] Taylor's retrospective evaluation was similar. "There was a great deal of rhetoric about coordination. . . . What we found was that the coordination people, the interagency people, the liaison people, who by and large came to these meetings, could not deliver their bureaucracies."[83] Even within HUD, efforts to coordinate its various fiefdoms proved time-consuming and often fruitless. As Taylor recalled, these difficulties in HUD delayed the entire process, because HUD's leaders felt that they could not ask the president for help before demonstrating that they had their own house in order.

The common thread running through agency intransigence was each fiefdom's desire to retain its turf. The other bureaucracies simply refused to earmark a portion of their appropriated funds for disbursement to the general accounts established under Model Cities. HEW even had its in-house lawyers write briefs to dispute HUD's authority to demand HEW's fiscal cooperation in carrying out the Model Cities law. OEO's administrators, in addition, feared that under the Model Cities program, CAPs might lose power, while bureaucrats in the Department of Labor worried about losing control of their manpower programs within Model Cities areas. Within HUD itself, Assistant Secretary Don Hummel accurately perceived Model Cities as a threat to urban renewal, which he oversaw.

When Taylor finally went to Wood and Weaver, and the three of them decided to seek White House intervention, the results were not as magical as the Task Force members apparently had anticipated in 1965. Califano, for Johnson, wrote a series of threatening memos to cabinet members and spoke directly to a few of them. Not much happened as a result. As Califano explained in 1972, the White House was "not equipped to maintain day-to-day relationship with only one program—no matter how important. . . . Model Cities, while important, could not compete on a continuous basis with key legislative, domestic and foreign policy crises." In any event, Califano believes, "even if staff had more time, it is doubtful whether . . . we could have done more."[84] Even had Johnson announced he was running for re-election, Califano added, "we could only bang heads at a certain level."

A question arises at this point: Why, given the fact that the White House "could only bang heads at a certain level," did not the "automaton" effect of ideological staffing come into play to assist in the coordination of the executive branch in the Johnson administration? Even though, as we saw in chapter 2, Johnson eschewed an overtly ideological appointments strategy, Haar, Wood, and Taylor were people of ideas and they had ideological peers in related agencies and departments. There were, however, several constraints on these people in this particular setting.

First, Johnson was far from being a venerated leader to the people of ideas laboring in his government. These people, therefore, had no reason to feel that they were actualizing the will of the president, as well as their ideology, when they labored for technocratic, apolitical coordination. They were thus denied a potential source not only of motivation but of clout as well. Being a mainstream liberal, in fact, might have compromised clout, as the academicians and intellectuals were frequently suspected by the White House of being Kennedy loyalists (at the same time as they were vilified by many of their intellectual peers outside of government for serving a "war-mongering" president). Second, mainstream liberal ideology had a weakly specified transfer culture. Systemic, comprehensive, logical coordination was not an easy mandate to translate into action. The ability of mainstream liberal ideology to act as a compass is undoubted, but the maps that it generates are fuzzy and indistinct. A third, and final, constraint was that there was another, competing group of people of ideas within the bureaucracy involved in Model Cities implementation. This group, furthermore, came closer to being a self-conscious cadre with an explicit transfer culture than did the mainstream liberals. The conflict between this cadre and the mainstream liberals further compromised the potential influence of the latter.

The Model Cities Act was engineered to avoid the radical excesses of the War on Poverty. But, as Wood recalls, "We let the genie of citizen participation out of the bottle with OEO programs, and now there was no way to put the cork back in."[85] In the first round of planning grants, applicants were generally neglectful of citizen participation as a part of their planning process. This got certain people within HUD jumping. The one who jumped the highest was Sherry Arnstein, H. Ralph Taylor's staff adviser on citizen participation. Arnstein was a "purist," in Weaver and Wood's terminology, and one of those Wood recalls as being "completely committed to ideology and participation."[86] She was committed, in the words of the leadership of one of the more radical Model Cities organizations, "to *help[ing] us do our thing*."[87] During the review of first-round applications, she circulated a paper within HUD that showed how to grade the citizen participation efforts of Model Cities applicants. This paper reportedly served to rally like-minded persons in government about this issue and "set the terms of an ensuing debate."[88]

The debate over what priority to assign citizen participation in Model Cities raged in the interagency process described above. The whole interagency process, of course, was somewhat illusory; that is, it was not supported or attended by those outside of HUD who were capable of "delivering their bureaucracies." But to Arnstein, it was an opportunity to get her ideas translated into policy. She "managed," according to two analysts of the process who were involved in the research and planning of Model Cities, "to have specialists with an orientation similar to her own review [the applications] on behalf of HEW, OEO, and the Justice Department's Community Relations Service."[89] These specialists all urged that greater citizen participation be demanded of applicants in future HUD guidelines. Their demands were adopted, for the most part, in City Demonstration Administration (CDA) letter number 3. According to this official letter of guidance issued by HUD, "cities would have to provide an organizational structure that brought neighborhood residents into the process of planning and implementation . . . the structure would be required to give them direct access to the decisionmaking processes of the City Demonstration Administration, with some form of technical assistance."[90] This was not everything Arnstein and her allies, such as Donald Hess of OEO, had wanted, but it was sufficient to spur the organization in some locales, such as Dayton, Ohio, of dissident citizen coalitions. Thus the program was sidetracked from giving top priority to planning to debating the division of power in Model City neighborhoods.[91]

Given Arnstein's intense demands, she could not be satisfied for long, and she resigned in September 1968. By that time, however, Haar had apparently lost all patience with Taylor and his deputy, Nick Farr, for having allowed Arnstein and her allies to influence policy up to that point. Thus, Haar wrote bitterly in his evaluation of the program of the youthful ideologues in HUD who valued the program "intrinsically."[92] (From the perspective of this chapter, of course, the differences between Haar and Arnstein were of degree, not kind, but it was characteristic of mainstream liberals not to see things this way.)

Who Controlled the Evaluation of Model Cities?

The persons most active today in evaluating Model Cities are the ideologues who designed the program. Haar and Wood have authored books detailing their experiences with Model Cities. Wood's MIT staff director, Bernard Frieden, along with urban policy consultant Marshall Kaplan, has also contributed a major volume to the literature on Model Cities. But the fact that these standard books on Model Cities were written by participants who were caught up in the Great Society crusade has not strengthened their original cause.

Haar's account is the most critical. He places a great deal of the blame for the program's difficulties on the Congress, wrongly so from the perspective of this research. He also, however, finds fault with the citizen participation proponents, who, as he sees it, interfered with the program's operation. Haar even finds some fault with himself and his liberal peers for their excessive confidence in the ability of the federal government, not to mention city governments, to engage in comprehensive, rational planning.

Wood blames American culture and the American pursuit of the war in Vietnam for what he considers the *apparent* failures of the program. The Model Cities program, from his vantage point, did not fail, but was "aborted" because the American people were never truly behind the Great Society. The Great Society, he notes, was aimed at helping economic and racial minorities, but the political culture of the United States is irrevocably "majoritarian." Wood further advances the argument, common in the press and among academic observers, that Johnson's pursuit of the Vietnam War also undermined the Great Society. Wood fuses these two lines of argument in writing that the Model Cities program was "based on the premise that paying Paul may not require robbing Peter."[93] That is, there was supposed to be enough money in the postindustrial society to do every noble thing. The poor and the black could be helped without hurting anyone else. When Johnson deepened American involvement in the war, a zero-sum perspective began to undermine efforts at interagency coordination.

More generally, the evaluation of Model Cities has been tied to the evaluation of all ambitious government efforts of the time to model and adjust human behavior. In the mid-sixties, Wood recalls, the social sciences were "on a behavioral high. . . . You had social scientists feeling terribly able to modify human behavior."[94] And because Wood and his colleagues took seriously the replacement of ideological conflicts by societal problems, they did not foresee how their own work was going to become embroiled in value choices and conflicts. For this reason, the liberal social scientists who built the Great Society programs were not well prepared to defend their efforts on the basis of principle. Instead, they instituted technical evaluation procedures in the most experimental agencies of government, such as OEO and, at the close of the Johnson administration and into the Nixon presidency, HUD as well. The technical evaluations of the experimental projects launched in the Great Society were, Henry Aaron has observed, typically highly critical.[95] In the case of Model Cities, the fact that inter-governmental coordination failed and that selection of Model Cities was not controlled by merit assured poor evaluations from a technical, planning perspective. Aaron believes that the social engineers of the 1960s should have stood their ground on the basis of principle, or ideology. They were doing what was right, and that is what should have mattered.

Lawrence Levinson takes the same position. In an interview, Levinson bridled at the term "chastened liberal." But for many of his peers the term is apt.[96] A decade after the passage of the act establishing the Model Cities program, a select group of Great Society architects was asked by the *New York Times* to evaluate how the perspective of liberal domestic policy entrepreneurs had changed since the Johnson administration. Charles Haar said: "You're more aware of the intractability of problems. I guess there's more modesty about what you can accomplish with integrity, computer analysis and hard work." And Gerson Green, an OEO veteran, thought he saw signs of an even deeper transformation: "The change I discern is that none of us know what to do. In those days we did. The country has taught the social engineers a lesson."[97]

Conclusion

The social engineers of the 1930s were seldom so repentant, even decades after their programs had failed, faded away, or been redirected in less ideological directions. But in the 1930s the plans of the ideologues were not so central to the plans of the president, nor were the ideologues given such a free hand as they were in the early stages of the Great Society to concoct comprehensive strategies for the realization of their utopian visions. The New Dealers, to put it bluntly, did not have so much to be sorry for, if only because their influence was kept under even tighter check than in the 1960s by the proponents and products of an anti-ideological, party-mediated system of policy realignment. The TVA, to be sure, is still with us, but in a form that would hardly be recognizable to its first chairman, Arthur Morgan. With a long-term debt of close to $20 billion and faced with increased competition from private utilities, the authority recently began a massive effort to create a more pragmatic, more businesslike organization.[98] The Model Cities program, by contrast, more intensely and more single-mindedly ideological from the beginning, met with a swifter fate.

"Model Cities—flush it," President Nixon told his close aide John Erlichmann days after his 1972 victory. In a follow-up meeting, Nixon reiterated the command: "Flush Model Cities and Great Society. It's failed. Do it, don't say it."[99] Nixon had been persuaded by White House aide Daniel Patrick Moynihan during his first term that he must move cautiously against Model Cities and other liberal inheritances. But after reelection, the president felt emboldened to reveal more of the "real" Nixon to his opponents and to the public. Model Cities, which had reached a funding level of $600 million by that time, was, according to Nixon's instructions, eliminated. In its place a new community-development grants program was instituted, with a promise that in the new program, localities, which were to be regular units of local government instead of special "participatory" constructs, might use their funds "with only a minimum of review by HUD."[100]

From the vantage point of the 1990s, it appears that in its domestic initiatives the Johnson administration was caught in the middle of the decay and growth of two patterns for the organization of influence in presidential politics. When it ventured beyond its party-based agenda to launch the Great Society, it was unable to find its footing in the emerging ideology-based patterns of personnel selection and executive branch management. The president himself unintentionally sabotaged what he had begun. Johnson's background in the Congress did not prepare him to understand the implementation requirements of the Great Society. The program was his in the sense that it matched his personal ambitions and style, but he did not understand its intellectual and conceptual roots.

Even if President Johnson had been the right leader for this movement, there were constraints upon the influence of the followers that transcended the limitations of Johnson and the system of strong party competition that molded Johnson's political style and expectations. Mainstream liberal ideologists were generally ill-prepared for the trench warfare of bureaucratic politics. They failed to foresee that their plans' assumptions regarding the coordination and planning capacities of the government were in fact assumptions, not statements of fact. They also, in part because of the absence in their ideology of an ascriptive component, underestimated the popular and political resistance their plans would face. This was not a problem for the Rooseveltian people of ideas. Nor would it hinder the conservative social engineers of Ronald Reagan's fiscal policy.

Chapter Five
Engineering a Supply-Side Revolution: The Reagan Administration

An air of disbelief lingers yet over some scholarly as well as lay discussions of the Reagan presidency. Could Ronald Reagan, an aging B-movie star from southern California, a man comfortable with certainty in an increasingly uncertain world, *really* have been our first two-term president since Eisenhower?[1] To Sidney Blumenthal, the Reagan years were a costly flight of mass fantasy, a long "national daydream"; to Michael Rogin, Reagan's presidency was a worrisome manifestation of the racism and paranoia that undergirds America's celluloid consciousness; to Diane Rubenstein, the Reagan years and their Bush epilogue are evidence of a crisis in male identity.[2] Why this reluctance to grapple with the ordinary, everyday reality of the Reagan administration?[3] Two reasons come to mind, both of which help to illuminate the significance of the Reagan years to an understanding of the ideologization of the presidency since the New Deal.

First, the Reagan presidency, if it did not come out of nowhere, clearly did not come from any mass, much less partisan, movement to install a new government, with a particular set of policies and a new agenda, in Washington. As noted in chapter 1, Reagan's election did not herald the arrival of the long-awaited "sixth" party system. In fact, when Reagan took office, there were only four fewer Democratic representatives in the House than when Lyndon Johnson left office, while the number of Republicans had increased by only five. Nor was Reagan's victory the result of any discernible rightward shift in the electorate's ideological self-identifications or policy preferences.[4] Second, Reagan's approach to the presidency defied what many experts assumed about the nature of presidential powers and responsibilities in the 1980s. According to the authors of *Memorandum for the President,* a lengthy volume published by a leading trade press in 1980, a modern president's "perspective must . . . approximate the reality of the world in which he operates." And the "distinguishing features of that world are complexity and breadth."[5] In domestic policy, the authors of this memorandum go on to advise, the president of the 1980s must be sensitive to both the "expanders" and the "managers." (The proponents of a third alternative, a conservative rollback of the welfare state, are simply not mentioned.) As to his relationship to the people, the president, regardless of his party, is advised to "educate the people on the limits you face in making things better."[6] Finally, about ideologues and the modern presidency, the less said the better, for "a top EOP [Executive Office of the President] position is the wrong place for . . . the ideologue who places policy objectives ahead of fair procedures."[7]

These possible explanations for the Reagan "surprise" highlight the ideological character of his presidency as well as underline what is at stake in its analysis. People of ideas are elite political operatives, not surrogate representatives of the people. What happens at the base of our polity no longer corresponds as closely as before to what happens at its apex. Hence the difficulty in incorporating the Reagan administration's achievements into frames of reference about the presidency as an accountable, partisan institution. Also, the Reagan presidency, in violating supposed laws or at least norms of executive politics, threatened the tenets of a competing ideology: the mainstream liberalism analyzed in chapter 4 and implicitly endorsed by the authors quoted immediately above. Finally, the converse implication of this analysis is also worth noting: the ideological thrust of Reagan's presidency should encourage us to rethink both the accountability of the contemporary presidency and the validity of a liberal, technocratic analysis of the institution.

In coming to terms with the ideological character of the Reagan presidency, a close examination of "Reaganomics" is crucial. The supply-side tax cuts at the heart of Reagan's economic agenda were central to the president's ambitions. When the Economic Recovery Tax Act of 1981 (ERTA) went into effect, lowering rates of marginal taxation in line with supply-side doctrine, the president felt that his destiny had been fulfilled. Thus, when ERTA was about to pass in the Congress, the president wrote in his diary, "Six months earlier, I'd come to Washington to put into practice ideas I'd believed in for decades. Now it was down to a few hours." "This on top of the budget victory," Reagan wrote following ERTA's passage, "is the greatest political win in half a century."[8] Yet among the broad public, the tax package had not been a major concern during the campaign. "Taxation/government spending" was, in fact, nominated as the "most important problem" facing the nation by fewer than one in ten voters during the entire campaign year, and only 23 percent of voters favored tax reductions of 30 percent or more, while 24 percent expressed a desire for no tax reduction at all.[9] The people were certainly brought into the legislative battle over this administration's fiscal policy—as a club with which the charismatic Reagan pummeled a frightened Congress—but they were not the driving force behind either the president's or his opponents' enthusiasm.

The driving force behind Reaganomics was ideology. Both ERTA and the complementary Omnibus Budget Reconciliation Act of fiscal year 1982 (OBRA) were conceived by supply-side conservatives and were seen through to their implementation by a coalition of people of ideas and partisan politicians in which the ideologists deserve star billing. There might well have been some innovations in fiscal policy in the early 1980s without the supply-siders, but they were essential in shaping the innovations that were actually pursued so that they constituted an attempted redirection in domestic policy of a magnitude associated in the past with critical partisan realignments. The supply-siders not only came up with the original ideas behind OBRA and ERTA but provided leadership in drafting and steering these bills through the Congress. They were able to exert such sustained influence in part because being ideologues, they were certain that their ideas were logically compelling, absolutely correct, and comprehensively efficacious and that they would usher in a new era in American and global prosperity and justice. Their ideology, in other words, provided intense motivation to the supply-siders and shielded them from factual threats to the soundness of their plan.

The Supply Side's Ideological Attributes

To the supply-sider, everything has its price. The price of an extra hour's work beyond the normal quitting time is whatever a person gives up in that hour. Supply-siders believe that in every decision made at the margin—whether to spend more time at the water cooler or get back to work, whether to apply for a promotion or wait for the boss to notice good work, whether to try to find the perfect words or to just say "and so on"—the worker considers the after-tax pecuniary reward of the "Work Harder" versus the "Take It Easy" decision path. This is why supply-siders insist on cuts in the *marginal* rate of taxation.

The difference between supply-side and familiar neo-Keynesian perspectives on the revenue effects of taxation is illuminated in the different meanings of *tax brake,* a supply-side concept, and *fiscal drag,* a neo-Keynesian idea. Bruce Bartlett and Paul Craig Roberts explain the difference as follows: "In Keynesian fiscal theory, taxation affects disposable income and aggregate demand. In supply-side theory, taxation affects relative prices that govern work-leisure and saving-consumption choices."[10] The difference is not just theoretical, as can be demonstrated with respect to the implications of these approaches for how best to deal with *bracket creep.*

Bracket creep is the gradual shift upwards due to inflation (minus indexing) of effective taxation burdens for taxpayers at all income levels. "Keynesians realized that the automatic rise in tax revenues from bracket creep siphons purchasing power away from consumers, and policymakers believed that this 'fiscal drag' had to be offset or it would choke off economic expansion. The favored offset was increased government spending." Supply-siders, by contrast, "argued that curing fiscal drag cannot cure the economy. Increased government spending can fill in for the consumer spending that is siphoned off by higher taxes, but it cannot replenish the incentives that are also siphoned off by higher tax rates."[11] Only by reducing marginal tax rates can incentives be restored.

So far, this sounds like an economic debate. But the supply side is more than equal to the sum of its economic propositions. Irving Kristol is an excellent guide to the maze of further meanings encompassed by the supply side. Kristol has put forth the thesis that supply-side economics is best understood at a political and ideological level. He acknowledges, to begin with, that "it is absurd economically to think in terms of such a choice" between supply and demand. "Beyond a certain point, a tax on production becomes a tax on consumption," and vice versa. And "a tax on commercial transactions and economic activity is always a tax on *both* production and consumption." But if supply and demand are "opposite sides of the same coin, coexisting of necessity," what is the point of a supply-side perspective? Kristol does not think the point is microeconomics instead of macroeconomics, or international exchange rate stability instead of tax cuts, but the implication of the theory for government policy: "Supply-side economics naturally gives rise to an emphasis on growth, not redistribution. It aims at improving everyone's economic circumstances over time, but not necessarily in the same degree or in the same period of time. . . . The supply side . . . is indifferent to the issue of equality. Its bias is consequently in favor of a free market for economic activity."[12]

And whether supply-side taxes make everyone work harder is not important. It is the entrepreneur that the supply side aims to help. Conventional models of the economy, Kristol complains, have been "utterly blind to entrepreneurship and innovation . . . what cannot be quantified they ignore." Among the nonquantifiables, Kristol places the reaction of entrepreneurs to the relaxation of taxation disincentives to work. As Kristol draws the necessary conclusions, "It does not matter in the least whether you or I will respond to a tax cut by sharpening our economic incentives. Some of us will not. What does matter is that there is, out there, in the real business world as distinct from the academic world of the economists, a minority who will respond in this way . . . it is the incentives of these 'economic activists' that are blunted by a heavy tax burden."[13] The fact that this makes the supply side impossible to test empirically—who can say who might emerge as an entrepreneur given the right top marginal tax rate, and thus, who can say whom to include in a sample of how people respond to economic incentives?—is probably not lost on Kristol. Kristol is a master ideologist, with an understanding of political realities to match his conviction in the ultimate truth of his thought. Unlike fellow supply-siders Lewis Lehrman and Jude Wanniski, that is, Kristol does not believe that truth necessarily wins out over falsehood. (Better to tip the scales beforehand than risk being repudiated?)

Kristol's defense of his doctrine is buttressed by the celebration of the entrepreneur in one of the supply side's weightiest books, George Gilder's *Wealth and Poverty*. Furthermore, Gilder's book, which takes the contributions of the entrepreneur as its theme, was not on the fringes of the supply-side movement when Reagan came to office (though that is where the professional economists among the supply side would like to see it today). Gilder's massive volume was funded in part by the same foundation that subsidized Wanniski's *The Way the World Works* (Smith Richardson, headed at the time by a Kristol protégé, Leslie Lenkowsky) and was reportedly a big hit with the president, who distributed copies of Gilder's work to congressmen and friends.[14] Many of the people who made up the Reagan team, and who dotted the top echelon of institutionalized conservatism, after all, were self-made millionaires, including Irving Kristol's professional peer, William E. Simon, and the members of Reagan's kitchen cabinet. This might have made an economic perspective that placed such individuals front and center especially intelligible to the Reagan team.

Applying the Ideal Type

The test of ideological thought can be applied to a collectivity in this case, as the supply side is a more clearly delineated movement than "Reaganism" or "conservatism." But to whom exactly should the test be applied? There appear to be great divides among the supply-siders. In fact, many are no longer on speaking terms with each other. (Wanniski does not speak with supply-side economist Arthur Laffer; David Stockman, who converted to the supply side before becoming Reagan's budget director, does not speak to anybody; supply-side economist Norman Ture thinks that his peer, Columbia University professor Robert Mundell, is now a Keynesian, and former congressman Jack Kemp an intellectual coward; and Roberts reportedly stormed out of one supply-siders' meeting muttering about socialists.)[15] But back in 1981, there was much greater harmony among these persons. Even today, though there are many factional disputes, there is only one serious divide on theory, that between the taxation economists and the internationalists. The other quarrels are personal, financial, and political.

Among supply-siders, however, what are essentially political (as well as personal and financial) rifts are commonly expressed in theoretical terms. This reflects the fact that the natural vocabulary for character assassination among sectarians is ecclesiastical. Thus, although in an interview Wanniski explained the personal and financial nature of the rift between himself and Laffer, in print Wanniski paints his former friend and business partner as that most horrid of things: a demand-sider. Except, then, as they inform the following case analysis, the factional disputes of supply-siders will be ignored. The ideal type of ideological thought is applied below, then, to the supply side as it has been discussed above—as a collectivity whose chief articulators are George Gilder, Jack Kemp, Irving Kristol, Paul Craig Roberts, Norman Ture, Jude Wanniski, and Arthur Laffer.

Does the supply side make the claims of an ideology? The supply-siders' claim to comprehensive explanation was demonstrated in chapter 1. That leaves open the claims to logical certitude and absolute truth. With respect to the former, though supply-siders may seek to justify their argument at times by citing the congruence of their views with mysterious intuitive precepts, the thrust of their efforts has been to persuade their critics through allegedly superior reasoning. That not one of the major works of the supply-side movement discusses evidence (or the lack of it) about the microeconomic proposition at the heart of the doctrine is powerful testimony to the insularity of supply-side reasoning. From this can be inferred the "close-mindedness" of supply-side thought. Jude Wanniski's close-mindedness is so intense, in fact, that when he was writing his book on the supply side, and Irving Kristol convinced him that his political and psychological models were wrong, he rebelled. He did so because he just *knew* that his economic propositions could not be wrong. As Sidney Blumenthal reports on his interview with Wanniski:

> "Irving said it was probably wrong. He said my economic theory was so innovative, so radical, that there was no reason to have it carry the extra burden of the political model. I thought Irving was right." Wanniski was depressed and confused; he felt that his work was being blocked. "Then," he said, "I thought if my political model was wrong, my economic model was wrong." And since he never believed that his economic model was in error, it followed that his political model must be correct, too.[16]

The significance of such close-mindedness is suggested by Irving Kristol's own insistence on the ideological imperatives of economic policy making. "Your first priority," he says, "is to shape the future of the society. And you don't listen to bankers, and you don't listen to economists." Kristol, who manages somehow to be both an admirer of the controversial elitist political philosopher, the late Leo Strauss, and a populist, goes on to suggest that what has been really important about Reagan's stewardship of the supply side is his ability to express in his policies the hopes of the masses:

> I don't think that production of more goods is all that important. The key is changing peoples' attitudes about economic activity. If people feel that they have opportunity—I mean this is the key to the United States. People must feel there is real opportunity out there; that's why I'm a supply sider. I think that in general, it leads to a more growing, dynamic economy, but really I'm more interested in its role of opening opportunities up.

In Kristol's view, even if no empirical evidence can be uncovered that supply-side tax cuts have their intended economic effects, they are still worth pursuing for their expressive benefits. "In fact," he states, "the macroeconomic statistics on income and so on are not that good in the past several years, but people feel better about the economy, and those feelings are real." Reagan's rhetoric, Kristol asserts, "corresponds with people's feelings, even if not with statistics compiled at MIT."[17]

As to whether or not the supply-siders claim absolute truth for their theories, the verdict must be split. The strictly economic supply-siders offer a dimly absolutist view of mankind. A particularly uninspiring vision of man as a calculator of marginal value is the foundation for their economic propositions. But many on the supply side do not think that this is sufficient. Thus, Kristol links the supply side to a general, antistatist conservative point of view wherein there is a transcendent obligation for individuals to be free from state coercion. But this still leaves the supply side somewhat uninspiring, if not actually demeaning. Where is the vision of man to match the vision of a global, inflationless economy or to compete with the chiliastic visions of intellectuals on the left? Jude Wanniski and George Gilder have grafted their own absolute beliefs onto the supply side and hence have made it potentially more inspiring.

Wanniski, as noted previously, even devotes the first part of his book to an exploration of developmental psychology from a supply-side point of view. The things children learn, from when to cry for help and when it is not worthwhile to how to frame a request for an increase in their allowance, are explicated from the point of view of a universal and innate supply-side intelligence. Gilder goes even further, to the point of contradicting the supply side's most basic tenet, namely, that people work for money.

Gilder saw in the supply side a way to link free-market economics with New Right morality. In *Wealth and Poverty*, he faulted conservatives for not creating a capitalist "theology" or vision of necessary "justice." Gilder sought to fill these gaps by imbuing entrepreneurial activity with sacred virtue. This he did by defining the rich in a tone of spiritual awe: "A successful economy depends on the proliferation of the rich, on creating a large class of risk-taking men who are willing to shun the easy channels of a comfortable life in order to create new enterprise, win huge profits, and invest them again." Profits to Gilder are, in this light, but "unexpected return." The "function of the rich" is not to become richer but to "foster opportunity for the classes below them in the continuing drama of the creation of wealth and progress." But by following this line of argument, Gilder divorces himself from the basic microeconomic propositions of the movement. It would appear, indeed, that the glory of the supply side to Gilder is the honor rather than the rewards it promises the wealth-makers.[18]

The ascriptiveness of ideological thought is evidenced even more plainly in supply-side thought. The supply side pays homage to the wealthy entrepreneur for making that extra effort—building that extra bridge or making that late-night deal. Meanwhile, those without cash have failed not only themselves but their nation and community as well. There are supply-siders, such as Lewis Lehrman and Irving Kristol, who possess a highly cultivated sense of the values of a civilization. These men are prone to believe that the wealthy entrepreneur who always chooses more work and more income over more leisure is only semiheroic, or merely useful to a society. As Kristol says of businessmen: "All they need to know is which side they're on and to give the money."[19] But there are many other supply-siders, such as David Stockman, Jude Wanniski, and George Gilder, who are strongly inclined to more expansive praise of the supply side's "good guys."

The pure ideologue, in addition to exhibiting the traits demonstrated above, will, I have stipulated, exhibit an imminent historical consciousness. Supply-siders, though they look back to the late-eighteenth-century philosopher Adam Smith and the early nineteenth-century economist Jean Baptiste de Say, intend to move the global economy forward to an abundance and harmony never before realized. Furthermore, supply-siders do not portray their ideal economy and society as a static order, but as a constantly expanding cornucopia. Growth, not utopian timelessness or a mythic return to bygone days, is the objective that inspires them. The transfer culture of the supply-siders, furthermore, is detailed, explicit, and designed to bridge rapidly the present with the future.

Finally, the "institutions" that count in establishing supply-side credentials are for the most part Ronald Reagan's campaign and early presidency and Jack Kemp's former congressional office. Two formal institutions important to the supply-siders from the 1970s into the 1980s were the Smith Richardson Foundation and the *Wall Street Journal*. Smith Richardson, mentioned above, had at the time an annual budget of about $3 million for grants to scholars and writers and funded the efforts of both Gilder and Wanniski. The *Wall Street Journal*, meanwhile, was edited by a Wanniski convert, Robert Bartley, who was the employer in the late 1970s of first Wanniski and then Paul Craig Roberts. When Roberts took his fight with the White House public in the first year of Reagan's administration, he did so by contributing stories to this reliably supply-side outlet.[20] Collectively, then, supply-siders, or significant factions among them, exhibit each of the traits in the ideal type of ideological thought and are, furthermore, sympathetic to the antistatist principles of conservatism more broadly defined.

OBRA and ERTA

Inception and Early Development

The groundwork for the legislative enactment of Reagan's fiscal policies was laid by people of ideas. Paul Craig Roberts, his one-time boss Kemp, and the coterie of supply-siders who surrounded Kemp in the late 1970s were the individuals most responsible for preparing the way for Reagan's innovations. These men, especially Wanniski, also helped take the idea public in intellectual and media circles, where its ideological implications were fully developed and debated.

Paul Craig Roberts joined Congressman Jack Kemp's staff in 1975 as a professional economist. In addition to being an expert on taxation, Roberts was a conservative in the broadest sense, being staunchly anticommunist and suspicious of bureaucratic intentions and capacities. Roberts had been a government intern in his early twenties and had run afoul of his superior by attempting to publicize what Roberts felt were undeniable facts about the harm being done to the Puerto Rican economy because of Washington's oversight. This experience left Roberts deeply disillusioned about Washington. Also, in his early adulthood Roberts visited the Soviet Union on a tour sponsored by a private organization. Roberts believed that those who ran this tour were liberal moral relativists. This alarmed him sufficiently to make him suspicious of American liberalism as well as Soviet communism from that time on. Thus, by the time he joined Congressman Kemp's staff, Roberts was interested in far more than the technical details of economic policy. To him, an economic policy change in a supply-side direction, if successful, would be a victory not just for a rather obscure group of economic theorists but for conservatism as a whole.[21] After impressing Kemp as a member of his personal staff, Roberts went to work in 1977 as the first chief economist on the minority staff of the House Budget Committee. Though Kemp was not on that committee, Roberts worked there more or less as "Kemp's man." Kemp, meanwhile (in 1975 and 1976), had been persuaded of the correctness of the supply side by the combined efforts of Roberts, Wanniski, and Laffer.[22] In the first congressional debate over fiscal policy in which a supply-side alternative was proposed, Kemp was the movement's leading spokesman, and Roberts, the chief staff member working behind the scenes.

Since the Congressional Budget and Impoundment Control Act of 1974, there had been at least two budget resolutions each year in each chamber of Congress. The third budget resolution for fiscal year 1977 was debated on the floor of the House in February 1977. At that time, John Rousselot, a freshman congressman from California, under the tutelage of Roberts, proposed an across-the-board tax cut of 5 percent for every taxpayer. Roberts acknowledges that this idea was supply-side only in disguise: it would actually have made the tax code more, not less, regressive. Despite this "drawback," the proposal would have reduced the top marginal rate, and the top rate is the bottom line to a supply-sider.

During the floor debate on Rousselot's proposal, he and the other Republicans had difficulty maintaining their conceptual clarity. The supply-side interpretation of how taxes affect the economy was a new idea that went against what had become reflexive Keynesian ways of thinking. The regular Republicans, Roberts believes, seemed generally not to understand that the supply side could be defended in terms of a broad vision of social as well as fiscal justice. Kemp's comments that day were the only bright spot for the supply-siders. He took the floor to explain to his colleagues the vision that animated Rousselot's proposal, that of a growing and stable economy. Though the Republican proposal was defeated 258 to 148, Jude Wanniski played up Kemp's principled stand in the losing effort in the next day's *Wall Street Journal*.

Roberts next went to work in the Senate, where the supply side was championed, again, by a freshman member of the body, in this case Orrin Hatch, Republican from Utah. Hatch and Roberts tried for months to get the Joint Economic Committee to fund a proposal from Michael Evans of Chase Econometrics to design an explicitly supply-side model of the national economy. Hatch, like Kemp and the others, was attracted to the supply side at least in part because of its symbolic logic. The supply side, he thought, made sense within a populist, conservative framework. The supply-siders understood, he told his colleagues, that it was not true that "the people who work and produce exist . . . only to fund our spending programs."[23]

The supply-side effort in the Senate and House continued into 1980 with movement toward acceptance of the supply side as one of the alternatives that might reasonably be pursued in fiscal policy. In the introduction to its 1979 report, in fact, the chairman of the Joint Economic

Committee, Senator Lloyd Bentsen, stated that there was "an emerging consensus in the Committee and in the country that the federal government should put its house in order and that the major challenges today and for the foreseeable future are on the supply side of the economy." And in 1980, when this committee held hearings on the econometric models used by government forecasters, the well-known mainstream economist Otto Eckstein not only testified about how his and other popular models neglected the supply consequences of fiscal policy but even seemed at one point to talk as a supply-sider himself, when he testified that "we are meeting here today at a rare moment of opportunity for supply-side economics."[24] Meanwhile, outside of the Joint Economic Committee, Senator William Roth, Jr., and Congressman Kemp were advancing a supply-side tax bill that would be endorsed by Ronald Reagan in his 1980 campaign, and Congressmen David Stockman and Phil Gramm were gaining valuable experience in preparing proposals for budget reductions.

In retrospect, it can be seen that though conservative ideology was likely beside the point to Bentsen and Eckstein, it was the motivating factor among the supply side's earliest and most consistent champions. The supply side's economists, as well as Senator Hatch and Congressman Kemp, were motivated by ideological zeal for the broad conservative world vision in which the specific propositions of supply-side economists were embedded. Without these people of ideas, including the two politicians, their staff man, Roberts, and the outside entrepreneurs and publicists, especially Laffer, Wanniski, Kristol, and Lenkowsky, there would have been no supply-side economic alternative to provide a rallying point for Hatch's and Kemp's nonideological peers on the Joint Economic Committee. Still, economic conditions and their political interpretation in the late 1970s significantly helped the supply-siders.

At the end of the Carter administration, the economy was in a puzzling stagflation, productivity declines in American industrial sectors were becoming a high-priority media item, and voter dissatisfaction with high property taxes seemed to presage a populist revolt against government. Under these conditions, the supply side appeared to some politicians of both parties to be a potential winning issue. What the supply-siders offered was an elaborate, specific, scientific-sounding plan in which they expressed absolute confidence and which promised amazing results. Though the political equation would not be sufficiently weighted in favor of passing the custody of the nation's fiscal policy to this cabal until after the 1980 elections, economic conditions in the late 1970s helped the supply-side ideologists gain entry into the marketplace of seemingly feasible ideas.

Foreseeing that to gain practical success, rather than just fleeting respect, they would have to launch their battle from the higher ground of the presidency, the supply-siders surrounding Kemp urged him to run in

1980. The possibility that Kemp might contend with Reagan for the conservative vote in Republican primaries that year of course placed pressure on the Reagan entourage to coopt the supply-side issue. The story of Kemp's pressure upon the Reagan campaign, beginning in 1976, is still obscure. What we do know is that in 1979 and 1980 the congressman consulted with Reagan at length on several occasions about adopting the supply-side themes of the Kemp-Roth bill in the coming campaign. Reagan, furthermore, allowed Kemp to send Wanniski and Laffer to instruct him in their doctrine.[25]

Jude Wanniski's first policy briefing with the candidate, a day-long classroomlike session on economics with Reagan and a score of other tutors, took place in Los Angeles in early January 1980. Wanniski and Laffer gave formal presentations on inflation, energy, and the historical perspective of supply-side thought. Kemp was one of the most vocal and consistent participants at all meetings. As Wanniski recalled the meeting in a memorandum to the clients of his consulting firm:

> The criticisms were along the lines that the ideas are theoretically correct, but no longer practical in the modern world. Reagan resisted such criticisms at every turn, and instead seemed to firmly reject counter proposals of a "practical" nature. He has the concept of economic growth, as opposed to the Malthusian idea [of the natural limits to growth], in his bones and thus finds himself extremely comfortable with supply-side ideas. . . . He has heard Kemp speak so many times by now, and has read so much of the supply-side material, that he was fairly sharp handling the ideas during the briefing.[26]

Wanniski's only complaint was that Reagan still tended to see foreign and energy policy as separate from the supply side, instead of "seeing the world as a closed political economy."

John Sears, Reagan's campaign manager for part of 1980, also had a role in persuading Reagan to focus more on supply-side ideas as the campaign progressed. Sears, no ideologue of any sort, was impressed by the near success of Jeffrey Bell in New Jersey's 1978 Senate race, a race in which he ran as a Jack Kemp look-alike. Bell had managed Reagan's 1976 campaign and was not an outsider in the Reagan camp in 1980. Sears, furthermore, worked behind the scenes for Bell in 1978. What was important in 1978, according to Wanniski, was that "Sears saw the appeal the supply side could have."[27] In Sears's words, "One thing that was wrong with all sides was that no one had any new handle, aside from the difference of opinion on who should pay the sacrifice. This was a new idea."[28] It also, of course, tied in well with the general appeal of tax busting (supply-side or otherwise), proven that same year in California's Proposition 13.

Although Sears, like some of the congressional allies of conve-

146

nience that Kemp had found useful before, was impressed most with the *secondary* qualities of the supply side, Ronald Reagan adopted it in an intensely ideological fashion. When Kemp and Reagan met to discuss their respective interests in the presidency, they met, after all, as combatants in the same army. Both were enemies of state expansion, and both were zealous in pursuit of their ideas. Reagan did not cynically attempt to coopt his fellow antistatist's idea. Rather, he incorporated it within his own conservative world-view, and made it his own most cherished goal.

The supply side, as Wanniski observed after his first meeting with the candidate, was "in Reagan's bones." Reagan's retrospective view of the supply side, in fact, is somewhat defensive. "During the 1980 campaign," he wrote in his memoirs, "a new term, *supply-side economics,* came into vogue. People said I embraced this theory, and several economists claimed credit for inventing its principles, which they said I had then adopted as the basis for my economic recovery program." According to Reagan, "that wasn't true." Rather, he reminds us that "at Eureka College, my major was economics." And in any event, "my own experience with our tax laws in Hollywood probably taught me more about practical economic theory than I ever learned in a classroom or from an economist." What happened in Hollywood was that Reagan, at the height of his career, faced a short-lived 90 percent marginal rate of taxation and, as a result, decided not to make as many movies each year as he might otherwise have made. "If I decided to do one less picture, that meant other people at the studio in lower tax brackets wouldn't work as much either." "The same principle," Reagan goes on to insist, "applied to people in all tax brackets. The more government takes in taxes, the less incentive people have to work."[29] Because Reagan has, as his friend William F. Buckley, Jr., says, a "penchant for the anecdotal,"[30] the fact that he could subsume the supply side under a powerful anecdote from the favorite years of his life allowed him literally to "possess" the idea and consequently to think of it as his own creation.[31] This would prove important because it was the ideologically motivated, including Reagan, who would stand firm behind the supply-side changes of 1981 during the recession that followed (chronologically if not causally; the matter is, of course, debated).

The Legislative Proposal

The decision to translate the general perspective of supply-side economics into the core of the Reagan team's agenda for the crucial first year in office was made during the transition. The most important influence here was probably the "Dunkirk" memorandum, written by Kemp, Stockman, and Lehrman and excerpted (after being leaked by Wanniski) in the *New York Times.* In this memo, these cabalists urged the president-elect to assault the failing economy with supply-side tax cuts and antistatist budgetary reductions. They called for "an Administration initiative in economic policy so bold, sweeping and sustained that it totally dominates the Washington agenda during 1981."[32] In terms of the budgeting process, this document urged a radical departure from standard practices. Reagan's first budget, these ideologists argued, should be for fiscal year 1982. Because of the time lag in budgeting, a budget for 1982 had already been prepared and presented to Congress by outgoing President Jimmy Carter, and there was very little time to prepare a comprehensive substitute. Quick action, consequently, was essential. This document helped to guarantee it. It also helped to secure its principal author his administration position, and Reagan his alleged revolution.

The work of Norman Ture, not a member of the Wanniski-Kemp-Stockman cabal, was also significant during the time the supply-side legislative proposals were being prepared. Ture had explored the macroeconomic rationale for reducing rates of marginal taxation several years before, while a staff economist at Martin Feldstein's National Bureau of Economic Research. Ture's monographs were surely not read by the incoming president, but his essay on tax policy in the widely publicized owner's manual to the White House, *Mandate*, published by the conservative Heritage Foundation, was known to the personnel office and those active in choosing the economic staff of the new administration, including Jack Kemp and Donald Regan, who became treasury secretary.[33] (The White House's "unrelenting" control of personnel selection, as explained previously, did not exclude cabinet secretaries entirely, and Kemp had earned his exceptional advisory role during the campaign.) Ture, in his *Mandate* contribution, proposed the creation within the Treasury Department of a new position, undersecretary for tax and economic affairs. The position, which was designed to provide a strategic advantage for supply-siders within the government, was created, and Ture was its first occupant. His subordinate at Treasury was Paul Craig Roberts, whose appointed aides were also supply-siders. This team maintained steady pressure to keep the supply side front and center as Reagan took office.

Thus, as the administration settled into office, the supply-siders remained in control of the economic policymaking process. In the Treasury Department, in OMB, and in the Oval Office, creating supply-side legislative proposals was perceived as the absolute priority of the new administration. Without, furthermore, the attraction of the individual ideologues in these positions to supply-side policies, it is unlikely that whatever tax "relief," "reform," or "stimulus" might yet have been pursued would have been in agreement with supply-side doctrine. The supply-side choice in cutting taxes was never self-evident. Indeed, the regular Republicans in the Congress during supply-side's trial run had great difficulty comprehending the uniqueness of the supply-side view.

After Reagan's inauguration, then, people of ideas remained in control. It was they who translated the Dunkirk memorandum, Ture's Heritage paper, Reagan's campaign speeches, the Kemp-Roth bill, and other supply-side documents into two pieces of proposed legislation. For strategic reasons, the budget bill was pursued first by the White House.

OBRA: Pre-Hill Battles

When, early in the preparation of the fiscal year 1982 budget, individual cabinet officers came to review their departments' budgets with the director of OMB, they came, for the most part, "individually to face a united White House front and Stockman's unequaled grasp of their agencies' budget numbers."[34] It was not so much that the White House was truly united as that Stockman had devised a strategy to minimize the influence of nonideologues in the budgeting process. After terminating the early practice of reviewing budgetary proposals at cabinet meetings, Stockman initiated his Budget Review Group. Though James Baker (chief of staff) and Edwin Meese (White House counselor) were members of this new institution, their participation was minimal. (As Stockman had anticipated, since the president himself would not be at these meetings, neither Baker nor Meese would attend.) Those who did participate, Stockman relates, were "hard-core anti-spenders," including Regan, domestic policy adviser Martin Anderson, U.S. trade representative William Brock, and chairman of the Council of Economic Advisers (CEA) Murray Weidenbaum.[35]

Anderson, in particular, a former protégé of Ayn Rand's, reportedly "came into his glory" in the "Cutting Room." In a typical encounter, after a secretary's civil service aide had finished a lengthy disquisition on the foolishness of OMB's proposed cuts, Anderson would draw the careerist into an account of his long service in the bureaucracy only to make the point that Anderson had "heard this same argument ever since I was in the Nixon Administration." "Delighted," he would reportedly say, "as I am to see it hasn't changed, it's still wrong." This routine was calculated to remind cabinet members that in Reagan's administration, one had to choose sides between the good guys and the bad guys. And the permanent government was on the wrong side in this heroic confrontation.[36]

Stockman and his allies gained a further advantage over the cabinet and the bureaucracy because among those appointees who had already assumed subcabinet positions at this time (and many posts remained unfilled months after Reagan took office),[37] only the ideologically pure were encouraged by OMB to participate in preparing budgets for their agencies. The others received the same treatment as the professional bureaucrats; they were ignored.

Thus, Joseph Wholey and his colleagues found that in the DOA, Labor, and HHS, departmental involvement in preparing the fiscal year

1982 budget was weak; elsewhere, those at the departmental level who were involved most heavily were among the most conservative of Reagan's appointees. In the Department of Labor, for instance, whereas in previous budget cycles the department's budget professionals had been solicited for policy analyses, program evaluations, and budgetary recommendations, the Reagan White House asked for nothing. Wholey quotes a Labor budget staffer as saying: "It has been a masterful performance of taking charge and cutting out things you don't like. Masterful! . . . They did this without a lot of paper. There was little guidance; mainly numbers from the Secretary or OMB to be met."[38] The assistant secretary in charge of the Employment and Training Administration, within Labor, however, who had impressive movement credentials, was brought into the budgeting process. The result was a series of reductions in force, hiring freezes, and reductions in salaries and expense account limits, which decimated the agency.[39]

Another instance in which the White House allowed ideological appointees exceptional access in the budgeting process was in welfare policy. For example, conservative subcabinet appointees in various parts of the government rewrote in the first months of the Reagan presidency the eligibility requirements for participation in the AFDC program, a prime target of criticism in the conservative reevaluation of the federal role in welfare provision. The moderately conservative, formerly liberal Richard Schweicker, secretary of health and human services, was left outside of this decisionmaking circle.

Those who took charge in this case—Robert Carleson, special White House assistant for policy development; David B. Swoap, undersecretary of health and human services; and John A. Svahn, commissioner of social security—had each at one time been in charge of Governor Reagan's welfare policies. From the time Reagan was elected governor until the time he was elected president, all three had gained national executive experience. Another item they had in common was a conservative perspective on income and welfare. "'Income belongs to the people who earn it,' Mr. Carleson says. 'It does not belong to the state, nor does it belong by right to any other segment of the population. . . . No threat of unrest . . . should be permitted to cow a government into transferring income . . . when that transfer is not justified by accepted social norms.'" And Mr. Swoap, answering a reporter's question "as to whether there should be equality of sacrifice by rich and poor," replied: "What is rich, what is poor, what is sacrifice? Most of the people whose benefits have been cut by the Reagan Administration are not poor."[40] It was through the coordinated work of this trio that the number of households receiving aid under AFDC (as under Medicaid and the food stamps program) held steady or was reduced in the 1980s, even though poverty and unemployment levels rose.[41] The new AFDC rules also took the nation's first coordinated step toward *workfare*, permitting states to require work in exchange for benefits. Most of the changes and reductions in AFDC and other welfare programs affected by OBRA were aimed, as the Reagan agenda dictated, at the *working poor.*

These stratagems were truly exceptional. OMB had never before assumed such exclusive authority in the budgeting process. Nor had the White House ever systematically sought alliances in budgeting with sympathetic subcabinet appointees, purposely undercutting the authority not only of the permanent bureaucracy but of recalcitrant cabinet secretaries as well.[42] The result was to get the blitzkrieg on its way. Indeed, in Stockman's accurate assessment of the early budgeting process, "The feverish work of January and early February 1981 was not policymaking, at least not in the normal sense. No basic policy options were appraised, discussed, or debated." Because "the fundamentals of the Reagan fiscal program . . . had been given *a priori.* The tumultuous work prior to February 18 was purely ministerial. It amounted to the translation of doctrine into the customary details, numbers, and formats of workaday policy."[43] Stockman's evaluation rings true for the next step in the policymaking process as well: the packaging of budgetary numbers within an overall economic forecast.

Normally, the CEA is in charge of forecasts. But from the perspective of Reagan and his top aides, the CEA was a nuisance, and by early January no one had been appointed to head this institution. The secretary of the treasury, meanwhile, thought of forecasts as bothersome formalities. The ideologists, by contrast, drawing on their congressional experience, recognized forecasting as an important battle ground. Consequently, those who took an active interest in forecasting at the outset included Stockman, his aide Lawrence Kudlow, Treasury appointees Ture and Roberts and Roberts's two supply-side deputies, Stephen Entin and Manley Johnson, and the Treasury's monetary expert, Beryl Sprinkel. Finally, though there is conflicting testimony as to the significance of their input, Arthur Laffer, Jude Wanniski, Lewis Lehrman, and Milton Friedman were in frequent contact with their allies in this group.[44]

This forecasting team was fairly small but large enough for a rift to appear. While the supply-siders wanted "*the biggest possible numbers for real growth,*" the monetarists (Sprinkel's clout was increased beyond his singular number by the reputation that the super-monetarist Friedman enjoyed as the "President's favorite economist") wanted "*the lowest possible numbers for money GNP.*" As Stockman observes, "When you brought the two camps together, it was the inflation number which took it in the neck." By compromising on inflation, they attained a temporary settlement that healed this rift without damage to supply-side dogma: "The Treasury supply siders wanted about 5 percent real growth; the monetarists wanted about 7 percent money GNP growth. Consequently, by the third or fourth year, inflation collapsed to 2 percent because that's what the arithmetic required."[45] The resultant forecast encapsulated the supply-side ideal of inflationless *and* recession-free expansion.

In February, a threat to the supply-siders' dominance of the forecasting battles emerged in the person of Murray Weidenbaum, the new chairman of the CEA. When he reviewed the proposed White House forecast, he demanded a higher inflation projection, threatening to take the issue to the president if it were not quickly resolved. Weidenbaum's demand represented a setback, in theory, to the supply-siders as well as the monetarists. In retrospect, however, it helped the original forecasters secure their legislative victory. The forecast that Weidenbaum forced on Stockman and his team, because of the obvious relationship of projected inflation to projected revenues before indexing was to take effect, made cutting taxes more acceptable to deficit-wary congressmen.

Some expert commentators, most notably Hugh Heclo and Rudolph Penner, have argued that their ability to compromise in this way shows that the supply-siders evolved a political as opposed to an ideological perspective on their agenda.[46] But this is an unnecessary distinction. For ideological dogmatism might itself have contributed to the willingness of the supply-siders to forge this and other compromises. The close-mindedness of ideological thought, that is, suggests that the supply-siders might have accepted compromises because their ideology made their core beliefs impregnable. To an ideologist, a compromise might seem like a way to shorten the path to the demonstration of the truthfulness of his beliefs. Thus, when Stockman had reservations as early as the second week of February about the reconcilability of the two halves of Reagan's fiscal revolution, the problem his forecast compromise with Weidenbaum helped to paper over, he did not seek to slow down the blitzkrieg but pushed ahead:

> I should have blown the whistle and called off the blitzkrieg. But a radical ideologue at the height of his powers does not stop, in mid-headlong rush, to wonder how history will judge him years from then. I had momentum, I had won victories, I would win more. The pace couldn't be slackened for a moment. To falter now would be to leave the Reagan Revolution stillborn and defeated.[47]

So long as his ideological blinders were on, what appeared to others as facts leaving the supply-side truth in question appeared to Stockman as merely political items, to be manipulated according to the dictates of his ideology. The ideologist's epistemological arrogance prevents him from treating his opponents with intellectual respect but does not prevent him from cutting political deals with his rivals. These deals were essential, furthermore, to Stockman's ability to move this case to its next stage, the fight on Capitol Hill for passage of Reagan's fiscal year 1982 budget bill.

OBRA: The Battle on the Hill

The congressional phase of the legislative process leading to OBRA began with the decision to use the reconciliation process in a novel way. This innovation forced votes in the Senate and the House on hundreds of authorizations and appropriations, including those for entitlement programs, in a single "up-or-down" vote. This innovative use of provisions contained in the 1974 Budget Act was the idea of Stockman and Senate Budget Chairman Pete Domenici. As Stockman explains in his memoirs, "Back then, I wanted to cut off the debate." With his ideology serving as a template, Stockman knew precisely what he wanted the Congress to do.

In struggling for passage of OBRA, Stockman had, to his further advantage, a clear perception of the stakes for Congress and the executive in pursuing the supply-side agenda. "Enacting the Reagan Administration's economic program meant rubber-stamp approval, nothing less."[48] In gaining his rubber stamp, Stockman was assisted, of course, by the partisan balance of the Ninety-seventh Congress. Especially in the newly Republican Senate, where the reconciliation process began, partisanship was significant. Still, the program would not have passed Congress had it not been for the acquiescence of the Democratic party's leadership in the House, who were brought along through skillful bargaining at the margins by the president with reluctant members of Congress and by the president's masterful manipulation of the traditional American contempt for those who govern them. As the Speaker, "Tip" O'Neill, recalls the contest, "Despite my strong opposition to the president's program, I decided to give it a chance to be voted on by the nation's elected representatives." Not only was this "how our democracy is supposed to work" but, O'Neill recalls, he "was afraid that the voters would repudiate the Democrats if we didn't give the president a chance to pass his program."[49] Or more plainly, as O'Neill said at the time, "I've been a politician long enough to know when to fight and when not to." Nineteen eighty-one was not a time for liberal Democrats to fight.[50]

There were two crucial votes in this process. The vote for the concurrent resolution (H.R. 115) in the Democrat-controlled House was passed by the substantial margin of 77 votes, 253–176. This followed weeks of intense lobbying by the president, political action committees, and the White House's highly professional legislative liaison office. OBRA's second crucial test also came in the House, when the House passed the reconciliation package, including changes in existing legislation affecting spending in all areas of the federal budget. To gain this latter victory, the president telephoned or telegraphed personally each of the 63 Democrats who had voted with him on the prior budget resolution, and his aides struck compromises when necessary to win votes for the administration's bill. The president also worked through Lynn Nofziger, a Reaganite ideologue on the White House staff, to rally conservatives to pressure wavering members of Congress in their home districts.[51]

After considerable legislative maneuvering and economic sophistry on both sides, Gramm-Latta II (H.R. 3982) passed the House with a vote of 232–193 on June 26. The vote on the corresponding bill in the Senate had not even been close; the administration had prevailed 80–15 the day before. The omnibus reconciliation package cut a total of $45.1 billion from the baseline established by the Congressional Budget Office for that fiscal year and was to have realized a total "savings" of $130.6 billion for fiscal years 1982 to 1984.[52] Even Stockman was pleased with the results at the time. The other supply-siders were especially happy that now they could move on to ERTA.

ERTA: Toeing the Line within the Administration

In fighting for supply-side tax cuts after OBRA won passage, people of ideas took the lead, though they shared responsibility with others. The key players, besides President Reagan, were Donald Regan, his ideological Treasury staffers, and Baker, his assistant Richard Darman, Meese, and Stockman. Within this group, battles were fought that are still obscure. Basically, it seems that Baker and Darman, being dedicated first and foremost to the success of Reagan as president, would have been happy to compromise on taxes, so long as an appropriate spin could be placed on the result. But Reagan signaled that he was not willing to compromise. Regan, meanwhile, as Stockman observes, "operated on the 'echo' principle. Whatever the President insisted on, he would try to get."[53] In effect, he became the chief administration salesman for the supply side and came to rely extensively upon his ideological subcabinet officials and their staffs. Stockman, of course, like the Treasury supply-siders, professed an absolute passion for a supply-side tax cut.

There was within this set of individuals influential in achieving passage for ERTA, a conflict, then, between those who viewed the supply side strategically, as a means toward an end, and those who valued it intrinsically, as an ideology, with Stockman straddling both groups. Stockman aside, the pragmatists considered the purpose of their policy efforts to be to achieve a dramatic political win for the president. The ideologues, by contrast, including (with occasional lapses) the president himself in the first year of his term, were there "to do whatever it takes"[54] to gain a true policy revolution. They were playing, after all, for what they took to be much larger stakes than public acclaim.

The pre-Hill phase of the interactions between these groups was marked chiefly by a contest between the pragmatists and the ideologues over whether to stick with the original plan of the Kemp-Roth tax bill adopted by Reagan or to dilute it in some way. Stockman had not yet joined tactically with the pragmatists and continued at least through the summer to toe the line on the desired structure and magnitude of the tax reductions. In part, he just could not let his leader down, at least not yet. Indeed, the success of the ideologists in pressing upon the Congress a true supply-side tax package was a victory for the efficacy in presidential politics of prophetic ideological leadership. President Reagan would, in subsequent years, side sometimes with the pragmatists on the issue of aggregate tax levels, but early in his presidency his steadfastness preserved administration influence for the ideologists in their struggle to send to the Hill and steer through Congress a pure supply-side tax bill.

The president's prophecy provided motivation as well as clout to the Treasury supply-siders operating in his name. According to Roberts, early in the battle for a supply-side tax bill, he realized, in an apparent epiphany, "that if the President was going to get anywhere with his economic program, I was going to have to take a lot of risks."[55] He would have to align himself, namely, with the "White House" against the imposters. And to Roberts, the "White House" meant only the true believers therein. Thus, Roberts exposed himself as a target to the pragmatists by contributing stories to the Op-Ed pages of the *Wall Street Journal*, whose editorial director was his former employer and supply-side convert, Robert Bartley. Roberts proudly recalls that "by the time I resigned . . . Bartley told me that I had earned a reputation as a guerrilla warring behind the lines of his own administration."[56]

If President Reagan had diluted his prophetic appeal at any time before the tax bill was sent to Congress, the pragmatists in the White House might have been able to push Roberts and the other Treasury Department supply-siders out of the policymaking circle. If the president had faltered at this stage, furthermore, Donald Regan would likely have sought to distance himself from the supply-side agenda and his supply-side aides. In less visible and less intensely contested arenas of domestic policy, ideological appointees could, at least negatively, assert influence on the direction of policy changes in the absence of strong prophetic communication from above. A nudge and a wink from the president seemed sufficient, for instance, to keep the social conservatives and antistatists in Education, Interior, and the EPA generally on track. But in the case of ERTA, Ronald Reagan sent a message not merely of comradeship but of unwavering certitude. Reagan's adamant stance on supply-side tax cuts sent signals throughout the government that where this issue was concerned, disloyalty was apostasy. And while a president might sometimes tolerate disloyalty, a prophet, unless he prefers martyrdom to earthly success, must be ruthless toward false apostles.

ERTA: Passing a Supply-Side Tax Bill

On the surface, ERTA was a legislative replay of the fight for OBRA. A Boll Weevil–GOP coalition was decisive in each instance. To maintain this coalition to pass ERTA, the president used his considerable powers of persuasion with members of Congress, as well as with the public, going "over the heads" of the Congress. There was, however, a significant difference in the legislative histories of these two bills.

The deals that had to be made in order to gain votes for budget cutting left more money in the budget. The deals that the White House had to strike to gain passage of ERTA, by contrast, took more money out of the government's revenue stream. Specifically, the supply-side tax bill, having already been merged with a business coalition's liberalized depreciation bill that had a slight resonance with supply-side theory, was saddled with "a cornucopia of tax ornaments" that could in no way be rationalized by supply-side ideas. According to David Stockman's calculations, "nearly a trillion dollars in tax revenue had to be spent on the business coalition plan and the congressional ornaments in order to pass a supply-side rate reduction costing almost an equal amount."[57]

As far as Ronald Reagan, Irving Kristol, Norman Ture, Jack Kemp, Paul Craig Roberts, and others were concerned, this was no great loss. President Reagan never did come to understand where his deficits came from, and the others did not care. In fact, the White House, to gain passage of ERTA, auctioned away billions of dollars in proposed fiscal year 1983 budget reductions, reflecting a clear priority for tax cuts over budget reductions—just the opposite of the priorities of the American public, as revealed in public opinion polls of the time.[58] Stockman, however, could not accept that this represented his peers' interests. Instead, he thought everyone else was acting "crazy."[59]

Crazy or not, the supply-siders were generally successful in maintaining control of this attempted major policy redirection. They had thought of the idea behind the legislative proposals, drafted the proposals, and even helped strike the political deals that enabled their passage in Congress. Before moving to examine the influence of people of ideas in implementing and evaluating OBRA and ERTA, though, it is important to clarify what was actually accomplished by the passage of this ideological program.

Summing Up

Objectively, what was accomplished, for the near term, in the Reagan fiscal revolution? According to one detailed analysis, "By December 1981, when the first session of the Ninety-seventh Congress ended, the effects of recissions, reconciliation, and appropriations actions could be totaled. All fiscal year 1982 budget authority had been reduced by $45.1 billion and all outlays by $44.1 billion below what they would have been if current policy had been continued. Nondefense budget authority had been reduced by $62.8 billion and nondefense outlays by $44.7 billion."[60] Overall, a reduction of several percentage points in the rate of nondefense government spending was achieved via Reaganomics. Discretionary domestic spending fell most precipitously. From a 1980 peak of 5.6 percent of GNP, by 1989 it had been reduced to 3.7 percent, roughly the same level, Paul Peterson has observed, as existed prior to the Great Society.[61] The changes in authorizations, meanwhile, allowed the administration to reduce entitlement expenditures, which do not require yearly appropriation action. And in these cuts, the biggest losers were, as they had to be for this to be a victory for the supply-siders, the working poor. According to R. Kent Weaver's calculations, in the first fiscal year of Reagan's second term, the accumulated changes in Reagan's first-term budgets resulted in decreases of 10.5 percent for AFDC, 13.8 percent for the food stamps program, 6.3 percent for Medicare, 39 percent for guaranteed student loans, and 28 percent for child nutrition.[62]

As for taxes, the essence of Kemp-Roth has survived into the 1990s: a multiyear reduction in marginal rates of taxation has taken effect. The major provisions for personal income taxes included a 5 percent reduction in individual income tax rates in fiscal year 1982, followed by two consecutive years of 10 percent reductions, for a total reduction of 23 percent by fiscal year 1984. Indexing, furthermore, was achieved for the purpose of alleviating bracket creep. In addition, incentives for savings in individual retirement accounts, pension plans for self-employed individuals, and increased exclusions for interest and dividend income were enacted, though they were largely eliminated in the Tax Reform Act of 1986. Finally, estate taxes were reduced under Reagan, as were corporate taxes, most prominently in the form of an accelerated cost-recovery system affecting depreciation allowances—not a supply-side victory but not unwelcome to the supply-siders outside of OMB.

Evaluation

Politically oriented appointees within the White House, especially Richard Darman (a former protégé of liberal Republican Elliot Richardson) and his boss, James Baker, began even before the fiscal year 1982 efforts were complete to engineer a rise in tax levels the following year, to compensate for what had not been achieved in the budget reductions. The supply-siders, especially those in the Treasury Department, recognized "demand-side" thinking in this line of argument and violently opposed any concessionary policy amendment. The pragmatists won an objective battle in terms of the White House proposals for fiscal year 1983 but lost the war for the mind of the president over the long term and, consequently, lost in their effort to rescind the fiscal year 1982 revolution. In the negotiations for a fiscal year 1983 budget, in fact, the president embarrassed his more pragmatic staffers by vetoing a compromise budget that they had worked out with congressional leadership.

The president, however, is not the only, or even the most important, audience for those intent on winning the contest to interpret the fiscal revolution of his administration. Now that Reagan has left office, the question remains whether his policies did indeed reshape domestic policy, and if so, whether that was good or bad. The answer could shape popular and elite opinion on the appropriateness of ideological influence in presidential politics and is thus of great interest to the supply-siders as well as to other, present and future persons of ideas and their observers.

In lay discussions, the supply side is probably most associated with the ballooning federal budget deficits of the Reagan years. Although the cabalists did not stake their claim to a positive evaluation on the ability of their tax cuts to "pay for themselves," huge deficits were certainly not supposed to result from the pursuit of their initiatives. The supply side's most rhetorically expansive figures (Wanniski and Laffer), furthermore, set the supply side up in 1980 and 1981 for criticism on the basis of the deficits by making claims as to the efficacy of supply-side tax cuts that Roberts, Ture, and Stockman took to be dangerously close to a "They'll pay for themselves" formulation. And regardless of what the cabalists said or wrote, Reagan himself was on record in the campaign and afterwards as saying that every time the government has cut taxes (as in 1964 and 1978), the result has been a net increase in revenues.[63]

Nevertheless, several alternative explanations of the deficits are currently in circulation. The one favored by the former president and associated in the 1988 campaign with the traditional Republican candidates for president, including his successor, is that the Congress failed to cut sufficient "fat" from the welfare state to balance its accounts. The explanation favored by supply-siders associated with the original Kemp-centered cabal focuses upon the "premature" collapse of inflation, and hence revenues, in the Federal Reserve Board–induced recession of Reagan's first term.[64] Coupled with the Fed's alleged villainy, these supply-siders find fault with Congress for delaying the dates when the successive reductions in personal income tax rates took effect.[65] David Stockman has offered a third alternative. The entire policy package, he argues, just never added up *politically.* Stockman realized, that is, after the fiscal year 1982 battles were complete, that tax cutting was too easy relative to budget cutting. The plan would not "add up," he foresaw, because congressmen would refuse, at least the first time around, to make it do so.

Some critics, including, again, Stockman, also see wishful thinking as an underlying problem. Reagan, especially, it is said, just refused to believe that the deficits were not of someone else's making. Others, less generous, argue that the formal policy was itself a hoax. The "real" policy, from this last point of view, is alleged to have been the creation of huge deficits so as to forestall policy activism in the Congress. This last perspective seems to possess a great momentum presently, particularly in the universities, and if it gains acceptance, it could ruin the supply-siders' chances for attaining for posterity a positive evaluation of their efforts in 1981.

The seeds of the planned-deficit hypothesis were planted by certain of the supply-siders themselves. Kemp argued back in the 1980 campaign that the supply side's value to Republicans was that it offered an alternative to the traditional gloominess of GOP pronouncements on the necessity of economic austerity. And a part of this gloom he associated with making a balanced budget too high a priority. We must not, he said on one occasion, "be bookkeepers for Democratic deficits." Irving Kristol, as observed above, similarly insisted that Republicans should not allow their fear of deficits to cause them to deviate from their package of increased military outlays along with society-shaping changes in the tax code. Spending borrowed money on one's own priorities with a devil-may-care attitude about the consequences was, he reasoned, the way the Democrats had kept the Republicans in minority party status for decades. The neoconservatives, he suggested, had come to the conclusion that two could play at that game.

After pressure was exerted on the supply-siders and the president to justify supply-side policies in the face of ballooning deficits, Reagan himself went on record with statements of a similar bearing. Thus, at a news conference on March 12, 1984, the president stated to the assembled press: "Very few of you have realized that for the last three years, unlike the last fifty, there haven't been arguments going on in Washington about whether or not and what to spend additional money on. The arguments have been on where do we cut."[66] And in his fifth State of the Union address, Reagan asked his friends to look on the bright side: "We must all realize," he said, "that the deficit problem is also an opportunity—an opportunity to construct a new, leaner, better focused and better managed Federal structure. Let's do it."[67] Finally, in his memoirs, Reagan spoke in a similar vein about his tax cuts. "I have always thought of government," he wrote, "as a kind of organism with an insatiable appetite for money, whose natural state is to grow forever unless you do something to starve it. By cutting taxes, I wanted not only to stimulate the economy but to curb the growth of government and reduce its intrusion into the economic life of the country."[68]

The revelations of David Stockman come closer than even the above to constituting a "smoking gun" in this case. Stockman's statements, picked up and amplified greatly by Senator Daniel Patrick Moynihan, suggest that although no identifiable figure in the policymaking process actually intended at the outset to unbalance the budget so as to achieve a stranglehold on costly welfare state experimentation, Stockman himself, as well as Richard Darman, quickly realized the antistatist virtues of a potential deficit crisis.

Stockman reports that he first recognized the political potential in a looming-deficit scenario as early as September 1980. It was then that he realized that if a supply-side tax and budget plan were implemented, as he thought they were supposed to be, with a complementary slow-growth monetary policy, the revenue effects of the tax cuts would be eroded by the collapse of inflation. This seemed an opportunity, not a cause for alarm. For "once Governor Reagan got an electoral mandate for Kemp-Roth . . . then we would have the Second Republic's craven politicians pinned to the wall. They would have to dismantle its bloated, wasteful, and unjust spending enterprises—or risk national ruin."[69] Of the many assumptions underlying this proposition, the one that later haunted Stockman was that the politicians would have the fortitude to keep the deficit in check by acceding to draconian budget cuts. This, he admitted in his memoirs, "wasn't arrogance of the normal sort, it was grandiosity of the historical variety."[70] Nevertheless, throughout the course of the fiscal year 1982 conflicts, Stockman maintained hope that this assumption would prove correct.

Senator Moynihan and *New York Times* columnist Tom Wicker, basing their assertions exclusively on Stockman's published account and a thirdhand report of a conversation between economist Friedrich Hayek and an unnamed White House aide, have made exaggerated claims about the extent to which the deficits of the 1980s were therefore intentional.[71] According to Wicker, the president himself planned the whole thing. In response, however, Stockman has made the curious statement, that "in truth *not six* of the six hundred players in the game of fiscal government in the spring and summer of 1981 would have willed this outcome" (emphasis added). In reply to the obvious question, who these five or so persons might be, if they exist, Stockman wrote to this author that "this [the sentence quoted immediately above] was a metaphor" and that "not a single senior official ever articulated or intended this."[72] Still, one wonders at Stockman's original statement and his attempt to clarify it. (In what way, for instance, can his statement be read as a *metaphor*? What is being compared to what?)

As to the president's alleged role in the planned-deficit scenario, those who know Reagan best find the idea that he in any way planned or anticipated his administration's legacy of deficits implausible. One senior adviser to the president reports that the notion that a Reagan insider told Hayek such a thing is itself "absolutely" plausible. But as for Reagan having been in on this idea: "He doesn't have ideas on much of anything." William F. Buckley, Jr., puts the matter more deferentially. He is certain that the deficit is Reagan's "greatest embarrassment." And although he cannot provide a presidential quotation to substantiate this opinion, Buckley finds it out of the question that Reagan would put the economy on such precarious footing for the achievement of a gain he hoped to secure anyway, in a more straightforward manner.[73] And by Stockman's account, Reagan never understood any of this, especially the relation between monetary policy, inflation, and the tax code.

What appears plausible, then, is that isolated insiders, aware of the possibility if not the likelihood of tremendous deficits arising from their actions, conspired, because of the value their ideology helped them to see in a looming deficit crisis, to keep their prescience to themselves until at least the passage of ERTA. This represents an extension of the influence of people of ideas in this case beyond what otherwise could be claimed, which itself is substantial. The exercise of conspiratorial influence in executive politics can, indeed, be seen as the logical outcome of a substantial breakdown of linkages between the electorate and elected officials in a democratic political system. President Reagan's first domestic policy adviser, and Hoover Institution fellow, Martin Anderson, in fact, recently went so far as to defend conspiracy as a preferred mode of policy making in presidential politics. Conspiracy, which he believes was essential, for instance, in launching Reagan's Strategic Defense Initiative, is, according to Anderson, "an American tradition as natural to us as breathing—and . . . it is good."[74]

Moving beyond the question of the deficits, the evaluation of OBRA and ERTA is likely to be affected by the ongoing reconstitution of the supply-side movement itself. The supply side has deep links, in the eyes of its earliest proponents, such as Robert Mundell, to global monetary policy. Ever since 1981, supply-siders have been returning to themes of worldwide inflationless expansion. This has, years later, been recognized by at least the *Wall Street Journal*.[75] And once the agenda of the supply-siders is recognized more widely as including monetary policy, the business of evaluating the supply-siders' success will be less dependent upon the consequences of OBRA and ERTA. Indeed, the record of Reagan appointments to the Federal Reserve Board, beyond the scope of this research, has already caused some observers to revise upward their evaluation of the supply-siders.

Finally, the supply side is surviving without its label. Bruce Bartlett, who left the Heritage Foundation to work on the domestic policy staff in the White House under Gary Bauer in 1987, Lewis Lehrman, and Federal Reserve Board Governor Manley Johnson are among those firmly identified since before 1981 with the supply side who disclaim the title today, although their economic and social views have not changed. Meanwhile, James Baker, supply-side nemesis in 1981, actually adopted the term to describe aspects of his policy agenda as Reagan's second-term secretary of the treasury, most likely in anticipation of a Kemp threat to his longtime friend George Bush's nomination as the GOP's presidential candidate in 1988.

In conclusion, then, the evaluation of the Reagan Revolution and its meaning is still in its early stages. It is not too early, however, to recognize that given the course of fiscal legislation since fiscal year 1982, and given the reality of enormous budgetary deficits, the supply-siders' attempt at a policy redirection of realignment magnitude promises to be at least a partial "success." Marginal tax rates remain low, while at least *liberal* social engineering programs, welfare payments to the working poor, and domestic policy initiatives generally continue to be crowded out by interest payments on the budget deficit.

Nor is it too early to begin thinking about the social and political costs of a partially successful policy realignment so dependent upon ideological activists and so weakly grounded in the decaying partisan integuments of the polity. Changes in the tax codes and budgets engineered by the supply-siders have contributed to a worsening economic situation for the poor, the near poor, and the working poor, while income levels for all but the wealthiest of American families have remained stagnant into the 1990s.[76] Kevin Phillips suggested, in a 1990 bestseller, that the result of our new "gilded age" will perhaps be a stunning partisan reaction akin to the New Deal realignment.[77] Paul Krugman (one of those MIT economists whom Irving Kristol wishes us to ignore), in an even more recent exploration of the American political economy, interpreted the results of the supply-side experiments as an indication of a revolution, downwards, in what most Americans expect of their government.[78]

My analysis suggests, contrary to both of these perspectives (which assume a near-steady state of mass-elite linkages and popular attentiveness to politics), that what happened in economic and more generally domestic policy in the 1980s was largely the result of elites maneuvering in a political environment in which ideological entrepreneurs are able to swing into action with both haste *and* forethought. Political circumstances favorable to bursts of ideological zealotry that leave their mark on the polity—the arrival on the scene of another "president of achievement"—can appear hastily, dependent as this still is on election returns. But when the ideologues do rush into government these days, they do so with plans evolved over years in extragovernmental organizations and forums. The policy results are neither democratic nor likely, given the inherent weaknesses of ideological thinking, to be effective at addressing the very real concerns of their experimental "subjects."

Conclusion

When Ronald Reagan sought to translate his revolutionary ideas into a policy realignment, he relied upon people of ideas. He had never been a regular Republican himself and was not inclined to become one as president. Thus, in even the legislative stage of Reagan's fiscal revolution, people of ideas took the lead. There had been, after all, no partisan realignment in 1980 to rely upon in congressional maneuvers. Whereas in traditional realignments, presidents of exceptional ambition had achieved their programmatic innovations through the pursuit of a partisan agenda in a realigned Congress, Reagan achieved his successes in a legislative "blitzkrieg" engineered and waged by a small band of intensely dedicated ideologues. Although the ultimate status of OBRA and ERTA as attempts of realignment magnitude must remain uncertain for now, it is already clear that in the Reagan administration the influence of people of ideas was intense.

One point that deserves amplification is the importance to the influence of people of ideas in presidential politics of the president's own standing as an ideologue. Even David Stockman, commonly seen as the Judas of this White House, was touched deeply by Reagan's prophecy. It was only when Stockman came to believe that Reagan had failed to live up to the demands of his prophecy that he began to work behind the scenes to sabotage Reagan's efforts. For at least the first year of Reagan's first term, Stockman was certain that he was doing the will of his ideological father figure. Thus, although Stockman complains that Reagan was as far above the details of his fiscal revolution as an imperial "monarch," he venerated the man for his ability to articulate the antistatist vision that they shared. This became important in preparing the budget bill because Reagan had delegated that task almost exclusively to Stockman, advising his budget director on numerous occasions that "we're here to do whatever it takes."

After the two bills under question were passed, however, Stockman decided that the president was too "soft-hearted" to lead a revolution. Consequently, Stockman joined tactically with the pragmatists in the White House in urging tax increases upon Reagan for the following year. Stockman understood that given the president's sentimentality and political sensibilities, as well as the collapse of inflation in the recession of 1982–83, a historic increase in the scale of the federal government's deficit was one likely result of the fiscal revolution of 1981. If even Ronald Reagan lacked the fortitude to make the two halves of the fiscal equation add up, there was no hope that the politicians in Congress would display any courage. For reasons that remain unclear but relate perhaps to his professional and personal assumption of responsibility as OMB director for the magnitude of the government's debt, Stockman was, therefore, willing after 1981 to renounce supply-side economic policies as politically impractical.

From the perspective of the other supply-siders, Stockman was unwittingly letting the tail (budget outlays and fiscal conservatism) wag the dog (cuts in the marginal rates of personal income taxation). In this, Stockman's ideological critics were essentially correct. Most supply-siders cared less about the program adding up than they did about getting the top marginal rate down. Thus, they stuck with Reagan through not only the first term but the Tax Reform Act of the second term as well. But when these other supply-siders accused Stockman of having turned away from the prophet in the Oval Office and from his creed, they were only half-right. As far as Stockman was concerned, the prophet had failed, not the prophecy. The prophet, most fundamentally, failed to comprehend the blueprint that his aides had derived from the antistatist ideology they all shared. As Stockman asserts in his memoirs:

> It would not have been loyal to the President to remain silent about the unfolding catastrophe. That he did not yet understand what was happening was unfortunate, but not reason enough to abandon him. So I joined with the politicians. There was no longer any revolution to betray, only a shambles to repair.[79]

Thus, in even the case of the White House's Judas, the basic point about Reagan's unique relationship with his appointees is reinforced. He was their ideological prophet, not just their chief executive. So long as this link remained secure, they were emboldened and empowered to do his will.

Chapter Six
The Radical's Dilemma
and the Future
of American Politics

People of ideas are here to stay in American politics. In this work, I have endeavored to show that such persons make up a unique cast of political actors and that they have become increasingly indispensable in the implementation as well as the design of the domestic programs that have helped to define the three presidencies of achievement since the 1930s. I have also argued that the will and the capacity of presidents to resist the offers of help tendered by people of ideas has undergone a complementary decline. Before assessing further the implications of this line of reasoning, a brief recapitulation of findings is in order.

In chapter 3, a close look was taken at the administrative, "output" side of the last partisan critical realignment in U.S. history. The TVA came into existence in President Roosevelt's famous first hundred days of office, that period of tremendous legislative accomplishment when a newly elected Democratic president led a reconstituted Democratic House and a newly Democratic Senate in carrying out a vague but deep mandate from the 1932 electorate. In assembling his proposal for a Tennessee Valley authority, President Roosevelt and Senator George Norris of Nebraska called upon the talents of various men, including the utopian planner Arthur E. Morgan. The bill these men wrote, which gained passage with virtually no debate on its planning passages or, for that matter, the philosophical implications of its controversial trust-busting provisions, promised a major departure from the standard practices of American government. In the TVA, the economic and social development of an entire multistate river valley was to come under the control of a presidentially appointed board of directors.

For his initial board, Roosevelt appointed Arthur Morgan as chairman. Morgan understood the mission of the TVA in terms of his and the president's interest in multipurpose planning. Morgan did not wish the TVA to battle the private utilities, for cooperation, not competition, was the path to progress. In all respects, including but transcending the power question, Arthur Morgan wished for the TVA to give life to his strongly held and intensely ideological principles. This became problematic, however, because President Roosevelt also appointed to the board Arthur Morgan's ideological opposite, David Lilienthal, a protégé of Felix Frankfurter and an admirer of the philosophy of government espoused by Justice Louis Brandeis. The third director, Harcourt A. Morgan, was also opposed on principle to the planning agenda of the TVA's chairman.

The direction in which this board should guide the TVA, and the people of the valley, was not indicated in the legislation that established the TVA nor strongly suggested in the law's legislative history. If the president himself had been willing to resolve the contradictions inherent in this law's provisions, he might have enhanced significantly the influence of people of ideas in his administration. To begin with, of course, he might have avoided the appointment of men with conflicting visions to head the TVA. But it would be a mistake to read this case as a story of missed opportunities for ideologues. To begin with, there would have been little chance whatsoever for people of ideas to attain influence in this or other New Deal programs had it not been for the critical election of 1932 and the tremendous impetus given by the ongoing critical realignment to major innovations in domestic policy. The TVA bill itself was a greatly expanded version of a bill that had been blocked for over a decade by split-party control of the government. Republicans, that is, held the White House as well as the Senate throughout the 1920s, and the House until the Seventy-second Congress. Only when Franklin Roosevelt and a host of other Democratic contenders won office in a Democratic landslide in 1932 was it possible for this bill, in a new form, finally to become law.

The fact that the law establishing the TVA rested upon a partisan base and was not the product of intensive debate and negotiation among ideological groups or task forces mitigated against its programmatic coherence and thus against the net influence of people of ideas in its creation and legislative passage. But could the president not have given people of ideas a more integrated and forceful role in implementing this keystone of his domestic agenda?

President Roosevelt might have done so, but he was not so inclined. The diversity of perspectives and potentialities encompassed within the TVA mirrored the diversity of the president's personal interests. Land use planning, even vaguely utopian schemes to restore a rural-urban "balance" to American civilization, were among the items represented in the TVA principally because the president happened to have an interest in such things. Thus, Roosevelt was inclined by his personal likes and dislikes, which did not add up to an ideology, to enlarge the relevant precedent so that it would include a "hunting license" for the planner, Arthur Morgan, whom Roosevelt selected to chair the new authority. But Roosevelt also had a longstanding interest in the sort of trust busting and grass-roots organization of local interests that the TVA law might contradictorily be construed to authorize. Thus, the president was drawn to follow his initial selection with the appointment of Dr. Morgan's eventual nemesis, David Lilienthal.

Finally, that President Roosevelt was as content to witness ideological incoherence and strife in the implementation of legislation as in its authorship is not merely an idiosyncrasy, for Roosevelt was, in this respect, an exemplary product of his environment. In the early part of this century, party ties and loyalties were the keys to a successful political career. Franklin Roosevelt was not trained or conditioned by his background to think in terms of ideological certitudes. In conclusion, the strong party system, in which Franklin Roosevelt prospered, gave opportunities during the New Deal realignment for the infusion of ideological plans and people of ideas into government but mitigated against their influence.

In the Johnson administration, the struggle of people of ideas, in this instance mainstream liberals of the Moyers, Goldman, Wood, and Haar set, to assert influence was considerably better structured at the front end of the policymaking process but just as devastatingly truncated during implementation as in the New Deal. The idea to build a Great Society, and to make Model Cities its centerpiece, was itself the product of ideological brainstorming. These noble deeds were to be based upon the twin pillars of Reason and Affluence, not upon party politics. By the time Model Cities was proposed, the formerly stalled agenda of the post–New Deal Democratic party had already gained passage, during Johnson's first year in office. The Great Society was to be a grand departure from this past; the Model Cities program, consequently, was written from the ground up, not on the skeleton of former legislative proposals. Its authors were a group of presidentially appointed professors and interest group leaders who worked as a task force, an integral institutional resource in the president's manic annual Search for Big Ideas. The report issued by this task force, which was closely followed in the drafting of the Model Cities legislation, was a classic of mainstream liberal thought. It was not, by consequence, ideologically incoherent as was the law establishing the TVA. Yet it, too, failed to cohere along ideological lines in its implementation.

In implementing Model Cities, the mainstream liberals ran up against two sorts of obstacles. The first was political. Anticipating congressional demands, the leaders of the Model Cities Task Force had amended their original plan so as to increase its distributive properties, thus diminishing its promise as an instrument of liberal experimentation. In the intensive congressional bargaining that preceded enactment of the Model

Cities program, its distributive characteristics were expanded further by behind-the-scenes promises from the White House to particular members of Congress that their votes would be remembered when the time came to select recipients of Model Cities grants. Indeed, in the selection of cities to receive funding to launch Model Cities demonstrations, politics predominated hands down over the interests of the academics ostensibly in charge of the program at the new Department of Housing and Urban Development.

Political factors created obstacles for the ideologically correct implementation of this program in another, quite distinct way. The 1964 elections had been a tremendous success for the president and his party, but they had not provided the government a mandate to build a Great Society liberals could be proud of. The 1960s was not an era of critical partisan realignment. Thus, there was no educative or aggregative link between the policy entrepreneurs who wanted to proceed with Model Cities in an ideologically appropriate fashion and the people in Model Cities districts, who wished to make either pork or revolution out of a legislative product that was intended to be neither.

A second set of problems mainstream liberals encountered in the implementation of Model Cities was ideological. The ideologies represented at the presidential level in the 1960s were far more coherent than those in the 1930s, but there was still room for fierce sectarian conflict. The authors of the Model Cities bill, and those who voted it into being, saw themselves as having resolved a potential conflict between leftist liberals and mainstream liberals in the latter's favor. But as long as both camps had adherents in the executive branch, as they did, it would require presidential initiative, short of popular direction mediated through well-organized partisan channels, to prevent this conflict from flaring up in the implementation of Model Cities. As in the case of the TVA, however, the president was not inclined to strive for ideological uniformity.

To Lyndon Johnson, a consummate man of politics, the Model Cities program represented, from its inception, much more than a chance rationally to experiment in urban policy. To begin with, the Model Cities bill was a favor for a political supporter, UAW president Walter Reuther. Thus, merely by proposing Model Cities, President Johnson scored a partial victory; he had fulfilled his promise to Reuther to try to get something started along the lines of an urban demonstration program. The subsequent passage of this bill represented another benefit to a president with a genuine passion for legislation. The distribution of program grants, finally, which the president personally oversaw, represented an opportunity to build political support for future legislative and electoral ventures. Lyndon Johnson, in other words, had already gotten a great deal out of this project by the time the mainstream liberals in HUD asked him to resolve the ideological tensions that they saw as wrecking the program's chance for "success."

The story of the Model Cities program points up the transitional nature of the Johnson administration in the developing influence of people of ideas. Devoid of either the strong interlocking base of a partisan realignment or the direction of an ideologically self-conscious White House, the Johnson administration's efforts at a policy innovation of the highest magnitude tell a story of great frustration.

The central feature of President Ronald Reagan's agenda when he entered office was the enactment of complementary tax and budget bills. Reagan's tax-cut proposal was based on the work, prior to 1981, of supply-siders such as Congressman Jack Kemp and his team of ideologists: Jude Wanniski, Paul Craig Roberts, and Arthur Laffer. And the budgetary changes that Reagan desired were those in accord with his basic antistatist philosophy of government. In translating the ideological propositions of supply-siders into law in 1981, furthermore, a handful of people of ideas were instrumental. Even the legislative battle itself was directed from the White House by David Stockman, who later proved his ideological devotion by turning on the president when he became convinced that Reagan had deserted their common cause. Overall, as Stockman, who was converted to the supply side through talking with Kemp and reading Wanniski's *The Way the World Works*, wrote, the legislative assault of fiscal year 1982 "was not policymaking, at least not in the normal sense." It was, rather, "the translation of doctrine into the customary details, numbers, and formats of workaday policy."

Reagan, furthermore, though almost certainly not a conscious participant in the game of "chicken" that Stockman and friends played in 1981 with the Congress to determine the course of the country's economic and social policy, was crucial to the influence of ideologues in his administration. Reagan supported the efforts of his kitchen cabinet, and of Edwin Meese and E. Pendleton James, to impose ideological standards upon the selection of appointive personnel. He supported, except when such support would be politically costly, the efforts that his appointees undertook to change the direction of social and regulatory policy without the democratic accountability and public debate that would have attended legislative struggles in such areas. He spoke proudly of the effort to "credential" as many conservative-movement followers as possible in his administration's lower ranks, so as to provide a pool of ideological talent irresistible to future Republican administrations. He firmly opposed the machinations of his pragmatic advisers with respect to reversing his supply-side tax cut of 1981. What is perhaps most significant, Reagan's mere presence at the center of government emboldened and directed those about him with conservative inclinations to do what they knew was "right." That Reagan, unlike Presidents Roosevelt and Johnson, sought to increase the influence in his administration of people of ideas is understandable in light of his associations and motivations. And by being an ideologue in the 1980s, Reagan was no more exceptional than were the decidedly nonideological Roosevelt and Johnson in their days.

Ronald Reagan, it is often said, is an utterly unique political being: a zealous ideologue who is at the same time a pragmatic politician and a tremendously popular, telegenic personality. If not for Ronald Reagan, this perspective implies, there would have been no attempt radically to redirect domestic policy in 1981; there would have been no concerted effort to stock the executive branch with people of ideas. There would, consequently, be no reason to talk and write of the recent importance of ideology in presidential politics.

There are two reasons to reject this seemingly prudent line of analysis. First, Reagan was no more eccentric than Roosevelt or Johnson. They were all presidents for their times. Reagan's party background was weak because he emerged out of California politics in the 1960s, when and where party competition took a back seat to personalist appeals and media-dominated campaigns. Reagan's philosophical certitude and consistency made for coherent, easily digestible symbolic projections on the campaign trail. What is even more significant, it was his ideology that bound Reagan to the kitchen cabinet, the source throughout his career of extensive fundraising and movement associations.

The second reason to reject the seeming prudence of the view that Reagan was unique is that other presidents have had their ideologues too. The New Dealers were not ideologically coherent as a group, and Roosevelt, of course, did not try to make them so. And the mainstream liberals of the 1960s are not typically characterized as members of the same fraternity as Ronald Reagan, Martin Anderson, and David Stockman. But the application of a systematic criterion for the identification of ideological traits demonstrates that the mainstream liberals do belong to the community of ideologues active in presidential politics, and the incoherence of Roosevelt's ideologues as a whole does not vitiate their status as people of ideas either. Thus, it is possible to see the Reagan administration as merely the latest in a set of presidencies of achievement, all of which have been influenced, though to differing degrees, by people who share objective traits with the Reaganites.

Implications

The most obvious implication of these findings is that people of ideas are indeed here to stay. The underlying decay and fragmentation of the polity that led to the observed trends show no sign of reversal. Party transformation continues, increasing room at the apex of our politics for policy intellectuals. Indeed, the recent near-appointment of a man of ideas, William Bennett (a neoconservative former professor of philosophy and protégé of Boston University president John Silber and, more recently, of Irving Kristol), to head the Republican party's national committee highlights the increasing importance in presidential politics of such actors and nicely illustrates the chasm between the partisan politics of old and party politics in the aftermath of the Reagan administration.

Similarly, the factors that have impelled persons of ideas actually to fill some of the vacuums left in presidential politics due to the decay of old-fashioned partisan linkages are not likely to dissipate any time soon. Life for political appointees in the executive branch continues to be complex and confusing, creating a need for frames of reference, including the ideological, that can provide cues for decision making. There is, in addition, no reason to expect a downturn in the numbers of institutions devoted to elaborating ideological world-views, such as think tanks, journals of opinion, and liberal and conservative lobbying organizations. Indeed, James Allen Smith showed in a 1991 publication on think tanks that liberal Democrats countermobilized during the 1980s with an increasing number and diversity of think tanks of their own. Smith reported that in 1990 there were over one hundred think tanks in the Washington, D.C., area alone. Only about one-third that number existed in Washington twenty years before.[1]

Yet another reason to project the trend toward ideologization of the presidency into the future is that "new ideas" may now be tied to regime legitimacy. As a consequence, people of ideas are going to be even harder to dislodge than before.[2] Even presidents such as George Bush, whose interests lie elsewhere than in redirecting the nation's domestic policy, are currently pressured to give at least the *appearance* of having new ideas. One reason for this is familiar: presidents since Franklin Roosevelt have been expected, not merely to maintain the safety net that was created under Roosevelt's stewardship, but to follow his lead in offering "new deals" to the public.[3] Another reason becomes clear through the study of ideological influence in presidential politics: people of ideas themselves exert pressure upon presidents to take their counsel, which by definition involves the articulation not simply of ringing themes (the Fair Deal, the New Frontier, the Great Society, and so on) but of transfer cultures that, when even partially implemented, have the potential to transform the lives of millions.

Furthermore, though it is beyond the scope of this study, there is also evidence of ideologization to be found among the administrations that would fall into the other categories identified by Erwin Hargrove and Michael Nelson. The trials and tribulations of people of ideas in the Bush administration, a "presidency of consolidation," are considered below, in the Epilogue. Brief observations on people of ideas in other post–New Deal presidencies of consolidation, as well as "presidencies of preparation," are perhaps in order here. It appears that the preparation phase of the ideological thrust of the three modern presidencies of achievement occurred largely in institutions outside the executive branch and, indeed, often outside the government as a whole. Franklin Roosevelt came to office, Hargrove and Nelson observed, without a preceding presidency of preparation. Cataclysmic shocks to the polity, such as the Great Depression, they argued, can break the cyclic flow of American politics.[4] And indeed, in the case of the TVA, insofar as the way was prepared for this achievement by prior government activity, the credit (or blame) belongs not to the Hoover administration but to the Congress. The ideas that led to the most innovative and most ideologically charged aspects of the TVA program, furthermore, came from sources outside the government as a whole.

The Reagan administration did follow a presidency of preparation, according to Hargrove and Nelson's classifications. Jimmy Carter's moral and fiscal restraint, his promotion of economic deregulation, and "an antibureaucracy posture that more than anything else accounted for his rise from obscurity to the Democratic nomination" made his a presidency of preparation.[5] But in terms of the relationship of ideological forces to the presidency, the action among conservatives was in the Congress, the think tanks, and the media from 1977 to 1981, while what ideological action there was within the Carter presidency, with the exception of economic deregulation, ran at cross-purposes with the interests of the ideologues who rushed into office after Carter returned to Georgia in 1981. Despite the conservative tone of Carter's presidency, in his own estimation he was an heir to the southern populist tradition in his desire to have the government "help the poor and aged, to improve education, and to provide jobs." He was also, in his own words, "quite liberal on such issues as civil rights, environmental quality, and helping people overcome handicaps to lead fruitful lives."[6] When Carter drew up plans for his new administration, consequently, making welfare more equitable and humane was included on a "must" list.[7] If the plan that the Carter administration eventually put forward to reform welfare helped prepare the way for the Reaganites, Martin Anderson showed curiously little gratitude in his appraisal of the program. "What is being proposed" in the Better Jobs and Incomes Plan, Anderson charged at the time, "is not a 'reform' of the current welfare system. What is being proposed is a radical, fundamental change in our entire approach to welfare." And indeed, under the plan, drawn up by a conflict-ridden interagency task force under the direction of one of the Great Society's leading defenders, Joseph Califano, "Americans were to be provided with a guaranteed minimum income by right irrespective of family status or geographic locale. Unemployed males and childless couples would have been eligible for welfare."[8] The program was never reported out of the House Ways and Means Committee, but on welfare, environmentalism, civil rights, and a host of other issues, the Carter administration was headed, not toward, but away from the conservative redirection in policy that occurred under Reagan.[9]

Even in the case of the Great Society, where a president of achievement followed a president of preparation from his own party, the preparation for the achieving president's most ambitious programs took place almost exclusively outside of government. The passage under Johnson's stewardship of the stalled Democratic party agenda from the 1950s and early 1960s was one thing, I have emphasized, the rush into the uncharted territory of building a "Great Society" quite another. (The important exception here would be the work of the participatory ideologues under the direction of Robert Kennedy in his brother's administration. These ideologues greatly influenced the direction of the War on Poverty undertaken by the Johnson administration, a story that has been told many times before.)[10]

A tale awaits telling with respect to the modern presidencies of consolidation. Hargrove and Nelson are surely right that during the presidencies of Truman and Eisenhower, and Nixon and Ford, the central "achievements" of, respectively, the Roosevelt and Johnson administrations were "not rejected but rationalized" and "slowed down."[11] A focus on the role of people of ideas in these presidencies of achievement, and the presidents who followed them, however, would suggest that Hargrove and Nelson's further claim that in presidencies of consolidation the achievements of their predecessors are "in effect legitimized for earlier opponents" deserves qualification. Despite the consolidation of antipoverty programs under the Nixon and Ford administrations, for example, the Reaganites flatly rejected the Great Society. Even the Great Society architects themselves rejected as a guide to future policy analysis what they saw as the hopelessly old-fashioned emphasis of the New Dealers on matters of quantity instead of quality. The inferences to be drawn from Hargrove and Nelson's observations on presidencies of consolidation seem to hold up much better, however, with respect to the struggles for influence that take place among people of ideas and others during such presidencies themselves. Though I cannot delve deeply here into the record of such administrations, it seems clear from what we know already that within these presidencies there are sometimes bouts of intense ideological activism and that that activism, though it often ends in outright failure and in any event does not issue forth in the sort of policy realignments that are the subject of my present inquiry, does tend to take a consolidative direction. In the Nixon and Ford administrations, the Family Assistance Plan of the former and the more grandiose plans of Vice President Rockefeller's domestic policy review groups in the latter were heading in at least the same general direction as that established during the Johnson administration.[12] As will become apparent in the Epilogue, however, the view from within the ideological niches that are found in such a presidency is not as tidy as might be suggested by the label "presidency of consolidation."

The big lesson to be taken away from this brief glimpse of ideological struggles within the administrations between the three presidencies of achievement dealt with in this book is that people of ideas, though only episodically central actors in the drama of American politics, do not simply disappear with the passage of each presidency of exceptional ambition and resources. How, then, might the presence of ideologues in presidential politics be incorporated into a broad perspective on the presidency? That such a synthesis or incorporation should take place is the second principal implication of my research. A few points about the potential synthesis can be hazarded at this juncture.

First, it is crucial to differentiate between ideology and expertise. Experts may or may not be ideologues. Donald Regan, for instance, was surely an expert on finance, but he failed to conform to the ideological ideal type. Robert Weaver and the civil service experts who drafted an interagency task force on urban problems for Lyndon Johnson were the equal in "expertise" of the ideologues who composed a much different agenda as members of the nongovernmental Model Cities Task Force of 1965. The role of ideology and ideologues cannot be captured by a perspective that fails to take such differences into account.

As a corollary, it will be important in bringing ideology into the mainstream of studies of the presidency to adopt a systematic approach to identifying persons as ideologues, or "people of ideas." The usefulness of the approach favored in this research—testing the expressed opinions and ideas of putative ideologues against an ideal type of the attributes of ideological thought—in identifying schools of thought that were important in the presidencies under question has been demonstrated. Beyond serving this "taxonomic" purpose, the ideal type employed in this work has provided the impetus for insights (which otherwise might have been missed) into the substantive character of particular ideologies. For instance, the fact that mainstream liberal ideologists diverge from the ideal type in terms of the "ascriptive" component of my definition led to insight into why mainstream liberals seem consistently to fall into the trap of not taking their opponents as seriously as they should. And the fact that the application of the ideal type forces the analyst to consider the underlying views of human nature that animate competing ideological cadres helps to uncover the larger stakes involved in the contests between alternative policy agendas.

With these points in mind, and with respect to presidential *leadership*, one approach toward a broader understanding of how ideology can affect the presidency might take as a starting point Peter Sperlich's effort to amend Richard Neustadt's influential analysis of the dimensions of presidential power. In Neustadt's famous formulation, "presidential power is the power to persuade." As a consequence, stress is rightly placed by scholars of the presidency, Neustadt argues, on a president's bargaining skills. "The power to persuade," Neustadt writes, "is the power to bargain."[13] What is largely left out of Neustadt's model, Sperlich has argued, is the potential efficacy of noninstrumental ties between a president and his governmental associates. "Neustadt does not consider," Sperlich notes, "the possibility that a person might accept influence and will do what is requested of him because he has come to identify with the individual who makes the request." "Altogether missing" from Neustadt's approach, Sperlich continues, "is a discussion of organizational ideology." And "there is no reason to think that ideology, at least within the executive branch, could not function as a power base."[14] Sperlich's observations might be given greater substance once explicitly ideological relationships are brought into focus, as they are in this research.

Barbara Kellerman, in *The Political Presidency*, suggests a complementary starting point for the same reevaluative work.[15] Kellerman, following independent paths suggested by her reading of social psychology, includes in her discussion of presidential leadership the concepts of "libidinal" authority and "inner-directed" motivation. Libidinal authority, as she applies it, encompasses leadership by "affective manipulation" and followership for the purpose of abiding by one's values and, thus, "reinforcing self-identity." The parallels to what I have called the automaton effect in presidential–executive branch coordination are clear. With reference to inner-directed motivation, Kellerman means to suggest, furthermore, that the successful president, in which category she places the Ronald Reagan of 1981, "should have a coherent political vision, arising out of strong convictions about the way things ought to be." She goes so far, in fact, as to suggest that "only this kind of an intellectual and ideological imperative will motivate the president to lead towards political ends." Interestingly, this leads her to see parallels, as I do, between Presidents Johnson and Reagan. "Both," she argues, "were other-directed in their behavior and inner-directed in their rather fierce determination to see a very particular policy become law."[16] Kellerman's insights, especially if conjoined with Sperlich's theorizing and the results of the present research into the explicitly ideological aspects of presidential politics, might provide a framework for extending the boundaries of presidential studies.

Sperlich and Kellerman seem, however, to leave out one thing: that presidential *leadership* is not a constraint upon "presidential" achievement. The lack of presidential commitment to an ideological perspective certainly hinders the impact that people of ideas can have in domestic policy, as we have seen, but people of ideas, just like other presidential appointees, do not come to life only when they are ordered, persuaded, or even inspired to do so by their chief executive. If the influence of people of ideas is most realistically to be incorporated into a broad perspective on the presidency, presidential *politics* will have to be understood, as it is in the present study, as denoting more than the personal leadership or power of individual presidents.

Should We Worry?

The indications of this research have relevance to some broad problematics of American politics. What is at least suggested in these pages, to begin with, is the gradual removal of national policy struggles of the most significant kind (those with the potential to realign the boundaries of policy outputs from the federal sector) from the realm of party-mediated politics. No partisan realignment provided Ronald Reagan with his initiatives or the resources to pursue them. Yet he attempted, and at least partly achieved, the sort of broadly encompassing yet polarizing innovations in policy historically associated with critical realignments. The same could be said, furthermore, of the Great Society agenda of President Johnson.

The critical realignment, to reiterate, was this nation's "substitute for revolution." It has been, more simply, the peculiar adaptation of the American political system to the demand within any representative, dynamic society for occasionally bringing before the people issues of great importance to permit their legitimate resolution. When, perhaps sometime in the late 1960s, party linkages reached the point at which realignments were no longer possible, the need for some such mechanism, on a variety of levels, did not also dissolve. At the level of the voter, who formerly was brought into and kept within the democratic system through periodic realignments and memories of critical elections (which always had more than a touch of an unforgettable crusade about them), the need for some process whereby citizens are mobilized and integrated into the political nation derives from the common understanding of democratic government. If it is accepted that broad participation is a prerequisite for a government in which the people are the ultimate repository of sovereignty, then this need is always at least latent in our civil society. At some time in the near future, it may become acute. For there is no reason to believe that modernization, with its attendant pressures for the creation of new categories of losers and winners, has run its course in the United States. How the cleavages resulting from America's continued economic, demographic, and cultural development might intersect a political system characterized by mass abstention at the base and intense ideological infighting at the top is, to say the least, problematic.

Partisan-mediated policy redirections fundamentally differ from ideological attempts at realignment. The movement from the former toward the latter involves a loss of accountability and, just as important, stability in the pursuit of major redirections in domestic policy. This is worrying whether or not one favors the basic policy thrust of a currently ascendant group of people of ideas. A major theme of this work has been, in fact, the *similarity* among groups of policy intellectuals generally considered to be quite distinct from one another. It is not so much the content of their ideas, I have argued, as the character of their thinking that suggests both the efficacy of and some of the problems involved with the empowerment of people of ideas.

Liberal as well as conservative, Brandeisian as well as Reaganite people of ideas, that is, are propelled into presidential politics by the same dynamic interaction of the attributes of their thought and the structures of modern politics. Their programs for redirecting domestic policy are all grounded in the hubris of the ideological world-view. While it might be good strategy for a future president of achievement to make use of the opportunities for automatic coordination among ideological appointees, that does not mean that such an occurrence would be good for the polity. Ideologues, like zealots of all kinds, get things done, but perhaps not what should be done. Is there, then, a way out of the further ideologization of presidential politics?

There might be two. The first would involve the promotion of an intellectually grounded yet nonideological influence in presidential politics. Perhaps, as in the application of James David Barber's well-known typology, one could apply the ideal type of ideological thought to the schools of policy advisers associated with presidential contenders. Those who were found to be the most ideological could be argued against on these grounds, with reference to the inherent limitations of ideological thought. I, however, would not recommend such an approach. It is not that I do not believe in the possibility of nonideological intellectual work; rather, I doubt that there exists a sufficient grounding in the structures of modern politics to support the infusion of nonideological intellectuals into presidencies of achievement. The very factors that make people of ideas suspect intellectually—their absolutism, hubristic certitude, and tendency to see the world through a polarizing ontology—are the factors that make them likely candidates for influence in the contemporary environment of presidential politics. These people, furthermore, represent a class interest that is on the rise in the United States.

People of ideas, I have argued in this work, are members of a professional/managerial, college-educated class that has attained a near monopoly over national government with the breakdown of the old party machines. The linkage between the class position of people of ideas as members of this group and the ideological attributes of their thought, however, should not be pushed too far. After all, people of ideas are but a subset of the set of all college-educated professionals and managers. They are even a subset of the smaller set of all such persons who earn their livelihood through the manipulation of symbolic knowledge. The core of the so-called New Class is composed, that is, not of policy intellectuals but of social workers, teachers, writers, editors, software programmers, and others. Nevertheless, the class position of people of ideas suggests what is lacking in the scenario that would see the rise of a competing, nonideological group of *intellectuals* with ideas about policy: a distinct class basis for such putative political actors.

This is important because the number of persons who rush into and out of government with each change of administrations in the United States is tremendous. Contrary to trends in other democratic governments, a substantial portion of ours is still built upon the distribution of spoils. The virtue of such a system, its representativeness, is also its vice. For a non-ideological intellectual elite to compete successfully for power in such a government would require the establishment of networks of influence for nonideological intellectuals commensurate with the networks of think tanks, journals of opinion, and ideological lobbies that promote the applications to government service of people of ideas. In the United States, the scramble for jobs and influence in contemporary executive politics requires the conscious mobilization of significant resources; one cannot place much reliance upon the bonds of a common aristocratic upbringing or post-secondary education, as one still can to a far greater degree in England, France, and Japan. Nor is it any more than wishful thinking to write of the day when the "organic intellectuals" of the poor and oppressed in the United States will rise up to threaten the "hegemony" of the broad middle class over the nation's political institutions. So long, then, as the institutional and class structure of national politics remains unchanged, it is doubtful that a nonideological group of policy entrepreneurs will emerge to compete successfully with those I call "people of ideas" for influence in future presidencies of achievement.

A second potential way out of the ideologization of presidential politics is suggested by what might be called the classic radical's dilemma: how simultaneously to be *"in* but not *of* the world."[17] The ideologues who battle for influence in presidential politics seek action on ambitious agendas that even the conservatives among them speak of as revolutionary. They do not want to make changes on the margins of public policy and are unimpressed with the prospects of muddling through. Yet, the closer such persons come to the seat of power, the greater the risk they expose themselves to as people defined by the character of their ideas. As sociologists have argued for over a century, there is a trade-off between political activism in a bureaucratized, nonrevolutionary society and the purity of one's ideas.

The tension between what might be termed the two horns of the radical's dilemma—to charge into politics and risk losing one's special, noncompromising identity as a person of ideas, on the one hand, or to remain steadfast in principle but ineffectual, on the other—has been particularly acute in the history of American ideological movements. The separation of powers and federalism that remain at the core of America's institutional design are such that compromise and conciliation are routinely demanded of our top elected officials. These are the persons, in the White House and Congress in particular, who must struggle daily with the consequences of the Founding Fathers' extreme distrust of strong government. To try to make such a system work is to place a premium (though not as exclusive a premium as is sometimes thought) on negotiation, instrumental bargaining, and other aspects of the politician's craft. These are the sort of activities that people of ideas find it difficult to tolerate in others, much less themselves, as the memoirs of David Stockman vividly illustrate. There is considerable room in such a government, of course, as has been indicated in these pages, for persons of ideas. Still, their situation is such that they are continually under great stress.

Some modern conservatives have not been able or willing to withstand such stress. Paul Gottfried, a political philosopher of the Right, has written forcefully against what he sees as the corruption of his brethren by their immersion in the secular realm of political revolutions. Gottfried's predecessors in the conservative movement are those such as Russell Kirk, who distanced himself from the *National Review* shortly after its founding precisely because he feared choosing the wrong, that is, activist, horn of the radical's dilemma. This brings to mind, on the Left, the struggles of the early twentieth-century American socialists to forge an electoral alliance. The effort was resplendent with factionalism and discord among the various organized parties—the Socialist Labor party; the Socialist party; and the International Workers of the World. Even within the Socialist party, the one most committed to secular activism, the constant tension between ideological expressionism and political realism imposed severe limitations upon practical success.[18]

There is, however, a way in which ideologues might transcend the radical's dilemma, and it should give us pause. By changing the nature of being *in* the world, by making the choice less severe between ideological purity and political efficacy, they might overcome the dilemma, to the detriment of democratic politics. Hints of this scenario were visible in the Reagan administration in the Iran-Contra affair. And although this example comes from the realm of foreign affairs, which is outside the scope of this book, it is too important to the overall picture of people of ideas in the presidency to be ignored.

The frustration felt by ideologues in the cumbersome American government was productive, specifically, of an attempt by Central Intelligence Agency chief William Casey and his partners to establish something along the lines of a miniature state secreted within the executive branch and thereby to transcend the choices heretofore evident in the radical's dilemma. "It was always the intention," star witness Oliver North (a Marine lieutenant colonel and staff member at the National Security Council) testified before Congress in its investigation of the Iran-Contra affair "to make this a self-sustaining operation and [to ensure] that there always be something there which you could reach out and grab when you needed it. Director Casey said he wanted something you could pull off the shelf and use at a moment's notice."[19] With the ability to pull military materiel "off the shelf" and use it "at a moment's notice," North, national security adviser John Poindexter, Casey, and their government and private-sector associates could move beyond a crisis-driven approach to their operations in Central America. The "Enterprise" moved toward its goal of self-sufficiency when North's associate, businessman Albert Hakim, established a secret bank account in Switzerland in the summer of 1985. From that time on, North, Casey, and Poindexter would not only acquire the funds for the Contras but spend them for them as well.[20]

As an additional prop to support the activities of the conspirators, North, Assistant Secretary of State for Inter-American Affairs Elliott Abrams, and his State Department colleague Otto Reich, eventually given the title ambassador, coordinated the work of the State Department Office of Public Diplomacy for Latin America and the Caribbean. In its efforts to shape public opinion, the office used government employees and outside contractors to, among other things, place Op-Ed pieces in major newspapers and to demonstrate to critics of the Reagan administration's Central American policy that "attacking the President was no longer cost free."[21]

As Martin Anderson has commented, this was "the ultimate fantasy of the old master spy," William Casey. "It was to be the ultimate covert activity, accountable to no one, yet all the time able to use the power and to invoke the glory of the United States in carrying out whatever activities it deemed appropriate." As Anderson, domestic policy adviser to President Reagan, sees it, this was a "rogue operation" and a "very bad idea." In fact, Anderson speculates, it may have been the result of the brain tumor that took Casey's life before he could testify about the events of the Iran-Contra affair.[22] It is suggestive, however, that in discussing the rise of the conservative movement as a whole, and in particular in recounting the highly secretive innovation of the Reagan administration's Strategic Defense Initiative, Anderson positively celebrates what he openly terms "conspiracy." "Above all," Anderson writes in the prologue to his book, "this is a story that says little in politics happens by chance, that virtually everything is carefully done, carefully plotted, sometimes years in advance, that conspiracy properly defined is an American tradition as natural to us as breathing—and that it is good."[23] From the perspective developed in this book, conspiracy —even of the sort witnessed in the Iran-Contra affair—may be an outgrowth of the impatient ambitions of people of ideas. Certainly not all persons of ideas would follow the example of North and Casey. But insofar as North and Casey did what they did because of who they seem to have been, people of ideas working on the foreign-policy side in a presidency of achievement, their example is one that should be studied carefully in anticipation of the future.

Epilogue:
People of Ideas in
the Bush Administration

Like surfers in a bathtub, people of ideas in the Bush administration have great ambitions but dim prospects for their realization. George Bush's presidency is not devoid of ideological activists, but their efforts have barely been noticed by the capital's journalistic scorekeepers and have faced outright hostility from the men closest to the president's office and, presumably, to his heart.[1] William Bennett and Jack Kemp were placed in charge of drug and housing policy, respectively, at the start of the new administration. Bennett has since departed government for private life, having failed to achieve more in the way of a war against drugs than he achieved in his war against the education establishment in the Reagan administration. Kemp, after laboring to extricate his department from the scandals of his predecessor's tenure there, has won only limited commitments from either the Congress or the White House for his cherished objective of launching a conservative war on poverty. The vice president, former Senator Dan Quayle, was chosen for his current position in part because of his appeal to conservative constituencies, and his office is a center for ideological lobbying within the White House. Quayle has failed, however, to win the public's confidence, and his potential as a conservative point man in this administration is circumscribed by that failure. In the White House's Office of Policy Planning, James Pinkerton and his aides produce a steady stream of position papers, but with little impact on the direction of domestic policy.

This might have been anticipated. There is no precedent for two domestically activist administrations in a row. Truman tried, but the programs that made up his Fair Deal had to await another president of achievement before finally making their way into law. Nixon did not even try. Rather, under the prodding of his domestic adviser, Daniel Patrick Moynihan, Nixon contented himself in his decisive first term with consolidating his activist predecessor's domestic programs. The most ambitious domestic policy initiative undertaken by the Nixon administration, furthermore, the Family Assistance Plan, failed to win necessary congressional backing. Looking farther back in history, finally, a parallel exists between 1988 and 1836, the last time that an incumbent vice president won the presidency in his own right. Like Bush, Martin Van Buren, who won the presidency in that year, was a thoroughgoing party professional from the Northeast with ambitions to consolidate, not eclipse, the achievements of his more remarkable predecessor. If we add ideologues to this pattern, the result is precisely what we witness in the early 1990s: the massive frustration in practice of what is in theory an impressively ideological agenda. The ideologues in this presidency want a costly new antidrug program,[2] an extension of resident management experiments and vouchers in housing, a government commitment to raise the morals of school children and welfare recipients—in short, an entirely "New Paradigm" for domestic affairs. The president, by contrast, spoke during his inaugural address of his "yearn[ing] for a greater tolerance, an easy-goingness about each other's attitudes and way of life," and expressed his hope that his presidency would contribute but "a small and stately story" to the book of history[3]—ambitions suited, it must be said, to a man who won the presidency in an election dominated by valence issues and capped by a sixty-four-year low in electoral turnout for presidential contests.[4]

George Bush's distaste for ideology is not lost on the ideologues who work in his administration. The president's sense of noblesse oblige and his dislike of zealotry came up spontaneously in several interviews with key ideological actors in this administration. The scion of a wealthy and prominent family, Bush grew up in Greenwich, Connecticut, before attending college at Yale, where he was selected for membership in that campus's most exclusive secret society, Skull and Bones. Bush's subsequent move to the Texas oil patch, and from there to Houston, did not make him a Texan. In the vernacular of his adopted region, Bush was and remains a Yankee. This is significant, not, of course, because conservative ideologues are necessarily men and women of humble origins from the periphery (though this happens often to be the case in today's Washington), but because the upper-class Yankee ethic of moderate Republicanism is decidedly anti-ideological.

In making his way to the White House, George Bush did not embrace conservative ideology, but he did accumulate some ties to particular people of ideas. The former vice president's first debt, of course, is to his predecessor. Because Ronald Reagan left office an elderly man and a diminished political figure, however, there is little chance that Reagan will exert the sort of influence over his more cautious successor that Theodore

Roosevelt attempted to exert over William Howard Taft, the daydreams of conservative editorialists to the contrary.[5] Bush did not need to be prodded, however, to choose Dan Quayle as his running mate in 1988 or to select Jack Kemp for his cabinet and William Bennett for the new position of coordinator of the government's antidrug efforts. Quayle was elected to the Senate as a free-market, social conservative candidate in a race that featured abortion as a prominent issue, and he continues to have the support of a broad range of New Right and neoconservative activists.[6] Kemp was and is a high-profile conservative contender for the presidency. By selecting the supply-side entrepreneur for his cabinet, Bush effectively silenced one of his most forceful critics on the Right, while positioning himself to share in whatever credit might accrue from his energy and ideas. The neoconservative Bennett, meanwhile, was given a thankless task "where any success [would] redound to Bush's credit."[7]

Chase Untermeyer, the president's director of personnel and a longtime Bush associate, calls the administration's approach to filling jobs an "entrepreneurial" strategy. With such entrepreneurs as Jack Kemp in the cabinet, "the president can pay attention to other things." In making plans for the new administration, Untermeyer recalls, HUD was not expected to be "of great importance to the Bush administration except insofar as Kemp made it so."[8] What Untermeyer reveals in these words is startling. It is virtually a matter of happenstance that there is an effort under way in this administration to reorient housing and welfare policy. Having new ideas for one's field of responsibility can help to propel a person such as Kemp into this administration, but it is not a formal or even informal criterion of selection.

The president's almost whimsical approach to domestic policy is even more clear in education. Bush's first secretary of education, Lauros Cavazos, was not known as a policy entrepreneur when Bush fulfilled a campaign pledge by selecting Cavazos, a Hispanic, for his cabinet. Cavazos made a weak impression in the cabinet and on Capitol Hill during his two years as secretary and was replaced by Lamar Alexander early in 1991. Alexander came to the administration from the presidency of the University of Tennessee and, before that, the governorship of the state. By the time of his appointment, he was well known as a conservative policy activist in the field of education. When his appointment was announced, the Heritage Foundation's executive branch liaison officer, David Mason, immediately went to work, steering résumés and reports to contacts within the department. While it is too early to gauge the results of Heritage's efforts, it is telling that the conservative people of ideas in Washington, including Mason, recognized the appointment of Alexander as a moment of opportunity.[9] And indeed, shortly after Alexander's appointment the administration announced a controversial plan for education reform, written by

Secretary Alexander with significant input from Chester Finn, a former Reagan administration appointee and frequent contributor to conservative journals. Their plan calls for, among other things, the use of vouchers and national examination standards in secondary education.[10]

Perhaps some people within the White House see school choice as an issue to push in the coming reelection campaign, in which case Alexander was selected in part for his ideas. Surely the president himself realized that given his pledge to be the "education president," he needed to demonstrate before 1992 that he had not neglected the topic. What is striking, however, is that Cavazos, by all accounts, was nudged out of the administration, not because of his ideas, or lack of them, but because he was deemed to be in "over his head" in Washington. Presumably, had Cavazos been more competent at his job, he could have stayed on, and Bush, perhaps after endorsing a comparatively cautious and moderate plan for education reform, could have continued to "pay attention to other things."

As befits a happenstance approach to domestic cabinet appointments, Kemp and most of his fellow cabinet members have had a relatively free hand under Bush to select their own "presidential" personnel. Untermeyer's role, as he sees it, is not to put a Bush stamp on the first- and second-tier personnel of the administration but to make sure that Bush's longtime supporters and friends are not forgotten in the disbursement of patronage at lower levels. He serves, in essence, as Bush's personal representative in the process, asking himself, he says, "Who would George Bush want doing this job?" Untermeyer is well-suited to carry out a job defined in so personalistic a way; he has been an associate of the president's longer than virtually anyone else in the White House.[11] He first worked for Bush during his college years, when he volunteered in Bush's campaign for Congress in 1966, and thereafter spent two summers as an intern on freshman Congressman Bush's Washington staff. Untermeyer, furthermore, began planning for the new administration during the 1988 campaign, and he enjoys high visibility in the administration, with a West Wing office and access to the president.[12]

Underscoring the personalistic nature of Untermeyer's role in the Bush White House, the person who comes closest to being Untermeyer's counterpart in the prior administration is not Pendleton James, Reagan's first personnel director, but Michael Deaver, the longtime family friend and associate who sought to ensure that the First Family's special friends and supporters shared in the bounty of presidential patronage. Thus Untermeyer asked the president's nephew Scott Bush to set up a special personnel operation in the White House after the transition to see that the new president's political backers and friends were not overlooked when persons were named to deputy assistant secretaryships, special assistantships, and similar positions below senatorial scrutiny. About seven hundred to eight hundred of these positions (one-half the total) were to be filled through this special operation.[13] It had been the innovation of Reagan's personnel operation to centralize control over such appointments within the White House. The purpose in 1981 had been to ensure that the number-one criterion in appointments, philosophical compatibility with the president, was not overlooked at this level. The use to which this innovation was turned in the Bush White House is highly suggestive of the diminished significance of ideology to this administration.

Still, in a happenstance presidency, ideologues have their place, or places. The people of ideas in the current administration may be divided functionally into two camps: the "stoppers" and the "doers." The former are the self-conscious consolidators of the Reagan Revolution. Reagan's legacy of scarce public funds and low marginal tax rates is not entirely self-sustaining; it has been helped along by the new administration in several ways. First, the budget deal worked out late in 1990 between the congressional rank and file and the White House set spending caps for various budget categories, effective through the reelection season. According to the terms of the agreement, all legislative initiatives must be considered in tandem with proposals for compensatory cuts in other programs within the same portion of the budget or for new taxes or fees. This helps mightily to keep in place the muzzle put on domestic policy initiatives in the Reagan years.[14] Also helpful is the work of Vice President Dan Quayle. Quayle, according to his chief of staff, William Kristol, has a distinct approach to the vice presidency: to use the office to see that ideas (as it happens, conservative ideas) that otherwise might not receive a hearing by the president are presented to him. As Kristol, a former Harvard professor and the son of the eminent neoconservative Irving Kristol, points out, there is a lot of government experience in the West Wing of the White House. Quayle is not needed to suggest political maneuvers or tactics that Chief of Staff John Sununu, Darman, or members of the cabinet might overlook. Rather, Quayle, who oversees a staff of some eighty-odd members, including "detailees" from the agencies, provides the results of independent analyses of policy issues.[15] In his capacity as chairman of the Council on Competitiveness, furthermore, the vice president seeks to mitigate the regulatory impact of environmental and health and safety legislation, including the much-touted 1990 clean air law.[16] In Kristol's view, "That's where we've really carved out a niche for ourselves."[17]

The "doers," who are also the more "red hot ideologues" (to use one of Lyndon Johnson's favorite epithets for those I call people of ideas), have been at odds with the "stoppers." Their ambitions remain nevertheless undiminished. Indeed, to James Pinkerton, who headed the domestic policy transition team for President-elect Bush and who now directs the Office of Policy Planning within the White House, the Bush years represent a historic opportunity. George Bush, according to Pinkerton, is "the first President to govern in the spirit of the New Paradigm."[18] The New Paradigm, according to Pinkerton, represents an antibureaucracy approach to government. In announcing the New Paradigm in a speech to the libertarian Reason Foundation, Pinkerton listed its tenets as: market orientation, choice, economic empowerment, decentralization, and an emphasis on what works. Additionally, Pinkerton emphasizes in conversation that a guiding principle of the New Paradigm is that "the government must not get bigger." The New Paradigm, he says, "is an effort to get more from less."[19] New Paradigm proposals, according to Pinkerton, include using vouchers in secondary education and housing, privatizing public housing, extending tax credits for childcare to low-income parents, reducing the capital gains tax, and lowering yet further marginal rates of personal income taxation. Even Operation Desert Storm, the U.S. war against Iraq in early 1991, was a victory for the New Paradigm, Pinkerton asserts.[20]

In domestic policy, the government's role in the age of the New Paradigm is to create or maintain incentives for the expression of what Pinkerton forthrightly identifies as "middle-class values of ownership and responsibility." Such values, Pinkerton believes, reflect not the historical experience of particular groups within the United States but "universalistic qualities of human nature." Essential to the inculcation of such values is "a decent economic system that encourages incentives," because "to try to impose values without a certain economic substrate—to borrow a phrase from a nineteenth-century German philosopher—is going to fail."[21]

If the New Paradigm sounds suspiciously like supply-side (or "voodoo") economics, the parallel is not accidental. Pinkerton himself returns repeatedly in explaining the New Paradigm to the core concept of the supply side: *incentives*. This emphasis reflects Pinkerton's intellectual background and convictions. The son of two liberal academics, whose first political memory was holding his mother's hand as he walked past a pro–Viet Cong rally on Massachusetts Avenue near Harvard, Pinkerton was, and remains, an opponent of the war in Vietnam.[22] At the same time as he opposed the war, though, he opposed "high taxes, socialism, and communism" as a high school student in Evanston, Illinois. Pinkerton recalls that as an undergraduate at Stanford he read an article in the *San Francisco Chronicle* about libertarians, who opposed the same array of government activities that he disliked, and thought, "That's what I am." Also as an undergraduate, Pinkerton encountered Jude Wanniski's supply-side opus, *The Way the World Works*. It had, he says, "a really huge impact" on his thinking, and Wanniski remains "a friend and an influence" in Pinkerton's work for President Bush.[23]

Pinkerton, according to Nicholas Lemann, "cuts a figure in Washington today a little like that of Stockman in the late 1970s."[24] Outside of

Washington, though, the person most closely associated with the ideas of the New Paradigm is HUD Secretary Jack Kemp, co-author of the supply-side tax cuts of the Reagan years. "I don't think things happen by accident," Kemp said in an interview. "I'm at HUD at this moment in history" to both clean up his department and "give it a higher mission." By using his position within the cabinet as a bully pulpit and by guiding legislation through the Congress, Kemp believes in fact that he can "fulfill some of the revolutionary goals, not only of Dr. King and Rosa Parks and the great civil rights struggles, but the ultimate revolution, which was the American revolution of Jefferson and Madison and Franklin."[25]

Secretary Kemp's ambitions for the administration center on his plans for his own department, to which I will turn momentarily. His portfolio was expanded, however, in September 1990, when the president created a White House Task Force on Economic Empowerment and selected Kemp to chair it. Kemp's brief experience with the task force is symptomatic of his experience within the administration as a whole. For as of the August congressional recess of 1991, the task force, operating under instructions to be "budget neutral" in its recommendations, had yet to produce even a report. Some task force members blame the war in the Persian Gulf for the slow pace of progress.[26] It may be, of course, that the president, his chief of staff, and his budget director simply do not want the task force to take the lead on domestic policy. The task force was created only after the strenuous efforts of Secretary Kemp, James Pinkerton, and their allies within the White House, and only after the *New York Times* published a front-page story by Robert Pear that alleged, in its headline, that "White House Spurns Expansion of Nation's Anti-Poverty Efforts." As Nicholas Lemann reported, "Inside the White House there was some desire to prove the *Times* story wrong—to counter, for reasons of election-year political expediency and East-Coast Republican gentility, the perception that the Bush Administration didn't care about the poor."[27] If this represents the White House's view on the Empowerment Task Force and its utility, it is not surprising that its role has thus far been restricted. Within Kemp's own department, however, as well as in the Department of Education, legislative programs have been launched that advance portions of the conservative "doers'" agenda. It is too early to report on the success or failure of the Alexander plan for school reform. It is not too early, though, to provide a preliminary analysis of the mixture of grand ambitions and deep frustration encountered by Kemp's efforts to launch a new war on poverty from a department created during the last one.

In November 1989 Jack Kemp spoke before the National Press Club on his vision of the Bush administration's domestic policy. "This is the 25th anniversary of the War on Poverty," Kemp observed, and "I want to recognize the good intentions of that effort as well as the architects who had such great hopes to help combat poverty." In fact, "our new war on poverty shares the goals of the original war on poverty: a hand up, not a hand out." The difference, according to Kemp, is that "we have learned something over the past 25 years. We know what works and we are beginning to know what doesn't work." "The President's strategy for combating poverty," Kemp told his audience, "we modestly call HOPE—Homeownership and Opportunity for People Everywhere . . . a dramatic, far-reaching, incentive-oriented approach to fighting poverty." HOPE rejects, Kemp went on to reassure the conservatives in his audience, "social engineering of people's lives and huge entitlement programs." Rather, HOPE "empowers people to take control of their own lives" by giving poor people "an equity stake in their neighborhoods" and by promoting economic growth in slums by relaxing tax and regulatory "barriers" to entrepreneurship. As part of the administration's overall approach to combating poverty, furthermore, the administration must continue to push, Kemp said, for capital gains tax reduction, because "we really can't help the Nation's poor if the Nation itself is becoming poor."[28]

The centerpiece of HOPE, which was signed into law by the president on November 28, 1990, as part of the Cranston-Gonzales National Affordable Housing Act, is the supply-side panacea of incentives, or "economic empowerment." Thus, in the president's remarks on signing the bill, he quite appropriately conjured a vision of a world transformed by carefully engineered economic incentives:

> When the people who live in public housing are in charge, the results are remarkable: more people pay their rent, maintenance improves, operating costs decline, and crime rates plummet. Employment goes up, more kids stay in school, and neighborhoods spring back to life. And the reason? Because each resident simply now has a stake in society—an equity stake—a chance to make a go of it, to live the American dream for themselves.[29]

"Empowerment," in the more succinct if less rhapsodical phrasing of HUD's press release on HOPE, "means incentivizing our housing and economic systems." Incentives would be created under HOPE primarily through a competitive grants program that would provide $1 billion over two years to local governments and nonprofit organizations with money of their own and plans to privatize public-housing stocks. Nonprofit organizations and units of local government with programs supporting resident management of housing facilities—turning "projects" into "coops"— would be given preference in the disbursement of these grants. Through the grants program, twenty-five thousand homeownership sales are anticipated over two years.[30] In addition, Kemp has promoted, as an adjunct to

HOPE, that the federal government continue to increase the proportion of vouchers in its housing subsidies. Finally, though killed in committee, Secretary Kemp's proposal to spur development in inner-city neighborhoods by relaxing taxation and regulation in "enterprise zones" was also proposed by the administration as part of the original HOPE package.

The incentives approach followed in HOPE is an outgrowth of Kemp's and his allies' supply-side convictions. In fact, two of Kemp's key aides at HUD who helped to design HOPE came to conservatism and government service as a result of their enthusiasm for supply-side ideas in the early 1980s. Thomas Humbert, a close aide to Kemp who followed him from his congressional office to the Heritage Foundation and from there to HUD, where he is deputy assistant secretary in charge of policy development, was first attracted to Kemp because of his economic principles. HOPE, as Humbert interprets the program, "is an extension of [the] sort of thinking" that Kemp became known for in his battle for a supply-side tax cut.[31] S. Anna Kondratas, assistant secretary at HUD responsible for community planning and development, was similarly drawn to the conservative movement by her introduction in the late seventies and early eighties to supply-side ideas. While Humbert learned a conservative approach to economics as a graduate student of business administration at the University of Chicago, Kondratas studied the same subject at George Mason University. GMU, a branch of the University of Virginia, grew in the 1980s into a highly visible intellectual force on the moderate Right. While studying at GMU, Kondratas took courses under two adjunct professors who played key roles in the supply-side case analyzed in chapter 5, Paul Craig Roberts and Steven Entin. Because her performance in these courses led to recommendations for employment in the conservative network after graduation, Kondratas started on the career path that brought her in 1988 to the attention of Kemp, and then to HUD.[32]

The housing program that these supply-siders designed passed the Congress by stunningly lopsided margins. In the House, the conference report of the bill was adopted by a voice vote, while in the Senate, it cleared by a tally of 93 to 6.[33] These tallies do not mean, however, that Kemp's new war on poverty is a success, or even a reality yet. For while the Congress overwhelmingly approved the new program at the end of 1990, there were strings attached to the Democratic Congress's support. First, the administration's conservative "stoppers" prevented Kemp from requesting of the Congress the level of budget authority that he wanted. As a Kemp ally, Barry Zigas, president of the National Low Income Housing Association told the trade publication *Housing Affairs Letter,* "He [Kemp] asked for a war on poverty, and Darman and Bush gave him ammunition only for a skirmish."[34] The number of housing units to be converted to private ownership through this "radical" plan's grants—about twenty-five thousand in

HUD's official estimate, "thousands" in President Bush's more vague pronouncement in signing the bill—is eloquent testimony to the limited scope of the administration's support of Kemp's ambitions. (There are presently over three million Americans in public housing.)

Second, the liberal Democratic members of Congress for whom the HOPE bill is actually named, Senator Allan Cranston of California and Congressman Henry B. Gonzales of Texas, along with the Democratic leadership of the Congress, exacted a price in exchange for their support of HOPE. "HOME"—the catchy name for a new block grants program designed to increase the housing stock for the poor through the acquisition and rehabilitation of affordable rental and ownership units as well as limited new construction—was accepted by the administration as the price of HOPE. The administration, in fact, agreed to funding levels for HOME that were slightly higher than those for HOPE. HOME was intended, not as a counterpart, but as a countervailing force to HOPE. HOPE, it was feared, might serve as a convenient cover for diminishing the government stake in housing the poor. HOME would approach the problem of affordable housing straightforwardly, by applying government funds to making more housing units available for incorporation in voucher and assigned-housing programs. The intention of the Congress in passing HOME in conjunction with HOPE was further revealed by the effort of the Congress to designate the housing commissioner within HUD as the person responsible for the new program. HUD intends for the assistant secretary of community planning and development, S. Anna Kondratas, to take charge of HOME. Congressional proponents of HOME, however, have fought HUD on this point, in part, as Kondratas herself acknowledges, because they do not trust a former Heritage analyst and a Reaganite conservative to administer *their* program.[35] Their preference was for the then housing commissioner within HUD, C. Austin Fitts, a former Wall Street investment banker with moderate views, to administer the program.[36]

A final "string" involved in the Congress's superficially enthusiastic approval of HOPE is that no funds have been appropriated for this keystone of the administration's new war on poverty. The appropriations subcommittees responsible for housing programs in the Senate and the House, headed, respectively, by the decidedly liberal Senator Barbara Mikulski (D, Maryland) and the equally liberal Congressman Robert Traxler (D, Michigan), are the apparent culprits. Specifically, their subcommittees have thus far denied the administration's request for a supplemental appropriation in the 1991 fiscal year to begin the HOPE program by consolidating and eliminating other HUD programs with a self-help orientation.[37] This denial may well prove to be temporary. Kemp pushed for the supplemental appropriation despite the fact that the nonprofit community organizations that would benefit from HOPE's grants programs, as well as local government lobbying organizations, were not enthusiastic about requesting operating funds until the following year. Also, Henry B. Gonzales and Congressman Traxler have given their assurances to persons at HUD that HOPE will eventually be funded.

Even if—or when—the administration's new war on poverty is funded, however, there are reasons to be skeptical of the impact that it might make, not only on the lives of the poor, but on the dynamics of the current administration. The funding levels being requested are relatively small, and their potential impact is diminished by the low visibility accorded this program by the White House and, consequently, the media. Also, of course, the program is minus its enterprise zones component, which Humbert calls the "indispensable economic component of what we were trying to do, so people would have the jobs by which they could afford to be homeowners."[38] Finally, the virtually utopian tones in which Secretary Kemp and even the president have described the program are grounded more in faith than in application of the New Paradigm's tenet of pragmatism.

There simply has not been sufficient experience with tenant management and ownership initiatives to support such claims as are routinely made in their behalf, according to Daniel J. Monti, an expert on the subject who conducted a major review of housing policy for a small think tank headed by a prominent Kemp ally from outside the government. Monti's report was never made public; its sponsors instead released a less ambivalent appraisal using in-house staff. What the Monti report could have taught the people at HUD, however, is that if the limited experience of the past is a guide, any attempt to make war on poverty through the national coordination of poor persons in subsidized housing communities grossly overestimates the number of sites capable of putting together the needed resources.[39]

Before George Bush became a wartime president, his political fortunes were flagging. In part this might simply have reflected the restlessness of a public that judges its presidents *right now,* not in the context of the cycle of presidential achievement and consolidation. Even so, Bush seemed to many observers to be doing even more poorly—despite broad but shallow support in the opinion polls—than was to be expected under his historical conditions. His vote-support scores in the Congress were by 1991 already the worst for any president since 1953, when *Congressional Quarterly* began tabulating such statistics.[40] Ironically, the apparent political as well as military success that Bush subsequently enjoyed in Operation Desert Storm might have done more than anything else to dampen the prospects that his go-slow approach in domestic policy would be shelved in favor of a more dynamic posture heading into the 1992 reelection season. Despite criticisms from liberal Democrats to the effect that Bush's heart bleeds only for victims of *foreign* crises, there are already indications that in 1992 Bush will stand on his domestic record, such as it is, and attempt to castigate the Democrats for having blocked some of the more innovative aspects of his programs.[41]

In conclusion, ideologues are in a weakly supportive and energizing environment in the Bush administration. They are not central to the apparent ambitions of President Bush, which seemed before the Gulf War to be directed more toward mere political survival than toward the redirection of government policy. But just because the ideologues are frustrated now does not mean that they will continue to be so forever. In fact, we might not have to wait as long as in the past for the return of another presidency of achievement capable of elevating people of ideas to positions of real influence in government. That is part of the bigger story and continuing problem that this book has addressed. Changes in domestic policy instituted through ideological maneuvers, relying only lightly on partisan dynamics, I have argued, are not likely to be as enduring as changes catalyzed (and tempered) by old-fashioned party realignments. If this proves to be the case for the Reagan Revolution, ideologues will almost certainly be leading actors in the eventual replacement of this revolution with another.

Despite the dreariness of these conclusions, I decline to close this epilogue with the usual call for alarmed intervention. It would be foolish to support political engineering in the service of dampening the ill effects of inadequately constrained social engineering. If we are to be made more secure (we do not exactly need to be "saved") from the consequences of the trends that I have charted here, though, it might help to keep in mind the relevant contrast. I cannot foresee any possibility that we shall ever witness an opportunity to rid our national politics of people of ideas. Ideology is a natural response to societal strains and is a centripetal force in a government subject to a great many centrifugal stresses. Ideological harmonization of executive branch personnel has its uses, as does, more broadly, ideology as a societal phenomenon. Ideologues, furthermore, often *do* possess at least a portion of what they profess: they have analyses, plans, blueprints, and ideas. A modern government cannot function without, in one form or another, just these things.

But while we cannot do without ideologues altogether, we could well do with a functional return to an older pattern of their integration into government. What has happened since the New Deal is not so much that we have been bombarded by *more* of these people; rather, they have become increasingly central actors in presidencies of achievement. Their plans have become the plans of presidents; their interests have begun to merge with the political interests of their "masters." The structural and institutional arrangements of national government can strengthen or, as in the New Deal and more weakly in the Great Society, temper and restrain the zeal of the ideologues. I do not know how to turn back the clock of party institutions, but we should be attuned to whatever possibilities might present themselves to alter institutional arrangements within our government so as better to channel the efforts of people of ideas. In that way, ideologues might once again become but one of a number of competing sets of presidential helpers, and the people the directing force in national politics.

Notes

Introduction

1. Jack Kemp, secretary of housing and urban development under President Bush, chairs the President's Task Force on Economic Empowerment and, along with James Pinkerton, a young White House assistant who directs the Office of Policy Planning, is the driving force behind the search for a "New Paradigm" in domestic policy. For more information, see the Epilogue.

2. "Presidencies of achievement" are, most generally, those in which presidents have unusually great objectives and exceptional resources with which to pursue them. The term is from Erwin Hargrove and Michael Nelson's *Presidents, Politics, and Public Policy* (Baltimore: Johns Hopkins University Press, 1984). During such presidencies, Hargrove and Nelson write, "great bursts of creative legislative activity occurred that altered the role of government in society in the service of some combination of purpose values of liberty and equality and process values of higher law and popular sovereignty." Such presidencies, they go on to note, are "made possible by overwhelming, if very general, popular mandates for change" and are "brief, sometimes lasting only two years" (p. 67; see also pp. 76, 197). On Reagan as a president of achievement, see idem, "The Presidency: Reagan and the Cycle of Politics and Policy," in *The Elections of 1984*, ed. Michael Nelson (Washington, D.C.: CQ Press, 1984), pp. 189–214. Compare with presidencies of "reconstruction," as developed by Stephen Skowronek, in his "Notes on the Presidency in the Political Order," *Studies in American Political Development* 1 (1986): 286–302. The "modern presidency" refers to the period since the New Deal. Because of the emphasis in this book on what happens within the executive branch in relation to domestic policy, it seems useful to follow the convention of considering the "modern" presidency as a unified era. Before the New Deal, the executive branch was a ghost of its present self; before 1939, in fact, the Executive Office of the President was but an idea in the minds of some progressive reformers (see Fred Greenstein, "Change and Continuity in the Modern Presidency," in *The New American Political System*, ed. Anthony King [Washington, D.C.: American Enterprise Institute, 1978], pp. 45–86). I have expressed my reservations about the wider relevance of the "modern presidency" paradigm in "Alternative Perceptions of the Presidency: Delegates, Trustees, and Non-Linear Models of American Political Development" (paper presented at the annual meeting of the Southwestern Political Science Association, Fort Worth, March 1990).

3. The term *political time* is Skowronek's (see n. 2 above).

4. Because Johnson came to office affiliated with the dominant party of his era, Skowronek would categorize him differently from Roosevelt and Reagan. Johnson would be a president of "articulation" instead of a president

of "reconstruction." Because of the extent to which Johnson stands out among the presidents between Roosevelt and Bush for his ambition to redirect domestic policy, however, I am more impressed by the similarity among Johnson, Roosevelt, and Reagan than by the admitted differences. Thus, I appropriate the terminology of Hargrove and Nelson (see n. 2 above), who type all three as modern presidents of achievement. My use of this term should not, of course, be interpreted to imply that only these three presidents since 1933 have achieved anything, for themselves or the nation! Perhaps a more precise term would be "presidents of exceptional resources and domestic-policy ambitions," but *president of achievement* has become part of the language of presidency studies and is obviously much more concise than my alternative.

5. On the New Dealers, for example, see Joseph Lash, *Dealers and Dreamers: A New Look at the New Deal* (New York: Doubleday, 1988); and Elliot Rosen, *Hoover, Roosevelt, and the Brain Trust* (New York: Columbia University Press, 1977). On the Great Society, see Henry Aaron, *Politics and the Professors: The Great Society in Perspective* (Washington, D.C.: Brookings Institution Press, 1978). On the Reagan administration, see Sidney Blumenthal, *The Rise of the Counter-Establishment* (New York: Times Books, 1986); Gillian Peele, *Revival and Reaction: The Right in Contemporary America* (Oxford: Clarendon Press, 1984); and M. Stephen Weatherford and Lorraine M. McDonnell, "Ideology and Economic Policy," in *Looking Back on the Reagan Presidency*, ed. Larry Berman (Baltimore: Johns Hopkins University Press, 1990), pp. 122–55. For a recent overview of the role of think-tank personnel in these and other twentieth-century presidencies, see James Allen Smith, *The Idea Brokers: Think Tanks and the Rise of the New Policy Elite* (New York: Free Press, 1991).

6. Joel Aberbach and Bert Rockman, with Robert Copeland, "From Nixon's Problem to Reagan's Achievement: The Federal Executive Reexamined," in Berman, *Looking Back;* John Kessel, "The Structures of the Reagan White House," *American Journal of Political Science* 28 (May 1984): 231–58; idem, "The Structures of the Carter White House," ibid. 27 (August 1983): 431–63. See also Colin Campbell, S.J., *Managing the Presidency: Carter, Reagan, and the Search for Executive Harmony* (Pittsburgh: University of Pittsburgh Press, 1986); Lawrence Herson, *The Politics of Ideas* (Homewood, Ill.: Dorsey Press, 1984); Anthony Downs, *Inside Bureaucracy* (Boston: Little, Brown, 1967); Paul J. Quirk, "In Defense of the Politics of Ideas," *Journal of Politics* 50 (February 1988): 31–41; and Paul Schulman, "The Politics of Ideational Policy," ibid. 50 (May 1988): 263–91. These studies offer a great deal, but either they fail to distinguish ideology from expertise or they employ extremely thin conceptualizations of ideology. Consider, for instance, that in Kessel's analysis, James Baker proves virtually indistinguishable from Edwin Meese in terms of their status as ideological actors (p. 237) and that from Downs's perspective, there is no way to distinguish between two hypothetical assistant secretaries of the Department of Health and Human Services (HHS), one a zealous advocate of revisions in departmental accounting practices, the other a zealous proponent of a libertarian state.

7. Robert B. Reich, ed., *The Power of Public Ideas* (Cambridge: Harvard University Press, 1988). See also Theodore J. Lowi, *The End of Liberalism* (New

York: Norton, 1969); Nelson W. Polsby, *Political Innovation in America: The Politics of Policy Initiation* (New Haven: Yale University Press, 1984); and John Kingdon, *Agendas, Alternatives, and Public Policies* (Boston: Little, Brown, 1984). The last is exceptional in its elaboration of a theory of the integration of expertise (whether ideological or not) into the policy process. Also relevant is the classic typology presented in James Q. Wilson, *The Politics of Regulation* (New York: Basic Books, 1980). These and other works in the tradition of policy analysis are of limited relevance to a study of ideologues, however, for not all experts are members of this unique subset of policy activists. For example, though Wilson emphasizes in his work cited above the contributions that intellectuals make to "entrepreneurial" policy making and the importance of generalized public opinion to "majoritarian" decision making, ideological politics cut across all four of Wilson's categories. The Tennessee Valley Authority (TVA), for example (the subject of chap. 3), mixed entrepreneurial and majoritarian debates, while the Model Cities program (chap. 4) was hampered by the president's perception of the program as an example of "clientele" politics. (The ideologues in the Johnson administration thought they had designed a majoritarian program.) And Reaganomics, finally (chap. 5), incorporated elements of majoritarian, clientele, entrepreneurial, and "interest-group" politics. Wilson himself acknowledges in a more recent work that the unique contributions, if any, that ideological personnel can make to presidential politics are open to question (Wilson, *Bureaucracy: What Government Agencies Do and Why They Do It* [New York: Basic Books, 1989], p. 262).

8. David McKay's subject in his informative book *Domestic Policy and Ideology: Presidents and the American State, 1964–1987* (Cambridge: Cambridge University Press, 1989) is actually not ideology, as I understand it, but rather the impact of a president's beliefs—whether "ideological" or not—on what happens in his administration. An important exception, however, is the ongoing project by M. Stephen Weatherford and Lorraine M. McDonnell to incorporate an ideological component within a model of the president's impact on economic policy making (see Weatherford and McDonnell, "Macroeconomic Policy Making beyond the Electoral Constraint," in *The Presidency and Public Policy Making*, ed. George C. Edwards III, Steven A. Shull, and Norman C. Thomas [Pittsburgh: University of Pittsburgh Press, 1985], pp. 95–113).

9. Shawn Rosenberg makes use of the same distinction in "Reason and Ideology: Interpreting People's Understanding of American Politics," *Polity* 20 (Fall 1987): 114–44.

10. There is convergence in a wide body of literature toward an understanding of the contemporary American regime as one in which the decay of mass partisan attachments and the subsequent functional though not organizational decline of party strength in government, along with other factors such as the rise of mass media and alternatives to party fund-raising, make national politics increasingly an elite activity. The person of ideas represents one type of elite actor. For a sampling of this literature, see the many works of Walter Dean Burnham, including his classic *Critical Elections and the Mainsprings of American Politics* (New York: Norton, 1970); Martin Wattenberg, "The Hollow Realignment: Partisan Change in a Candidate-centered Era," *Public Opinion Quarterly*

51 (Spring 1987): 58–74; Burdett Loomis's study of the new Congress, *The New American Politician: Ambition, Entrepreneurship, and the Changing Face of Political Life* (New York: Basic Books, 1988); Theodore Lowi's analysis of the new presidency, *The Personal President: Power Invested, Promise Unfulfilled* (Ithaca: Cornell University Press, 1985); and Benjamin Ginsberg and Martin Shefter's analysis of the machinations of elites in both branches, *Politics by Other Means: The Declining Importance of Elections in America* (New York: Basic Books, 1990).

11. See Lowi, *The Personal President*, pp. 24–30.

12. The Reagan presidency was not exceptional in this regard (see James W. Ceaser, "The Reagan Presidency and American Public Opinion," in *The Reagan Legacy: Promise and Performance*, ed. Charles O. Jones [Chatham, N.J.: Chatham House, 1988], pp. 172–210).

13. Byron Shafer, *Bifurcated Politics: Evolution and Reform in the National Party Convention* (Cambridge: Harvard University Press, 1988), p. 293.

14. See the exchange between Paul Herrnson and Stephen C. Craig, "Do Political Parties Really Matter?" a *Polity* Forum, in *Polity* 20 (Summer 1988): 705–19.

15. The increased partisan homogeneity and intensity in Reagan's appointees was impressive. See Harold Stanley and Richard Niemi, *Vital Statistics on American Politics* (Washington, D.C.: CQ Press, 1988), table 8-15 (p. 225); and Linda Fisher, "Fifty Years of Presidential Appointments," in *The In-and-Outers: Presidential Appointees and Transient Government in Washington*, ed. G. Calvin Mackenzie (Baltimore: Johns Hopkins University Press, 1987), pp. 12–13. On the narrowing of the ideological spectrum of the Republican party, see Nicol Rae, *The Decline and Fall of the Liberal Republicans* (New York: Oxford University Press, 1989); and Warren E. Miller and M. Kent Jennings, with Barbara G. Farah, *Parties in Transition: A Longitudinal Study of Party Elites and Party Supporters* (New York: Russell Sage Foundation, 1986), pp. 247–48.

16. See Smith, *The Idea Brokers;* R. Kent Weaver, "The Changing World of Think Tanks," *Political Science and Politics: PS* 22 (September 1988): 563–78; Samantha L. Durst and James A. Thurber, "Studying Washington Think Tanks: In Search of Definitions and Data" (Paper presented at the annual meeting of the American Political Science Association, Atlanta, August 1989); and Winand Gellner, "Political Think Tanks: Functions and Perspectives of a Strategic Elite" (Paper presented at the annual meeting of the American Political Science Association, San Francisco, August 1990).

17. That these people and their schools of thought were ideological can be substantiated with reference to the ideal type introduced above. See chap. 1 for details.

18. The BYM files are with John Macy's papers in the Lyndon Baines Johnson Library and were opened for review in the course of this research.

19. In the classic realignments punctuating the American party systems, candidates were widely separated on the issues (see Burnham, *Critical Elections*, p. 10; and David Brady, *Critical Elections and Congressional Policymaking* [Stanford: Stanford University Press, 1989]). By contrast, in the 1964 election, polls indicated that Johnson successfully presented himself as a consensus-seeking middle-of-the-road candidate. Johnson might plausibly have inter-

preted this victory as a mandate to carry on with the stalled Medicare and civil rights bills associated with the Truman and Kennedy administrations, but there was little basis in that election for a more dramatic break with the past in the nation's social policy (see Thomas Benham, "Polling for a Presidential Candidate: Some Observations on the 1964 Campaign," *Public Opinion Quarterly* 29 [Summer 1965]: 185–99).

20. The use of the epithet "trained seals" was reported by Fred Greenstein in his edited volume, *The Reagan Presidency: An Early Assessment* (Baltimore: Johns Hopkins University Press, 1983).

21. I borrow this metaphor from Peter L. Berger's classic critique of development theories, *Pyramids of Sacrifice* (New York: Doubleday, 1974).

Chapter One Ideology: Attributes and Significance to Presidential Politics

1. A similar strategy was adopted by Robert Putnam in his pioneering work "Studying Elite Political Culture: The Case of 'Ideology,'" *American Political Science Review* 65 (September 1971): 651–81; see esp. table 1 (p. 655).

2. See Herbert McClosky and John Zaller, *The American Ethos: Public Attitudes toward Capitalism and Democracy*, Twentieth-Century Fund Report (Cambridge: Harvard University Press, 1984), table 7-1 (p. 192).

3. See Peter L. Berger, *The Capitalist Revolution: Fifty Propositions about Prosperity, Equality, and Liberty* (New York: Basic Books, 1986), pp. 68–71; and Frank Heuberger, "The New Class: On the Theory of a No Longer Entirely New Phenomenon," in *Hidden Technocrats*, ed. Hansfried Kellner and Frank Heuberger (New Brunswick, N.J.: Transaction Press, forthcoming).

4. Berger, *Capitalist Revolution*, p. 51.

5. That the New Deal is the relevant dividing line here is suggested for reasons discussed in detail by Theodore Lowi in his analysis of the multiple revolutions engendered in national politics by the Roosevelt administration (see Theodore J. Lowi, *The Personal President: Power Invested, Promise Unfulfilled* [Ithaca: Cornell University Press, 1985], chap. 2, "The Legacies of FDR"; see also Hugh Heclo, "The Executive Office of the President," in *Modern Presidents and the Presidency*, ed. Marc Landy [Lexington, Mass.: Lexington Books, 1985], pp. 73–78).

6. Ayn Rand, *Atlas Shrugged* (New York: Random House, 1957).

7. See Claude Brown, *Manchild in the Promised Land* (New York: Macmillan, 1965); see also Brown's testimony before Congress, 29 August 1966, as reprinted in *Congressional Quarterly Almanac, 1966* (Washington, D.C.: CQ Press, 1966), p. 236.

8. Philip Converse, "The Nature of Belief Systems in Mass Publics," in *Ideology and Discontent*, ed. David E. Apter (London: Free Press of Glencoe, 1964), pp. 206–61; Gabriel Almond and Sidney Verba, *The Civic Culture* (Princeton: Princeton University Press, 1963).

9. Richard Cox, ed., *Ideology, Politics, and Political Theory* (Belmont, Calif.: Wadsworth, 1969), p. 12.

10. David Stockman, *The Triumph of Politics: Why the Reagan Revolution*

Failed (New York: Harper and Row, 1986), p. 21.

11. Ibid., p. 31.

12. Ibid., pp. 31–35.

13. Ibid., p. 39.

14. Jude Wanniski, personal interview, 5 November 1986.

15. Jude Wanniski, *The Way the World Works: How Economies Fail—and Succeed* (New York: Basic Books, 1978).

16. Wanniski, personal interview.

17. William E. Simon, *A Time for Truth* (New York: Reader's Digest Press, 1978), p. 25.

18. William E. Simon, personal interview, 4 December 1986.

19. James F. Lea, *Kazantkis: The Politics of Salvation* (University: University of Alabama Press, 1979).

20. Lea calls his ideal the "redistributivist state" (ibid., pp. 44 and 45 n. 27). "There is an immense gulf," in Lea's view, "of principle, between the welfare state and the redistributivist state" (just as there is a chasm, in Simon's view, between the welfare state and the good state).

21. Nathan Glazer, "The Social Policy of the Reagan Administration," in *The Social Contract Revisited: Aims and Outcomes of President Reagan's Social Welfare Policy*, ed. D. Lee Bawden (Washington, D.C.: Urban Institute Press, 1984), pp. 221–40.

22. See Michael B. Katz, *The Undeserving Poor: From the War on Poverty to the War on Welfare* (New York: Pantheon, 1989).

23. Some scholars of ideology, such as Hayward Alker and David Sylvan, have made this the core element of their definition of the term. The attractiveness of their approach is that it permits one to distinguish ideological thought as a matter of syntax. There are distinct ways syntactically to express polarities in the English language. The ways in which ideologues tend to interpret events so that they fit within a polarizing gestalt can, therefore, be represented as a logically coherent set of inference rules. Because I am committed to a semantic analysis and interpretation of ideology and to a semantic, even literary approach to reading texts, I do not follow the "dialecticians," but I do wish to note the partial complementarity of their view and mine. See Hayward R. Alker, Jr., "Some Attributes of Ideo-Logical Thought," Project Working Paper, Center for International Studies, MIT (Cambridge, 1979); and David J. Sylvan, "Ideological Constraints in Economic Policy" (Paper presented at the annual meeting of the American Political Science Association, New Orleans, August 1985).

24. Ralph Nader, Introduction to *Reagan's Ruling Class*, by Ronald Brownstein and Nina Easton (New York: Pantheon, 1983), pp. xv–xxvi.

25. Clifford Geertz, "Ideology as a Cultural System," in Geertz, *The Interpretation of Cultures* (New York: Basic Books, 1973), pp. 194–205.

26. Chalmers Johnson, *Revolutionary Change*, 2d ed. (Stanford: Stanford University Press, 1982); Anthony Wallace, *The Death and Rebirth of the Seneca* (New York: Alfred A. Knopf, 1970).

27. Antonio Gramsci, "The Intellectuals," in *Selections from the Prison Notebooks of Antonio Gramsci*, ed. and trans. Quintin Hoare and Geoffrey Nowell

Smith (New York: International Publishers, 1971).

28. For recent statements by both Gottfried and Kirk, see *Intercollegiate Review* 21 (Spring 1986): 18–21 and 25–28.

29. William F. Buckley, Jr., *Quotations from Chairman Bill*, comp. David Franke (New York: Pocket Books, 1971), p. 44.

30. See John Rawls, *A Theory of Justice* (Cambridge: Harvard University Press, Belknap Press, 1971). The most celebrated "response" to Rawls's book was Robert Nozick's *Anarchy, State, and Utopia* (New York: Basic Books, 1974).

31. See the profile of James Baker in Brownstein and Easton, *Reagan's Ruling Class*, pp. 647–50.

32. Ibid.

33. Profile of Edwin Meese in ibid., pp. 643–47; see also Sidney Blumenthal, *The Rise of the Counter-Establishment* (New York: Times Books, 1986).

34. Brownstein and Easton, *Reagan's Ruling Class*, p. 34.

35. Donald Regan is also profiled in Brownstein and Easton, *Reagan's Ruling Class*, as well as in the *Current Biography Yearbook* (New York: H. W. Wilson, 1982). See also Regan's memoirs, *For the Record: From Wall Street to Washington* (San Diego: Harcourt, Brace, Jovanovich, 1988).

36. Brownstein and Easton, *Reagan's Ruling Class*, p. 4.

37. See the testimony and public statements of Treasury Department officials in the first several months of the administration, available in the Treasury Department Library.

38. Regan, *For the Record*, pp. 142–44, 157–59.

39. This fourfold plan was originally spelled out by Reagan in a speech to a Chicago business audience during the campaign. The text of the speech is reprinted in Paul Boyer, ed., *Reagan as President: Contemporary Views of the Man, His Politics, and His Policies* (Chicago: Ivan Dee, 1990), pp. 106–9.

40. Regan's testimony before the Joint Economic Committee, 19 February 1981, p. 1, as bound in volumes of testimony in the Treasury Department Library.

41. I refer to a speech in which Regan explained the Economic Recovery Tax Act to a business audience at Columbia University in March 1981. The text is available in a press release bound with other department releases at the Treasury Department Library.

42. Ibid.

43. E. Pendleton James, personal interview, 15 December 1986.

44. Simon, *A Time for Truth*.

45. Ibid., chap. 2.

46. Ibid., p. 73.

47. Ibid., p. 44.

48. Ibid., p. 55.

49. Ibid., p. 198.

50. Ibid., p. 57.

51. Simon, personal interview.

52. Walter Dean Burnham, *Critical Elections and the Mainsprings of American Politics* (New York: Norton, 1970), p. 10.

53. See Walter Dean Burnham, *The Current Crisis in American Politics* (New York: Oxford University Press, 1982), and idem, "Revitalization and Decay: Looking toward the Third Century of American Electoral Politics," *Journal of Politics* 38 (August 1976): 146–72. See also J. Clubb, W. H. Flanigan, and N. H. Zingale, *Partisan Realignment: Voters, Parties, and Government in American History* (Beverly Hills: Russell Sage Foundation, 1980); Benjamin Ginsberg, "Critical Elections and the Substance of Party Conflict: 1844–1968," *Midwest Journal of Political Science* 16 (November 1972): 603–25; and David Brady, *Critical Elections and Congressional Policymaking* (Stanford: Stanford University Press, 1989).

54. Burnham, *Current Crisis,* p. 1.

55. The New Deal realignment was perhaps something of an exception in this regard, being based in part on a surge to the polls by previously inactive voters. This continues to be debated, however (see Richard P. McCormick, "The Realignment Synthesis in American History," in McCormick, ed., *The Party Period and Public Policy* [New York: Oxford University Press, 1986], p. 77).

56. See Brady, *Critical Elections,* on the importance of partisan polarizations among members of Congress to the policy shifts that followed critical elections. See also David Brady, with Joseph Stewart, Jr., "Congressional Party Realignment and Transformations of Public Policy in Three Realignment Eras," *American Journal of Political Science* 26 (May 1982): 333–60.

57. See Burnham, *Current Crisis,* esp. the first two selections.

58. On Jackson's reelection campaign as one that bound him to the voters as a "majoritarian delegate of instruction," see Thomas S. Langston, "A Rumour of Sovereignty: The Head of State as an Agent of American Political Development" (Paper presented at the annual meeting of the American Political Science Association, San Francisco, August 1990).

59. Everett C. Ladd, "Commentary: Like Waiting for Godot: The Uselessness of Realignment for Understanding Change in Contemporary American Politics," *Polity* 23 (Spring 1990): 511–25.

60. Cornelius P. Cotter et al., *Party Organizations and American Politics* (New York: Praeger, 1984); Xandra Kayden and Eddie Mahe, Jr., *The Party Goes On: The Persistence of the Two-Party System in the United States* (New York: Basic Books, 1985).

61. Self-identified "independents" overtook Republicans as a percentage of the electorate in 1968, a lead they have held since. "Independents" overtook Democrats in 1988 (see Martin Wattenberg, *The Decline of American Political Parties, 1952–1988* [Cambridge: Harvard University Press, 1990], table 9.1 [p. 140]). On the tremendous contemporary strength of the "party" of nonvoters, see Harold Stanley and Richard Niemi, *Vital Statistics on American Politics* (Washington, D.C.: CQ Press, 1988), p. 64.

62. David Price, *Bringing Back the Parties* (Washington, D.C.: CQ Press, 1985), pp. 16–17.

63. Seymour Martin Lipset, "The Elections, the Economy, and Public Opinion, 1984," *Political Science* 18 (Winter 1985): 35.

64. See Martin Wattenberg, "The Hollow Realignment: Partisan

Change in a Candidate-centered Era," *Public Opinion Quarterly* 51 (Spring 1987): 58–74; and James W. Ceaser, "The Reagan Presidency and American Public Opinion," in *The Reagan Legacy: Promise and Performance*, ed. Charles O. Jones (Chatham, N.J.: Chatham House, 1988), pp. 172–210.

65. See "Conservative Tide That Swept Reagan May Be Subsiding," *Christian Science Monitor*, 20 August 1985, p. 1.

66. Wattenberg, "Hollow Realignment," p. 67.

67. Gallup reported that "Reagan backers this year [1984] cited his economic policies as their main reason for choosing him" (quoted in Ceaser, "The Reagan Presidency and American Public Opinion," p. 194).

68. Quoted in Lipset, "The Elections," p. 29.

69. Byron Shafer, "The Notion of an Electoral Order: The Structure of Electoral Politics at the Ascension of George Bush" (Paper presented at the annual meeting of the American Political Science Association, Atlanta, August 1989).

70. See Benjamin Ginsberg and Martin Shefter, *Politics by Other Means: The Declining Importance of Elections in America* (New York: Basic Books, 1990).

71. Karl Mannheim, *Ideology and Utopia: An Introduction to the Sociology of Knowledge*, trans. Louis Wirth and Edward Shils (New York: Harcourt, Brace, 1936).

72. Ibid., pp. 159–60, from his chapter entitled "The Prospects of Scientific Politics."

Chapter Two   The Recruitment and Management of People of Ideas

1. See James McGregor Burns's account of Franklin Roosevelt's political career, *Roosevelt: The Lion and the Fox, 1882–1940* (New York: Harcourt, Brace & World, 1956).

2. Ibid., pp. 30–50; Ted Morgan, *FDR: A Biography* (New York: Simon and Schuster, 1985), pp. 123–24, 193; Edward J. Flynn, *You're the Boss* (New York: Viking Press, 1947).

3. See, e.g., Cabell Phillips, *From the Crash to the Blitz: 1929–1939*, A New York Times Book (New York: Macmillan, 1969), p. 73.

4. The story is told in Morgan, *FDR*, p. 343.

5. William Safire gives the term "brain trust," as opposed to "brains trust," his imprimatur in *Safire's Political Dictionary* (New York: Random House, 1978). According to Cabell Phillips, *From the Crash to the Blitz*, p. 108, the term was originally used in this way by the man credited with applying the term first to Roosevelt's academic advisers, John Keran, an Albany reporter for the *New York Times*.

6. Arthur M. Schlesinger, Jr., *The Coming of the New Deal*, vol. 2 of *The Age of Roosevelt* (Boston: Houghton Mifflin, 1958), pp. 180–84.

7. See Raymond Moley's own account of his service with Roosevelt, *After Seven Years* (New York: Harper Brothers, 1939).

8. See Donald Brand, *Corporatism and the Rule of Law: A Study of the*

National Recovery Administration (Ithaca: Cornell University Press, 1988).

9. See Kim McQuaid, "Corporate Liberalism in the American Business Community, 1920–1940," *Business History Review* 52 (Fall 1978): 342–68.

10. Raymond Moley, as quoted by E. Francis Brown in *Increasing the President's Power*, comp. Julia E. Johnsen, The Reference Shelf, vol. 9, no. 2 (New York: H. W. Wilson, 1935).

11. Beatrice Bishop Berle and Travis Beale Jacobs, *Navigating the Rapids, 1918–1971: From the Papers of Adolf A. Berle* (New York: Harcourt, Brace, Jovanovich, 1973), p. 62. The quotation is from Berle's draft of the speech Roosevelt delivered at the Commonwealth Club in San Francisco on September 23, 1932. For Berle's in-depth analysis of the economy, see his classic work (written with Gardiner C. Means), *The Modern Corporation and Private Property* (New York: Macmillan, 1931).

12. The contrasting phrase is borrowed from John Kenneth Galbraith's less radical study of industrial concentration, *The New Industrial State* (Boston: Houghton Mifflin, 1967).

13. Berle and Jacobs, *Navigating the Rapids*, p. 62.

14. Rexford Guy Tugwell, *The Industrial Discipline and the Governmental Arts* (New York: Columbia University Press, 1933), p. 218.

15. Ibid., p. 145.

16. Rexford Guy Tugwell, *Roosevelt's Revolution: The First Year, a Personal Perspective* (New York: Macmillan, 1977), p. 145.

17. Tugwell, address before the Federation of Bar Associations of Western New York, June 24, 1933, as reprinted in Johnson, *Increasing the President's Power*, p. 88.

18. As quoted in Schlesinger, *Coming of the New Deal*, p. 184.

19. Tugwell, *Roosevelt's Revolution*, p. 7.

20. See Lewis A. Coser, *Men of Ideas: A Sociologist's View* (New York: Free Press, 1965), contrasting the New Dealers with the Fabians. Coser cites as the principal source for the theoretical aspects of his argument about the New Dealers' relative lack of effectiveness Robert K. Merton's "Role of the Intellectual in Public Bureaucracy," in *Social Theory and Social Structure* (Glencoe, Ill.: Free Press, 1949), pp. 161–78.

21. Bruce Allen Murphy, *The Brandeis/Frankfurter Connection: The Secret Political Activities of Two Supreme Court Justices* (New York: Oxford University Press, 1982), p. 123.

22. Murphy, *Brandeis/Frankfurter*, pp. 38–103.

23. Bruce Allen Murphy, "Brandeis, FDR, and the Ethics of Judicial Advising," in *The Roosevelt New Deal: A Program Assessment Fifty Years After*, ed. Wilbur J. Cohen (Austin: Lyndon Baines Johnson School of Public Affairs, 1986), p. 247.

24. Quoted in Joseph Lash, *Dealers and Dreamers: A New Look at the New Deal* (New York: Doubleday, 1988), p. 115.

25. Brandeis's comments come from a letter to Robert Bruere, reprinted in Donald Richberg, "The Industrial Liberalism of Justice Brandeis," *Columbia Law Review* 31 (November 1931): 1098, as reprinted in *The Curse of Bigness: Miscellaneous Papers of Louis D. Brandeis*, ed. Osmond K. Fraenkel, as

projected by Clarence M. Lewis (Port Washington, N.Y.: Kennikat Press, 1934), p. 271.

26. Walter Isaacson and Evan Thomas, *The Wise Men: Six Friends and the World They Made: Acheson, Bohlen, Harriman, Kennan, Lovett, McCloy* (New York: Simon and Schuster, 1986), pp. 125–26.

27. Brandeis, quoted in ibid.

28. H. N. Hirsch, *The Enigma of Felix Frankfurter* (New York: Basic Books, 1981), pp. 104–5; see also pp. 21, 40–41.

29. Lash, *Dealers and Dreamers*, p. 105, from a letter written to Walter Lippmann after the 1933 inaugural.

30. On the differences between mythical, ideological, and utopian perspectives on time, see Willard Mullins, "On the Concept of Ideology in Political Science," *American Political Science Review* 66 (June 1972): 498–510.

31. Berle and Jacobs, *Navigating the Rapids*, p. 72.

32. Moley, *After Seven Years*, pp. 82–84. See also Bernard Sternsher, *Rexford Tugwell and the New Deal* (New Brunswick, N.J.: Rutgers University Press, 1964), pp. 90–102. According to Sternsher, Tugwell wanted the brain trusters' campaign functions to be assumed by a federally sanctioned planning agency, which would become a "Fourth Power" within the government. Public hearings and a legislative "check" would ensure that the Fourth Power remained democratic. On popular suspicions, see Richard Hofstadter, *Anti-Intellectualism in American Life* (New York: Vintage Books, 1962), pp. 214–23; and Phillips, *From the Crash to the Blitz*, p. 114.

33. These appointments are typically termed *competitive* and appraised as conducive to the president's personal control of his administration. For the leading instance of this analysis, see Richard Neustadt, *Presidential Power* (New York: John Wiley and Sons, 1960). From the perspective of ideological identifications, *contradictory* seems a more apt term.

34. James Farley, Oral History Interview, Lyndon Baines Johnson Library (hereafter "LBJL").

35. As a result, the top choices were largely Roosevelt's (Laurin Henry, *Presidential Transitions* [Washington, D.C.: Brookings Institution Press, 1961], p. 420).

36. Alfred B. Rollins, Jr., *Roosevelt and Howe* (New York: Alfred A. Knopf, 1962), p. 389.

37. As a consequence, party endorsements were simply lacking entirely for some appointees (Harold Brayman, "Roosevelt and the Spoilsman," *Current History*, October 1934, p. 22; Henry, *Presidential Transitions*, pp. 204, 231–33, 422).

38. James Farley, *Behind the Ballots: The Personal History of a Politician* (New York: Harcourt, Brace and Company, 1938), p. 233.

39. See chaps. 3 and 4 in Schlesinger, *Coming of the New Deal*.

40. Ibid., p. 16.

41. Tugwell, *Roosevelt's Revolution*, p. 256.

42. Murphy, *Brandeis/Frankfurter*, p. 38.

43. Frankfurter considered his greatest gift to be the management of

human affairs, which encompassed these personnel efforts and which he called "personalia" (Hirsch, *Enigma*, p. 108).

44. See Lash, *Dealers and Dreamers*, p. 178.

45. Liva Baker, *Felix Frankfurter* (New York: Coward-McCann, 1969), p. 163.

46. Murphy, *Brandeis/Frankfurter*, p. 253.

47. Baker, *Frankfurter*, p. 163.

48. Flynn, *You're the Boss*, p. 123.

49. Hirsch, *Enigma*, p. 103; Farley, Oral History Interview.

50. Henry, *Presidential Transitions*, pp. 400–417.

51. Farley, Oral History Interview.

52. In the first sixteen months alone, Roosevelt's administration dispensed about 150,000 jobs, divided almost equally between replacements and persons filling new positions (see Henry, *Presidential Transitions*, p. 432).

53. Lyndon Baines Johnson, *The Vantage Point: Perspectives on the Presidency, 1963–1969* (New York: Holt, Rinehart, and Winston, 1971), pp. 103–4.

54. Jeff Fishel, *Presidents and Promises* (Washington, D.C.: CQ Press, 1985), pp. 31–40.

55. Thomas W. Benham, "Polling for a Presidential Candidate: Some Observations on the 1964 Campaign," *Public Opinion Quarterly* 29 (Summer 1965): 185–99. Benham polled for Goldwater.

56. William Safire, in his *Political Dictionary*, credits Adlai Stevenson, Jr., with coining the term "quality of life." John Kenneth Galbraith popularized the term "affluent society" in *The Affluent Society* (Boston: Houghton Mifflin, 1958). Arthur M. Schlesinger, Jr., in numerous works, praised the "toughminded" path of intellect, consciously elaborating upon the vision of American pragmatist William James (see the discussion of Schlesinger in Christopher Lasch, *The New Radicalism in America, 1889–1963: The Intellectual as a Social Type* [New York: Norton, 1965], pp. 308–10). "Vigor" was a much-admired Kennedy trait, and the president's pronunciation of the term a presidential trademark. Daniel Bell, finally, famously proclaimed "the end of ideology" in his book by that title (Glencoe, Ill.: Free Press, 1960).

57. Bell, *The End of Ideology*; Arthur M. Schlesinger, Jr., *A Thousand Days: John F. Kennedy in the White House* (Boston: Houghton Mifflin, 1965), chaps. 24 ("A National Agenda") and 28 ("The Politics of Modernity").

58. Schlesinger uses the term repeatedly in *The Crisis of Confidence* (Boston: Houghton Mifflin, 1967).

59. Eric Goldman, *The Tragedy of Lyndon Johnson* (New York: Alfred A. Knopf, 1969).

60. Goldman, *Tragedy*, p. 163.

61. Harry McPherson, Oral History Interview, LBJL.

62. Unless otherwise noted, the quotations in this section are from the Great Society speech, which can be found, with a brief commentary, in Theodore Windt, ed., *Presidential Rhetoric: 1961 to the Present*, 3d ed. (Dubuque, Iowa: Kendall/Hunt, 1983), pp. 61–64.

63. See *Safire's Political Dictionary*, s.v. "quality of life."

64. Richard Goodwin was a holdover from the Kennedy administra-

tion who became one of Johnson's favorite speechwriters. For Goodwin's own views, see *The American Condition* (Garden City, N.Y.: Doubleday, 1974); and *Remembering America: A Voice from the Sixties* (Boston: Little, Brown, 1988). Harrington, Manciewicz, and Jacobs worked on the task force that recommended the programs launched as the War on Poverty.

65. Robert Wood later admitted as much in his book looking back on the Great Society, suggestively entitled *The Necessary Majority: Middle America and the Urban Crisis* (New York: Columbia University Press, 1972).

66. Windt, *Presidential Rhetoric,* p. 62.

67. Lasch, *The New Radicalism,* p. 290.

68. John P. Roche, *Sentenced to Life* (New York: Macmillan, 1974).

69. John P. Roche, personal interview, 19 June 1987.

70. Doris Kearns, *Lyndon Johnson: The American Dream* (New York: Harper and Row, 1976), p. 294.

71. Roche, personal interview.

72. Kearns, *Johnson,* p. 54.

73. Memorandum, Valenti to LBJ, with Johnson's handwritten reply, 28 December 1963, John Macy files, LBJL.

74. Kearns, *Johnson,* p. 41. This is also the impression of retired University of Texas professor of government Carl Leiden, whose request to interview Johnson in his retirement was rebuffed with invective against all intellectuals (Carl Leiden, personal interview).

75. Lists of members of Domestic Affairs Brains Trust, arranged alphabetically and by subject of expertise, John Macy files, box 897, "Brain Trust" folder, LBJL.

76. John Macy et al., *America's Unelected Government: Appointing the President's Team* (Cambridge: Ballinger, 1983), p. 31.

77. John Macy, Oral History Interview, LBJL. As to this administration's efforts at affirmative-action hiring, it is worth recalling that Johnson had become acquainted with Macy through their joint work on President Kennedy's Committee on Equal Employment Opportunity, as noted by G. Calvin Mackenzie in *The Politics of Presidential Appointments* (New York: Free Press, 1981), pp. 33-36.

78. Even so, the number of people with Ph.D. degrees selected for top government jobs in the 1960s did increase sufficiently to merit the attention of Kenneth Prewitt and William McAllister ("Changes in the American Executive Elite, 1930-1970," chap. 5 in *Elite Recruitment in Democratic Polities: Comparative Studies across Nations,* ed. Heinz Eulau and Moshe M. Czudnowski [Beverly Hills: Sage, 1976]).

79. The BYM files are with Macy's files in the LBJL; they were opened for review for the first time in the course of this research.

80. Memorandum, Kearns to LBJ, 31 October 1968, with attachments, EX/PE 12 4/22/67, folder PE 12 10/1/68, LBJL.

81. "Of the Week," *U.S. News & World Report,* 5 February 1968, pp. 16-17.

82. James C. Gaither, Oral History Interview, LBJL.

83. Matthew Coffey reports that this was true for at least a while ("A

Death at the White House: The Short Life of the New Patronage," *Public Administration Review* 34 [September–October 1974]: 440–45).

84. Macy read the citation in his Oral History Interview.

85. Mackenzie, *Politics of Presidential Appointments*, p. 39.

86. Macy, Oral History Interview.

87. On the list of contacts, see Matthew Coffey, Oral History Interview; Dan Fenn, Oral History Interview, LBJL; and Macy et al., *America's Unelected Government*.

88. Macy et al., *America's Unelected Government*, pp. 31–35.

89. Memorandum, Marvin Watson to Cliff Cater, 20 August 1965, EX/PL 1/22/63, box 1, LBJL. In other memoranda, White House personnel are shown in 1965 struggling to get hold of prestige appointments, because, in the words of one official, "until all of these from the various Departments are clearing your desk, we can not really make the President's Club function as it should" (memorandum, Dick Maguire to Marvin Watson, 3 May 1965, EX/PL 11/22/63, box 1, "Political Affairs 8/7/64–6/28/65" folder, LBJL. See also memorandum, James Jones to Marvin Watson, n.d., ibid., reflecting Jones's suspicion that Califano's office was trying to "run" away with the selection of persons to prestige appointments).

90. Macy, Oral History Interview.

91. Mackenzie, *Politics of Presidential Appointments*, pp. 36–40.

92. Macy files, LBJL; a copy of the memorandum is in the author's possession.

93. *U.S. News & World Report*, 5 February 1968, pp. 16–17; Lawrence E. Levinson, telephone interview, 9 July 1987, in which he discussed the roles of some of these BYM. See also memorandum, Macy to Moyers, 14 May 1966, White House Central Files, Aides, Moyers, "Personnel" folder, LBJL.

94. Johnson, *Vantage Point*, pp. 328–29, 76.

95. Harry McPherson, *A Political Education* (Boston: Little, Brown, 1972).

96. As reported in Thomas Cronin, *The State of the Presidency*, 2d ed. (Boston: Little, Brown, 1980), p. 303.

97. Richard Tanner Johnson, *Managing the White House: An Intimate Study of the Presidency* (New York: Harper and Row, 1974).

98. See George Reedy, *Lyndon B. Johnson: A Memoir* (New York: Andrews and McMeel, 1982).

99. A common story about President Johnson, as recounted by MIT Professor Lucian Pye (personal interview).

100. Lou Cannon, *Reagan* (New York: Putnam, 1982), p. 17.

101. Bayard Boyarsky, *Ronald Reagan: His Life and Rise to the Presidency* (New York: Random House, 1981), pp. 93–97.

102. William Rusher, *The Rise of the Right* (New York: William Morrow, 1984). See also Garry Wills, *Confessions of a Conservative* (Garden City, N.Y.: Doubleday, 1979).

103. According to Reagan's comments at the thirtieth-anniversary celebration of the *National Review*, seen by this author on videotape.

104. William F. Buckley, Jr., personal interview, 11 October 1986.

105. Buckley's regular conversations with Malcolm Muggeridge on Buckley's public television interview program, "Firing Line," hammer away at this point.

106. Buckley, personal interview.

107. Lewis Lehrman, personal interview, 20 November 1986. See also Michael Kramer, "Who Is This Guy Lew Lehrman?" *New York*, 5 April 1982, p. 25; and Thomas O'Donnel, "Return of the Golden Rule?" *Forbes*, 8 June 1981, p. 33.

108. Lehrman, personal interview, 16 December 1986.

109. Lehrman Institute, *History and Current Programs, 1986–87* (New York, 1986).

110. David Stockman, *The Triumph of Politics: Why the Reagan Revolution Failed* (New York: Harper and Row, 1986), p. 75.

111. Lewis Lehrman, "The Right to Life and the Restoration of the American Republic," *National Review*, 29 August 1986, pp. 25–28. The analogy between slavery and abortion was also favored by Ronald Reagan in Ronald Reagan, *Abortion and the Conscience of a Nation*, with afterwords by C. Everett Koop and Malcolm Muggeridge (Nashville: Thomas Nelson Publishers, 1984), pp. 19–20, 27.

112. Personal interviews, Leslie Lenkowsky, 3 November 1986, and William E. Simon, 4 December 1986.

113. With reference to his earlier, technocratic writing, Kristol says: "As an editor of *The Public Interest*, I stand by it; as an editorial writer for the *Wall Street Journal*, I've changed my mind" (Irving Kristol, personal interview, 16 December 1986).

114. Kristol, personal interview.

115. Irving Kristol, "Reflections of a True, Self-Confessed Neoconservative," in *Reflections of a Neoconservative: Looking Back, Looking Ahead* (New York: Basic Books, 1983), p. 76.

116. Kristol, personal interview. When Kristol founded *The Public Interest* with Daniel Bell in 1965, they both hoped that a nonideologized politics was becoming possible, given the apparent eclipse of Marxist-inspired ideology in Western countries. Bell's statement on why he resigned from the magazine ten years later is interesting on this point: "Kristol," he writes, "had begun to believe that all modern politics is inescapably ideological because these views are competitions to control the shape of the future, and that the liberal culture is a frail reed against the compulsions of the utopian or eschatological claims which drive Western culture to the destruction of liberty" (Bell, *End of Ideology*, new afterword to the 1988 reprint, pp. 443–44).

117. Kristol, *Reflections*, p. 76.

118. Ibid., pp. 41, 92.

119. Ibid., p. 74. For biographical profiles of Kristol and several of his associates, see Peter Steinfels, *The Neoconservatives: The Men Who Are Changing America's Politics* (New York: Simon and Schuster, 1979).

120. Kristol, *Reflections*, chap. 3, "The Adversary Culture." For a similar argument, see Brigitte Berger and Peter Berger, "Our Conservatism and Theirs," *Commentary* 82 (October 1986): 62–67.

121. Fred Greenstein, "Reagan and the Lore of the Modern Presidency: What Have We Learned?" chap. 6 in *The Reagan Presidency: An Early Assessment,* ed. Greenstein (Baltimore: Johns Hopkins University Press, 1983).

122. Reprinted in Paul D. Erickson, *Reagan Speaks: The Making of an American Myth* (New York: New York University Press, 1985).

123. Ronald Reagan, "A Time for Choosing," 27 October 1964, reprinted in ibid., pp. 124–45.

124. Ronald Reagan, *Ronald Reagan: An American Life* (New York: Simon and Schuster, 1990), pp. 715, 473.

125. Reagan, speech before the National Association of Evangelicals, Orlando, Fla., 8 March 1983, in Erickson, *Reagan Speaks.*

126. According to Speaker of the House Tip O'Neill, Reagan retold one such tale so often that Joseph Califano researched it, found it to be false, and wrote to the president with his findings on at least three separate occasions (See Thomas P. O'Neill [with William Novak], *Man of the House: The Life and Political Memoirs of Speaker Tip O'Neill* [New York: Random House, 1987], pp. 347–48).

127. Reagan, *Reagan,* pp. 67–69.

128. See the complementary analysis of liberals as the objective allies of communists in ibid., p. 205.

129. Ronald Reagan, interview with Thomas Winters, *Human Events,* 26 February 1983, p. 1.

130. Reagan, *Reagan,* p. 316, diary entry of 28 January 1982.

131. Reagan, *Human Events* interview. Also on this issue, see Stanley Rothman and S. Robert Lichter, "How Liberal Are Bureaucrats?" *Regulation: AEI Journal on Government and Society* 7 (November–December 1983): 16–22.

132. "Operation Legacy," *New York Times,* 7 May 1987.

133. See James P. Pfiffner, *The Strategic Presidency: Hitting the Ground Running* (Chicago: Dorsey, 1988); see also G. Calvin Mackenzie, "The Reaganites Come to Town: Personnel Selection for a Conservative Administration" (Paper presented at the annual meeting of the American Political Science Association, New York, August 1981).

134. Meese was named a fellow of the academy during the early years of the Reagan administration, a decision that was highly controversial at the NAPA (Paul Light, personal interview, November 1986).

135. Carl Brauer, *Presidential Transitions: Eisenhower through Reagan* (New York: Oxford University Press, 1986), p. 227; corroborated by E. Pendleton James in a personal interview, 15 December 1986.

136. James, personal interview.

137. Pfiffner, *Strategic Presidency,* p. 79.

138. As noted by Mackenzie, "Reaganites Come to Town," p. 25.

139. Ibid., pp. 12–13.

140. For details, see Dom Bonafede, "The White House Personnel Office: From Roosevelt to Reagan," in *The In-and-Outers: Presidential Appointees and Transient Government in Washington,* ed. G. Calvin Mackenzie (Baltimore: Johns Hopkins University Press, 1987), p. 50; and more generally, "The Decisionmakers," *Congressional Quarterly Weekly Report,* special report of 25 April

1981, pp. 673–768. My best estimate, based primarily upon the descriptions provided in this special report, is that approximately 69 of the 350 appointees profiled there came to work for the Reagan administration with conservative organization credentials, as opposed to backgrounds in business or in regular Republican politics. On second-term appointees, see *Congressional Quarterly Weekly Report*, special report of 18 May 1985, pp. 1069–1208.

141. *National Journal*, 20 February 1982, p. 506.

142. See Mackenzie, "Reaganites Come to Town"; and "Reaganites Make the Bureaucracy Toe the Line on Policy," *Wall Street Journal*, 10 February 1982, p. 1. See also Richard Waterman, *Presidential Influence and the Administrative State* (Knoxville: University of Tennessee Press, 1989); Robert Rector and Michael Sanera, eds., *Steering the Elephant: How Washington Works* (New York: Universe Books, 1987); Jerry Hagstrom, *Beyond Reagan: The New Landscape of American Politics* (New York: Norton, 1988), pp. 86–92; and "Environmental Report," *National Journal*, 5 November 1983, pp. 2306–9.

143. Linda Fisher, "Appointees and Presidential Control: The Importance of Role" (Paper presented at the annual meeting of the American Political Science Association, Washington, D.C., August 1986). The NAPA survey, Fisher indicates, was based on "biographical data obtained from published sources on 1285 individuals who held 1528 presidentially appointed, Senate-confirmed positions from 1965–1984" and from a questionnaire completed by 532 respondents.

144. Ibid. See, more generally, the edited volume of papers based on the NAPA survey, Mackenzie's *In-and-Outers*.

145. Nadine Cohodas, "Reagan's Legacy Is Not Only on the Bench," *Congressional Quarterly*, 26 November 1988, p. 3393.

146. David McKay, *Domestic Policy and Ideology: Presidents and the American State, 1964–1987* (Cambridge: Cambridge University Press, 1989), table 5 (p. 192).

147. Sheldon Goldman, "Reaganizing the Judiciary: The First Term Appointments," *Judicature* 68 (April–May 1985): 313–29; Ronald Brownstein, "With or Without Supreme Court Changes, Reagan Will Reshape the Federal Bench," *National Journal*, 8 December 1984, pp. 2338–41; James, personal interview; "Conservatives Pressing to Reshape Judiciary," *Congressional Quarterly Weekly Report*, 7 September 1985, p. 1759.

148. See the comments of presidential counsel Fred Fielding, as quoted in Brownstein, "With or Without Supreme Court Changes."

149. Reagan figures are my calculations, based on U.S. Congress, Senate, Committee on the Judiciary, "Confirmation Hearings on Federal Appointments—Hearings before the Committee on the Judiciary," 99th Cong., 2d sess., 1989. The other figures are from Goldman, "Reaganizing the Judiciary," p. 324.

150. Goldman, "Reaganizing the Judiciary," table 3 (p. 324).

151. Robert Bork, "Tradition and Morality in Constitutional Law," as quoted in Everett Carl Ladd, *The Ladd Report*, no. 7, "The Political Battle for the Federal Courts" (New York: Norton, 1988): 12. See also Antonin Scalia, "The Doctrine of Standing as an Essential Element of the Separation of Powers,"

Suffolk University Law Review 17 (Winter 1983): 881–99; Ralph K. Winter, Jr., "Changing Concepts of Equality: From Equality before the Law to the Welfare State," *Washington University Law Quarterly,* Summer 1979, esp. pp. 754–55; Patrick E. Higginbotham, "Introduction: A Brief Reflection on Judicial Use of Social Science Data," *Law and Contemporary Problems* 46 (Fall 1983): 7–12; and J. Harvie Wilkinson III and G. Edward White, "Constitutional Protection for Personal Lifestyles," *Cornell Law Review* 62 (March 1977): 563, 625.

152. Robert Bork, "Neutral Principles and Some First Amendment Problems," *Indiana Law Journal* 47 (Fall 1971): 3, 11.

153. See Frank Easterbrook, "The Court and the Economic System," foreword to "The Supreme Court, 1983 Term," *Harvard Law Review* 98 (November 1984): 4–60; Kenneth Starr's comments in "Judicial Review of Administrative Action in a Conservative Era: A Panel," *Administrative Law Review* 39 (Summer 1987): 353–98; Starr, "Judicial Review in the Post-*Chevron* Era," *Yale Journal of Regulation* 3 (Spring 1986): 283–312; and Richard Posner, "The Meaning of Judicial Self-Restraint," *Indiana Law Journal* 59 (Fall 1983): 8.

154. Frank Easterbrook, "Ways of Criticizing the Court," *Harvard Law Review* 95 (February 1982): 802–32.

155. Donald Regan, *For the Record: From Wall Street to Washington* (San Diego: Harcourt, Brace, Jovanovich, 1988), esp. pp. 227–30.

156. Larry Speakes, *Speaking Out: The Reagan Presidency from Inside the White House* (New York: Charles Scribner's Sons, 1988), pp. 109, 305.

157. Joseph Sobran, in *American Spectator,* October 1986, p. 18.

Chapter Three   Defining a Mission for the TVA: The Roosevelt Administration

1. A useful compendium of pro– and anti–New Deal rhetoric of the time, containing numerous rhetorical references to these isms, is Julia E. Johnsen, comp., *Increasing the President's Power,* The Reference Shelf, vol. 9, no. 2 (New York: H. W. Wilson, 1935).

2. On the inaptness of the terms *pragmatic* and *experimental* to the New Deal, see Barry Karl, *The Uneasy State: The United States from 1915 to 1945* (Chicago: University of Chicago Press, 1983), p. 127.

3. In a recent book on the philosophical and historical roots of Roosevelt's presidency, Philip Abbott characterizes the TVA as representing the "Jeffersonian" streak in Roosevelt's makeup (see Abbott, *The Exemplary Presidency: Franklin D. Roosevelt and the American Political Tradition* (Amherst: University of Massachusetts Press, 1990), pp. 91–100.

4. George W. Norris, *Fighting Liberal: The Autobiography of George W. Norris* (New York: Macmillan, 1945).

5. Arthur M. Schlesinger, Jr., *The Coming of the New Deal,* vol. 2 of *The Age of Roosevelt* (Boston: Houghton Mifflin, 1958), pp. 322–23; Norris, *Fighting Liberal,* p. 160.

6. Norris, *Fighting Liberal,* pp. 160–61; on pp. 248–49 he calls the profiting from electricity "unconscionable."

7. Judson King, *The Conservation Fight: From Theodore Roosevelt to the*

Tennessee Valley Authority (Washington, D.C.: Public Affairs Press, 1959), p. 265; Thomas McCraw, *TVA and the Power Fight: 1933–1939* (Philadelphia: J. B. Lippincott, 1971), p. 28.

    8. McCraw, *TVA and the Power Fight,* p. 28.

    9. Ibid., p. 31.

    10. Ibid., p. 35.

    11. As reported in Paul K. Conkin, "Intellectual and Political Roots," in *TVA: Fifty Years of Grass-Roots Bureaucracy,* ed. Erwin C. Hargrove and Paul K. Conkin (Urbana: University of Illinois Press, 1983), pp. 22–23.

    12. As C. Herman Pritchett pointed out, there was indeed "no prototype for the T.V.A. as planner" (*The Tennessee Valley Authority: A Study in Public Administration* [Chapel Hill: University of North Carolina Press, 1943], p. 117).

    13. McCraw, *TVA and the Power Fight,* p. 35.

    14. Morgan himself is the source of the interpretation that gives him credit for being the sole author of the planning sections of the legislation (see Arthur E. Morgan, *The Making of the TVA* [Buffalo: Prometheus Books, 1974], pp. 6–7; and Thomas McCraw, *Morgan versus Lilienthal: The Feud within the TVA* [Chicago: Loyola University Press, 1970], in which personal interviews with Morgan are the source of the same interpretation). Ted Morgan, *FDR: A Biography* (New York: Simon and Schuster, 1985), and Kenneth Davis, *FDR, the New Deal Years, 1933–1937: A History* (New York: Random House, 1986), follow Arthur Morgan's lead as well but do not provide their sources. Ted Morgan writes on p. 91, for instance, that "FDR had been in favor of public power as Governor of New York. He read an article on a unified river system by Dr. Arthur Morgan . . . and decided to act on it." He goes on to assert, on the same page, that Roosevelt was "perhaps most greatly helped" to see the planning potential of the TVA by a long conversation with Arthur Morgan. But Arthur Morgan, in his own book, *Making of the TVA,* pp. 6–7, informs us that his first conversation with FDR occurred after the Congress was already considering a TVA bill with planning provisions based on FDR's statements in Warm Springs and his message to Congress.

    15. Schlesinger, *Coming of the New Deal,* p. 319.

    16. Michael J. McDonald and John Muldowny, *TVA and the Dispossessed: The Resettlement of Population in the Norris Dam Area* (Knoxville: University of Tennessee Press, 1982), p. 10.

    17. Schlesinger, *Coming of the New Deal,* p. 319; see also Conkin, "Intellectual and Political Roots," pp. 24–25. According to Schlesinger (p. 320), Roosevelt knew that his back-to-the-land enthusiasms might contribute to fears harbored by some of his critics of a class uprising among the urban proletariat, but the evidence for this line of thinking dates from 1934, after passage of the TVA Act.

    18. Morgan's authorship of this provision was indicated on the floor of the Senate by Senator Norris on May 1 (see *Congressional Record,* 73d Cong., 1st sess., 1933, 77, pt. 3:2634. That Norris was not, however, very familiar with Morgan at this time is revealed, incidentally, on the same page, where Norris mistakenly identifies Morgan as the "head of the Engineering Department" of Antioch College. Morgan was actually president of the institution).

19. Conkin, "Intellectual and Political Roots," p. 28. For the president's words, in his message requesting the legislation to establish the TVA, see *The Public Papers and Addresses of Franklin Delano Roosevelt,* comp. Samuel Rosenman, 13 vols. (New York: Random House, 1938–50), 3:122.

20. Roosevelt, *Public Papers and Addresses,* 3:122.

21. These remarks may be found in *Congressional Record,* 73d Cong., 1st sess., 1933, 77, pt. 2:2176, 2179, 2196, 2262, 2200.

22. See C. Herman Pritchett, "The Development of the Tennessee Valley Authority Act," *Tennessee Law Review* 15 (1938): 128–41.

23. The promised "tightening up" never did occur (House Committee on Military Affairs, *Muscle Shoals: Hearings,* 73d Cong., 1st sess. 1933).

24. *Congressional Record,* 73d Cong., 1st sess., 1933, 77, pt. 2:2250–51.

25. Ibid., 77, pt. 6:6214.

26. See the remarks of Senator King in ibid., 77, pt. 3:2634.

27. James McGregor Burns, *Roosevelt: The Lion and the Fox, 1882–1940* (New York: Harcourt, Brace & World, 1956), p. 179.

28. Donald Davidson, *The Tennessee,* vol. 2, *The New River: Civil War to TVA* (New York: Rinehart, 1948), pp. 216–18. This attitude was expressed nicely, and not untypically, by Alabama congressman Miles C. Allgood on the first day of hearings. "I have listened to hearings on Muscle Shoals for ten years," Allgood began. "I doubt if there is very much new that can be brought before the committee. I have not had the time nor the opportunity to study this bill, but I know to a certain extent what is included in it" (House Committee on Military Affairs, *Muscle Shoals: Hearings,* p. 45). Similarly, Sam D. McReynolds, Democrat from Tennessee, said: "I feel, from a hurried glance at this bill, that it is the greatest bill, the best bill that we have ever had for the solution of this problem," the "problem" being the "proper disposition of Muscle Shoals" (ibid., p. 10).

29. King, *Conservation Fight,* pp. 268–75.

30. 48 Stat. 69.

31. Ibid.

32. Executive Order 6161, as reprinted in 16 *United States Code, Annotated,* sec. 831u.

33. It was presumably up to the president, for instance, whether the authority's chairman would have power independent of the other two board members and whether a general manager might be appointed to carry out the board's plans.

34. Morgan, *Making of the TVA,* p. 6.

35. See the following works by Arthur E. Morgan: *The Long Road* (Washington, D.C.: National Home Library, 1936); *The Small Community: What It Is and How to Achieve It* (New York: Harper and Row, 1942); *Edward Bellamy* (New York: Columbia University Press, 1944); and *Nowhere Was Somewhere: How History Makes Utopias and How Utopias Make History* (Chapel Hill: University of North Carolina Press, 1946).

36. Morgan, *Making of the TVA,* pp. 40–41.

37. Ibid.

38. Ibid., p. 54.

39. Ibid., p. 189.

40. "In my endeavor to build a foundation of mutual trust and respect with him [i.e., Lilienthal], I deliberately put in his hands power that could be used against me. . . . Because from long experience I had found that I could sometimes turn adverse human relationships into good ones" (ibid., p. 29).

41. Ibid.

42. See memoranda, Arthur Morgan to David Lilienthal and Harcourt Morgan, and Lilienthal's response to Morgan, July 1933, PSF 187, "TVA" folder, 3d file, Franklin Delano Roosevelt Library, Hyde Park, New York (FDRL).

43. Memoranda, Arthur Morgan to FDR, 12 April 1933, and FDR to Morgan, 18 April 1933, PPF 290, "Arthur E. Morgan" folder, FDRL.

44. Telegram, Arthur Morgan to Marvin McIntyre, the White House, 30 May 1933, OF 42, box 1, "TVA, 1933," folder, FDRL.

45. Ibid. See National Popular Government League, bulletin 183, 17 March 1938, for King's retrospective analysis (OF 42, box 6, "Arthur Morgan" folder, FDRL).

46. McCraw, *Morgan versus Lilienthal*, p. 13.

47. Ibid.

48. Harcourt A. Morgan, commencement address, University of Western Ontario, London, Ontario, 7 June 1939, PPF, box 4958, "Morgan, Dr. Harcourt," folder, FDRL. See also Erwin Hargrove, "The Task of Leadership," in Hargrove and Conkin, *TVA*, esp. pp. 96–97.

49. Daniels wrote at the time of the feud: "Many of us will prefer a sloppy South to a South planned in perfection by outlanders. We know out of our past that the worst carpet baggers were the ones who came down here to improve us" (quoted in Schlesinger, *Coming of the New Deal*, p. 331).

50. McCraw, *Morgan versus Lilienthal*, p. 17.

51. David E. Lilienthal, *The Journals of David E. Lilienthal*, 4 vols. (New York: Harper and Row, 1964–69), vol. 1, *The TVA Years, 1939–1945: Including a Selection of Journal Entries from the 1917–1939 Period.*

52. Telegram, Arthur Morgan to McIntyre, 30 May 1933. Morgan also remarked that the Jewish Lilienthal's "racial characteristics were not obtrusive." Whether this reflected anti-Semitism and/or Arthur Morgan's pseudo-scientific habits of thought is unclear.

53. Actually, the president decided to offer the appointment to Lilienthal the day before Morgan's favorable telegram arrived at the White House. Roosevelt was anxious to act and apparently trusted that he had sufficient information already. Perhaps this is why Morgan came to believe that FDR was intent on appointing Lilienthal regardless of his advice (see telegram, McIntyre to Morgan, 29 May 1933, OF 42, box 1, "TVA, 1933," folder, FDRL).

54. He did not know, however, that he was inviting a protégé of Felix Frankfurter and Louis Brandeis into his fold. Frankfurter's pleasure at the appointment was communicated in a glowing congratulatory note to the president. "Not often," he wrote, "does one get such a combination of training, courage, understanding and youthful ardor as Lilienthal represents. It is a truly great appointment" (Frankfurter to FDR, 6 June 1933, ibid.).

55. McCraw, *Morgan versus Lilienthal*, p. 18.

56. Morgan, *Making of the TVA*, p. 30.

57. McCraw, *Morgan versus Lilienthal*, pp. 21–23; see also H. N. Hirsch, *The Enigma of Felix Frankfurter* (New York: Basic Books, 1981). This is ironically similar to Arthur Morgan's own early career. Morgan had chosen his vocation of dam building because he judged it to be a wide-open field in which an ambitious man might quickly make a name for himself.

58. McCraw, *Morgan versus Lilienthal*, pp. 21–23.

59. See Lilienthal, *Journals*, 4 September 1917 and 25 December 1920, 1:3–4 and 11–13, respectively.

60. For an indication of Lilienthal's relationship with Thomas Corcoran, see Joseph Lash, *Dealers and Dreamers: A New Look at the New Deal* (New York: Doubleday, 1988), p. 153; and for an indication of Corcoran's interest in the TVA, see Henry Hamill Fowler's reminiscences in *The Making of the New Deal: The Insiders Speak*, ed. Katie Louchheim (Cambridge: Harvard University Press, 1983), pp. 228–35.

61. As quoted in Morgan, *Making of the TVA*, p. 56. See also David E. Lilienthal, *TVA: Democracy on the March*, rev. ed. (New York: Harper and Row, 1953).

62. See Lilienthal, *TVA*, chap. 9, "Democracy at the Grass Roots." Ironically, the notion of "grass roots" democracy was originally articulated by "Alf" Landon, the 1936 Republican candidate for president (Steven M. Neuse, "TVA at Age Fifty—Reflections and Retrospect," *Public Administration Review* 43 [November–December 1983]: 492).

63. FDR to Lilienthal, 1 September 1944, PPF 5891, "David E. Lilienthal" folder, FDRL. "Your book," the president wrote, "is in a sense an epic of what you call 'dreamers with shovels.' We all really belong in that category."

64. Lilienthal, *TVA*, p. 190.

65. David E. Lilienthal, *Management: A Humanist Art* (New York: Carnegie Institute of Technology, 1967), pp. 20–21.

66. David E. Lilienthal, *This I Do Believe* (New York: Harper and Brothers, 1949), p. 91; see also pp. 81, 83, 86.

67. Philip Selznick, *TVA and the Grass Roots: A Study in the Sociology of Formal Organization* (Berkeley: University of California Press, 1953).

68. Rexford Guy Tugwell and Edward E. Banfield, "Grass Roots Democracy—Myth or Reality?" *Public Administration Review* 10 (Winter 1950): 47–55.

69. Morgan, *Making of the TVA*, p. 54.

70. McCraw, *Morgan versus Lilienthal*, p. 26. See also p. 19, where McCraw comments on Lilienthal's "series of almost incredibly ingratiating letters" to a man he earlier wished to cultivate, Frank P. Walsh. For Morgan's assertion regarding office design, see ibid., chap. 4.

71. Ibid., p. 33.

72. Memorandum, Arthur Morgan to Lilienthal, 21 July [1933?], PSF 187, "TVA" folder, 3d file, FDRL.

73. Ibid.

74. Memorandum, Lilienthal to Morgan, in ibid.

75. They supported each other, in fact, in all further decisions of the Board in which both took part (McCraw, *Morgan versus Lilienthal*, p. 32).

76. Quoted in ibid., p. 34.

77. Paul Hutchinson, "Revolution by Electricity," *Scribner's Magazine*, October 1934, pp. 193–200; and "Address of David E. Lilienthal before the Rotary Club," Memphis, Tenn., 17 October 1933, OF 42, box 1, "TVA, 1933," folder, FDRL.

78. Lilienthal, address before the Tennessee Lawyer's Club, Atlanta, Ga., 10 November 1933, OF 42, box 1, "TVA, 1933," folder, FDRL. See also David E. Lilienthal, "Business and Government in the Tennessee Valley," and Arthur E. Morgan, "Purposes and Methods of the Tennessee Valley Authority," in *Annals of the American Academy of Political and Social Sciences* 172 (March 1934): 45–49 and 50–57, respectively.

79. McCraw, *Morgan versus Lilienthal*, p. 34.

80. Ibid., p. 48. See also Morgan, "Purposes and Methods of the Tennessee Valley Authority," pp. 51–55.

81. Julian Huxley, *TVA: Adventure in Planning* (Cheam, Surrey: Architectural Press, 1943), p. 119.

82. Davidson, *The Tennessee*, 2:324.

83. McDonald and Muldowny, *TVA and the Dispossessed*, pp. 170–72.

84. North Callahan, *TVA: Bridge over Troubled Waters* (New York: A. S. Barnes, 1980), p. 30.

85. See the photographs of Norris in *Pencil Points*, November 1939, pp. 40–41.

86. McDonald and Muldowny, *TVA and the Dispossessed*, pp. 225–27.

87. Callahan writes that "He [God] at first was left out of the program" of Norris's town life, and "this showed that the TVA did not understand the people of the valley. They wanted God and murmured about the lack of Him at Norris. TVA called a vote among the townspeople, and almost unanimously they asked for a preacher. On Thursday nights several hundred of them gathered in the auditorium to hear a sermon and sing for an hour" (Callahan, *TVA*, p. 32; see also McDonald and Muldowny, *TVA and the Dispossessed*, pp. 230–31).

88. Davidson, *The Tennessee*, 2:229.

89. Ibid.; cf. Huxley's glowing account of Norris in *TVA*, pp. 56, 105.

90. For figures on TVA expansion, see *Annual Reports of the Tennessee Valley Authority for the Years 1934–1967*, with an introduction by Edward S. Mason (New York: Arno Press of the New York Times, 1969). Note that a shift took place with the dismissal of A. E. Morgan, from downplaying the power program to emphasizing it. Cf. esp. pp. 2–3 of the 1934 report and p. 5 of the 1936 report with pp. 1–3 of the 1939 report.

91. Quoted in McCraw, *Morgan versus Lilienthal*, p. 40.

92. *Public Papers and Addresses of Franklin D. Roosevelt*, 3:461, 462–63. Characteristically, just days later, at a Warm Springs press conference, Roosevelt switched gears and explained that "power is really a secondary matter. What we are doing here is taking a watershed with about 3 and a half million people in it, almost all of them rural, and we are trying to make a different type

217

of citizen out of them from what they would be under their present conditions" (p. 466).

93. Lee S. Greene, "Personnel Administration in the Tennessee Valley Authority," *Journal of Politics* 1 (May 1939): 171. To this day the TVA is statutorily exempted from civil service requirements in the employment of its professional staff.

94. Morgan, *Making of the TVA*, chap. 6, esp. pp. 82–84.

95. Ibid., chap. 12.

96. Harold L. Ickes, *The Secret Diary of Harold Ickes*, 3 vols. (New York: Simon and Schuster, 1953–54), vol. 1, *The First Thousand Days*, esp. pp. 566–67, regarding the events of 30 April 1936.

97. Lilienthal, *Journals*, 12 May 1936, 1:61–62.

98. FDR to Morgan, n.d., FDRL, copy in possession of author.

99. McCraw, *Morgan versus Lilienthal*, p. 58.

100. Ibid., p. 61.

101. FDR to Morgan, 11 July 1936, PPF 290, "Arthur E. Morgan" file, FDRL.

102. Morris L. Cooke to FDR, 7 July 1936, ibid. (filed along with Roosevelt's subsequent letter to Morgan), FDRL.

103. Quoted in McCraw, *Morgan versus Lilienthal*, p. 64.

104. Ickes, *Secret Diary*, vol. 2, *The Inside Struggle*, p. 67.

105. Lilienthal, *Journals*, 12 September 1936, 1:66.

106. Ibid.

107. McCraw, *Morgan versus Lilienthal*, p. 81.

108. Lilienthal, *Journals*, 3 March 1938, 1:70. FDR spoke on this date of his former embarrassment at "having a befuddled old man on our hands."

109. McCraw, *Morgan versus Lilienthal*, p. 86.

110. These charges were laid out in a series of articles in popular journals of the time. See the analysis by Harcourt Morgan and David Lilienthal of Arthur Morgan's "Public Ownership of Power" (*Atlantic Monthly*, September 1937, pp. 339–46), attached to Harcourt Morgan to FDR, 13 September 1937, PSF, box 187, "TVA" folder, 3d file, FDRL.

111. "And finally," the working papers of Lilienthal and Harcourt Morgan stated, "we believe Mr. Morgan's methods are wrong because the doctrine of 'rule or ruin' cannot coexist alongside the doctrine of majority rule and minority responsibility" (memorandum, Harcourt Morgan and David Lilienthal to FDR, 17 January 1938, ibid., p. 5).

112. "Stenographic Transcript of the Conference Held Today in the President's Office," 11 March 1938, ibid., 1st file.

113. Ibid.

114. FDR to Morgan, 22 March 1938, OF 42, box 5, "TVA, March–December, 1938," folder, FDRL.

115. Ibid.

116. "Under the Constitution . . . ," n.d., PSF, box 187, "TVA" folder, 1st file, FDRL.

117. FDR to the Speaker, 9 April 1938, OF 42, box 187, "TVA, March–December, 1938," folder, FDRL.

118. Davidson, *The Tennessee*, 2:319.

119. The TVA's power programs took center stage after A. E. Morgan's dismissal (see *Annual Reports of the TVA*).

120. Callahan, *TVA*, p. 34. Norris was by that time evolving into a bedroom community of nearby Knoxville, sought after by young professionals and their families, who appreciated its schools and gardens (see McDonald and Muldowny, *TVA and the Dispossessed*, pp. 233–35).

121. Tugwell and Banfield, "Grass Roots Democracy," p. 47.

122. My attribution of the handwriting on this document to President Roosevelt, which must be tentative, is based on the content and context of the humorous plea being made by the writer. A comparison of the handwriting with other examples known to be the president's proved inconclusive. The president did not normally write in block letters, as he did on this occasion, making comparison difficult. For a rare example of block writing, not inconsistent with the handwriting in question, in what is known to be Roosevelt's hand, see "FDR to ER," 17 March 1933, in Roosevelt Family Papers Donated by the Children of Franklin and Eleanor Roosevelt, box 12, "FDR to ER" folder, FDRL. Bob Parks, of the Franklin D. Roosevelt Library, located this latter document for me.

Chapter Four   Creating Model Cities: The Johnson Administration

1. The story of CAP has been told many times before (see Daniel Patrick Moynihan, *Maximum Feasible Misunderstanding: Community Action in the War on Poverty* [New York: Free Press, 1969], and Allen J. Matusow, *The Unraveling of America: A History of Liberalism in the 1960s* [New York: Harper Torchbooks, 1984], chaps. 4 (pp. 97–130) and 9 (pp. 243–74). On David Hackett and John Knowles, see Nicholas Lemann, *The Promised Land: The Great Black Migration and How It Changed America* (New York: Alfred A. Knopf, 1991), pp. 123–24.

2. Matusow, *Unraveling*, p. 125. Johnson draws the NYA parallel in his memoirs, *The Vantage Point: Perspectives of the Presidency, 1963–1969* (New York: Holt, Rinehart, and Winston, 1971), pp. 72–73.

3. Matusow, *Unraveling*, p. 270, from a *Washington Post* story of 23 January 1969.

4. Johnson, *Vantage Point*, pp. 324–25.

5. For a generally balanced, scholarly assessment of the Model Cities legacy in several California locations, see Rufus P. Browning, Dale Rogers Marshall, and David H. Tabb, *Protest Is Not Enough: The Struggle of Blacks and Hispanics for Equality in Urban Politics* (Berkeley and Los Angeles: University of California Press, 1984).

6. The name Demonstration Cities reminded some congressmen of urban demonstrations. The president took note and introduced the alternative term at the bill's signing ceremony.

7. For an example of the use of such language in describing the program, see Johnson, *Vantage Point*, p. 339.

8. Before Model Cities, the thrust of urban policy was urban renewal. In practice, renewal replaced low-income tenants with middle-income tenants and homeowners. As a consequence, urban renewal came under increasing criticism in the 1960s (see esp. Raymond Vernon, *The Myth and Reality of Our Urban Problems* [Cambridge: Harvard University Press, 1962]; Lewis Mumford's 1962 *New Yorker* criticisms of urban renewal, as discussed in Bernard J. Frieden and Marshall Kaplan, *The Politics of Neglect: Urban Aid from Model Cities to Revenue Sharing* [Cambridge: MIT Press, 1975]; and Theodore Lowi's classic political science text, *The End of Liberalism* [New York: Norton, 1969]).

9. Johnson, *Vantage Point*, p. 324.

10. Ibid., p. 339.

11. On the task forces of Johnson and Kennedy, see Norman C. Thomas and Harold L. Wolman, "Policy Formulation in the Institutionalized Presidency: The Johnson Task Forces," in *The Presidential Advisory System*, ed. Thomas E. Cronin and Sanford D. Greenberg (New York: Harper and Row, 1969), pp. 124–43; and Lester M. Salamon, "The Presidency and Domestic Policy Formulation," in *The Illusion of Presidential Government*, ed. Hugh Heclo and Lester M. Salamon (Boulder: Westview Press, 1981), pp. 177–202. "Blue sky planning" was a phrase adopted in HUD as a directive to cities in their planning efforts.

12. See Thomas and Wolman, "Policy Formulation," p. 129.

13. Lawrence E. Levinson, telephone interview, 9 July 1987. Johnson's personal view on the search for ideas is suggested by Eric Goldman, who wrote that to Johnson, "an idea was a suggestion, produced on the spot, of something for him to do tomorrow . . . a point to be made in a speech, an action, ceremonial or of substance, for him to take promptly, a formula to serve as a basis for legislation to be hurried to Congress" (quoted in James Allen Smith, *The Idea Brokers: Think Tanks and the Rise of the New Policy Elite* [New York: Free Press, 1991], p. 145).

14. Documentation of these "academic dinners" is in the Lyndon Baines Johnson Library (LBJL), White House Central Files, Aides, James C. Gaither, "Academic Dinners" folders, boxes 213, 286, and 287. For an official White House account of the entire legislative development cycle, see "Policy Formulation during Johnson's Administration," ibid., box 300, "Policy Formulation during the Johnson Administration" folder.

15. Levinson, telephone interview.

16. James C. Gaither, Oral History Interview, LBJL.

17. Ibid.

18. Discussed in Frieden and Kaplan, *Politics of Neglect*, pp. 37–39, 48–49, corroborated by Robert C. Wood, personal interview, 2 June 1987.

19. Memo, Califano to LBJ, with attachment, Legislative Background, Model Cities 1966, box 1, "Early Origins" folder, LBJL.

20. Reuther was one of those whom Johnson called immediately after the assassination to ask for his support (see the account in Frank Cormier and William J. Easton, *Reuther* [Englewood Cliffs, N.J.: Prentice-Hall, 1970], chap. 28, pp. 380–92).

21. On the president's fifty-seventh birthday, August 27, 1965,

Reuther, a dedicated liberal, wired the following comrade-in-arms message: "May you be blessed with continued good health so that the people and the nations of the world may share the blessings of peace, freedom, social justice and brotherhood, the goals to which you have dedicated your life and committed your leadership. I want also to report that I am on the job" (Name File, Walter P. Reuther, LBJL). Reuther's reputation within the White House corroborates the impression suggested by this telegram. In December of the same year, McPherson discussed in a memorandum to the president the possibility of appointing Reuther to head the new Department of Housing and Urban Development. The nomination of Reuther, McPherson wrote, would "no doubt . . . raise problems with the builders and the mortgage people, as well as the Birchers." It would, however, "certainly indicate your [the president's] intention to make HUD a major social, as well as brick-and-mortar department" (13 December 1965, in ibid.). See also Jean Gould and Lorena Hickok, *Walter Reuther: Labor's Rugged Individualist* (New York: Dodd, Mead, 1972).

22. Discussed in Frieden and Kaplan, *Politics of Neglect*, p. 38, corroborated by Wood, personal interview.

23. Memorandum, Reuther to LBJ, 13 May 1965, Legislative Background, Model Cities 1966, box 1, "Early Origins" folder, LBJL.

24. The exact date of the meeting is not recorded. As is the case with an unknown number of White House meetings, no record was made (see note in ibid., "preliminary outline," placing the meeting "somewhere in the summer of 1965").

25. Charles Haar to Richard N. Goodwin, 9 June 1965, ibid.

26. "Califano's Notes on Early Staff Meeting," n.d., ibid., "Origins and Deliberations of the Wood-Haar Task Force" folder.

27. Reuther to LBJ, partial copy in ibid.

28. Califano to LBJ, 9 October 1965, ibid., "Early Origins" folder.

29. Ibid., n.d.

30. Charles Schultze's sole document prepared for the Task Force, "Outlines of Subjects to be Considered by the Task Force on Cities," n.d., ibid.

31. Levinson, telephone interview.

32. Wood, personal interview.

33. Bernard J. Frieden, personal interview, 7 July 1987; H. Ralph Taylor, Oral History Interview, LBJL.

34. See Califano to LBJ, 13 October 1965, Legislative Background, Model Cities 1966, box 1, "Origins and Deliberations" folder, LBJL.

35. Wood, personal interview, corroborated by Charles Haar, Oral History Interview, LBJL.

36. Wood, personal interview; previously reported in Frieden and Kaplan, *Politics of Neglect*, p. 48.

37. "New towns" were considered at the highest levels (see EX LG 11/22/63, box 1, "LG 9/18/65–6/9/66" folder; see also Carl Stover to Douglas Cater, 31 July 1964, "Urban Extension Corps," in ibid., "11/22/63–8/30/65" folder). Johnson mentioned this idea in a televised speech from the University of California at Irvine (see generally the September 1965 *Scientific American* and articles of the period collected in Bernard J. Frieden and Robert Morris's thick

compendium, *Urban Planning and Social Policy* [New York: Basic Books, 1968]).

38. Harold Wolman found that a majority of housing experts in the United States believed these to be the underlying foci of urban policy (Wolman, *Politics of Federal Housing* [New York: Dodd, Mead, 1971]).

39. See their books of this period: Edward C. Banfield and James Q. Wilson, *City Politics* (Cambridge: Harvard University Press, 1963); Edward C. Banfield, *The Unheavenly City: The Nature and Future of Our Urban Crisis* (Boston: Little, Brown, 1970); and Martin Anderson, *The Federal Bulldozer: A Critical Analysis of Urban Renewal, 1949–1962* (Cambridge: MIT Press, 1964).

40. Frieden, personal interview.

41. Frieden and Kaplan, *Politics of Neglect*, p. 3.

42. Levinson, telephone interview.

43. Internal Working Papers, n.d., Legislative Background, Model Cities 1966, box 1, "Origins and Deliberations" folder, LBJL.

44. Notes on first meeting, Califano's office, 15 October 1965, and notes on luncheon meeting with Wood, Haar, and Rapkin, 17 October 1965, ibid.

45. Notes on first meeting, ibid.

46. See Bernard Frieden and Marshall Kaplan, "Community Development and the Model Cities Legacy," Joint Center for Urban Studies, MIT and Harvard, Working Paper no. 42, November 1976, pp. 9–10, available at the HUD Library.

47. Wood, personal interview; plus documents from Legislative Background, Model Cities 1966, box 1, "Origins and Deliberations" folder, LBJL, esp. relating to OSTP's interest in the project.

48. See esp. staff paper no. 1, "A Framework for Center City Demonstration Projects," by Chester Rapkin and Grace Milgram, in Legislative Background, Model Cities 1966, box 1, "Report of Wood-Haar Task Force" folder, LBJL.

49. The first three items are adapted from Frieden and Kaplan, *Politics of Neglect*, pp. 43–44; the fourth from Charles M. Haar, *Between the Idea and the Reality: A Study in the Organization, Fate, and Legacy of the Model Cities Program* (Boston: Little, Brown, 1975), p. 47.

50. This is the impression one gets from talking with the participants, and it is corroborated in Haar, *Between the Idea and the Reality* (see esp. his statement of the tenets of his liberal belief on p. 48). Wolman's *Politics of Federal Housing* also suggests the overwhelmingly liberal world-views of the mid-1960s housing experts. For his part, however, Robert Wood writes that "I am always bemused when I am termed a liberal in any strict ideological sense. . . . It is true that I am an anxiety-ridden optimist, but my operative code is simply that there are groups of people that need help in a capitalist society, that the marketplace cannot or will not help them, that the government sometimes can, and that we should try, always understanding that remedies are a series of approximations and reapproximations" (letter to the author, 3 January 1989).

51. Wood, personal interview.

52. Wood to Rapkin, 14 November 1965, Legislative Background, Model Cities 1966, box 1, "Origins and Deliberations" folder, LBJL: "My

counsel is to shut off all sources of input except the Task Force, its staff, and your consultants, relying on your recent activities and those of Bill Wheaton to be sufficient diplomacy. The job now is to think and write and to reconcile conflicting inputs . . . try to see if you can take a little bit of something from everyone."

53. As reported in Frieden and Kaplan, *Politics of Neglect*, p. 45.

54. Task Force staff paper no. 1 (Rapkin and Milgram, "Framework for Center City Demonstration Projects") specified the "slumless city" as the long-range goal of the program.

55. Frieden and Kaplan, "Community Development," p. 13.

56. Haar, *Between the Idea and the Reality*, pp. 52–53.

57. "Ribicoff made a good contribution. His main concern, however, will not be reflected in the report. He has a practicing politician's fear of a 'contest' in which some cities win, and others lose. He was inclined to escalate the demonstration program into a come-one, come-all program" (McPherson to Califano, 13 December 1965, in EX LG 11/22/65, box 1, "LG 9/18/65–6/1/66" folder, LBJL).

58. Legislative Background, Model Cities 1966, box 2, "HUD TF" folder, LBJL.

59. See letter of transmittal, Weaver to Califano, 1 September 1965, attached to report, in ibid.

60. U.S. President, *Message Transmitting Recommendations for City Demonstration Programs* (26 January 1966), 89th Cong., 2d sess., H. Doc. 368.

61. Califano to LBJ, 27 January 1966, EX LG 11/22/63, box 1, "LG 9/18/65–6/9/66" folder, LBJL.

62. See various documents in Legislative Background, Model Cities 1966, box 2, "Legislative Struggle" folder, esp. memoranda, Sidney Spector to Weaver, 24 May 1966, and Weaver to Califano, also 24 May 1966, LBJL.

63. Levinson, telephone interview.

64. Kennedy's remark was made in testimony of August 17, 1966, during proceedings by the Senate's Government Operations Subcommittee on Executive Reorganization (*Congressional Quarterly Almanac*, 1966, pp. 232–33).

65. Ibid.

66. R. Douglas Arnold, *Congress and the Bureaucracy: A Theory of Influence* (New Haven: Yale University Press, 1979), pp. 168–69.

67. *Congressional Quarterly Weekly Report*, 26 August 1966, pp. 1827–29.

68. H. Ralph Taylor, "Model Cities?" *IUD Agenda*, 5 March 1967, pp. 8–11, a publication of the AFL-CIO, available on microfiche at the HUD Library.

69. See "HUD's Advisory Committee on Demonstration Program Development, Report to the President on the Demonstration Cities Program," published 20 October 1966, available from the HUD Library. The program guide, entitled "HUD Program Guide: Model Neighborhoods in Demonstration Cities December, 1966," is also available from the HUD Library.

70. "Report to the Secretary," p. 1.

71. Robert C. Weaver, "HUD at Two: A Program Review," *Nation's*

Cities: The Magazine of the National League of Cities 5 (November 1967): 7–11.

72. Robert Wood to the author, 3 January 1989. As Wood recalls in this letter, he was "quoted in replying to a reporter on why a Tennessee city, sponsored by the Chairman of the Appropriation Committee, was chosen as saying 'It's a small, city, but there are those who love it.'"

73. Lashman to Sanders, 8 November 1968, Personal Papers of Harold Barefoot Sanders, Jr., box 26, "Model Cities" folder, LBJL. Neither Poteet nor Crystal City, however, was actually funded in that round.

74. Califano to LBJ, 10 July 1967, with attachment; and memorandum, Lashman to Sanders, 19 August 1968, both in ibid..

75. Califano to LBJ, 4 March 1968, in ibid.

76. Ibid.

77. Sanders to LBJ, 9 December 1968, with attachment, in ibid.

78. Memorandum, Sanders to LBJ, 4 September 1968, ibid., detailing the "Johnson support scores" of the representatives from districts sending in Model Cities applications.

79. Ibid.

80. Arnold, *Congress and the Bureaucracy*, pp. 198–99.

81. Haar, *Between the Idea and the Reality*, p. 159.

82. Ibid., p. 161.

83. Taylor, Oral History Interview.

84. From Frieden and Kaplan, *Politics of Neglect*, p. 109.

85. Wood, personal interview.

86. Wood, personal interview; Robert Weaver, Oral History Interview, LBJL.

87. See the fascinating account of the North Philadelphia Model City Neighborhood Organization, "Maximum Feasible Manipulation," as told to Sherry R. Arnstein, *Public Administration Review* 32 (September 1972): 377–89; the quotation is from p. 377.

88. See Frieden and Kaplan, *Politics of Neglect*, pp. 74–77.

89. Ibid.

90. Ibid.

91. Taylor, Oral History Interview.

92. Haar, *Between the Idea and the Reality*, p. 147.

93. Robert C. Wood, *The Necessary Majority: Middle America and the Urban Crisis* (New York: Columbia University Press, 1972).

94. Wood, personal interview.

95. Henry Aaron, *Politics and the Professors: The Great Society in Perspective* (Washington, D.C.: Brookings Institution Press, 1978). See in this regard Arthur D. Little, Inc., *Strategies for Shaping Model Cities* (Boston, 1967), and a similar evaluation report from General Electric's "think tank," TEMPO, *Model Neighborhood Program Planning*, Report no. 53957, draft of 21 July 1967, prepared for HUD by P. Ginsberg. Both are available at the HUD Library.

96. For a diversity of mainstream liberal perspectives on the whole Johnson social policy experience, however, see Marshall Kaplan and Peggy L. Cuciti, eds., *The Great Society and Its Legacy: Twenty Years of U.S. Policy* (Durham, N.C.: Duke University Press, 1986).

97. "Johnson Anti-poverty Aides Look to Possible Roles under Carter," *New York Times*, 27 November 1976. It should be noted that in the 1980s, however, some voices were raised to defend the work of the liberal social engineers. With regard to Model Cities, the best such work would be Browning, Marshall, and Tabb, *Protest Is Not Enough*. For a review of some of the important works in this genre, see Edward J. Harphan and Richard K. Scotch, "Rethinking the War on Poverty: The Ideology of Social Welfare Reform," *Western Political Quarterly* 41 (March 1988): 193–208. See also the highly influential conservative critique of welfare from the 1980s, Charles Murray, *Losing Ground: American Social Policy, 1950–1980* (New York: Basic Books, 1984).

98. "TVA," *National Journal*, 10 June 1989 (special ed.), p. 1539.

99. Lemann, *The Promised Land*, p. 218.

100. *Budget of the U.S. Government, FY 1977* (Washington, D.C.: GPO, 1976), p. 115.

Chapter Five Engineering a Supply-Side Revolution: The Reagan Administration

1. James Ceaser suggests the difficulty that some intellectuals encounter in understanding the Reagan administration when he writes, "When, contrary to the intellectuals' expectations, Reagan was elected, the prospect that he might actually be successful was more than impossible. It was unacceptable" ("The Reagan Presidency and American Public Opinion," in *The Reagan Legacy: Promise and Performance*, ed. Charles O. Jones [Chatham, N.J.: Chatham House, 1988], p. 179).

2. Sidney Blumenthal, *Our National Daydream* (New York: Harper and Row, 1988); Michael Paul Rogin, *Ronald Reagan, the Movie and Other Episodes in Political Demonology* (Berkeley and Los Angeles: University of California Press, 1987; Diane Rubenstein, "The Mirror of Reproduction: Baudrillard and Reagan's America," *Political Theory* 17 (November 1989): 582–606; idem, "Bush Disfigured" (Paper presented at the annual meeting of the American Political Science Association, San Francisco, August 1990). See also Garry Wills, *Reagan's America: Innocents at Home* (New York: Doubleday, 1987).

3. Even "mainstream" political scientists were generally taken by surprise by the Reagan presidency. For an overview, see Bert A. Rockman's "What Didn't We Know and Should We Forget It? Political Science and the Reagan Presidency," *Polity* 21 (Summer 1989): 777–92.

4. Seymour Martin Lipset and William Schneider, "The Confidence Gap during the Reagan Years, 1981–1987," *Political Science Quarterly* 102 (Spring 1987): 1–23.

5. Ben W. Heineman, Jr., and Curtis A. Hessler, *Memorandum for the President: A Strategic Approach to Domestic Affairs in the 1980s* (New York: Random House, 1980), p. xviii.

6. Ibid, p. 13, and see p. 55n.

7. Ibid., p. 201.

8. Ronald Reagan, *Ronald Reagan: An American Life* (New York: Simon and Schuster, 1990), pp. 287, 288.

9. Warren E. Miller and Merrill Shanks, "Policy Directions and Presidential Leadership: Alternative Interpretations of the 1980 Presidential Election," *British Journal of Political Science* 12 (July 1982): 322.

10. Paul Craig Roberts and Bruce Bartlett, "The Basis and Origin of Supply-Side Economic Policy," *Value Line Investment Survey*, 11 October 1986. For a different perspective, see Jude Wanniski, "An Authentic Guide to the Supply Side" (Morristown, N.J.: Polyconomics, May 1980, photocopy). The best overview of the economics of supply side is Richard H. Fink, ed., *Supply-Side Economics: A Critical Appraisal* (Frederick, Md.: University Publications of America, 1982).

11. Roberts and Bartlett, "Basis and Origin."

12. Irving Kristol, "Ideology and Supply-Side Economics," *Commentary*, April 1981, p. 48.

13. Ibid., pp. 51–52.

14. George Gilder, *Wealth and Poverty* (New York: Basic Books, 1981); Personal interviews, Leslie Lenkowsky, 3 November 1986, and Jude Wanniski, 5 November 1986.

15. Personal interviews, Wanniski, and Norman Ture, 26 December 1987.

16. Sidney Blumenthal, *The Rise of the Counter-Establishment* (New York: Times Books, 1986), p. 196.

17. Irving Kristol, personal interview, 16 December 1986.

18. Quoted in Blumenthal, *Rise of the Counter-Establishment*, pp. 207–9.

19. Kristol, personal interview.

20. Paul Craig Roberts, *The Supply-Side Revolution: An Insider's Account of Policymaking in Washington* (Cambridge: Harvard University Press, 1984).

21. Paul Craig Roberts, personal interview, 11 June 1987.

22. There is considerable bickering among supply-siders over who "converted" Kemp. In his campaign biography, Kemp gives the credit to Wanniski (Jack Kemp, *An American Renaissance* [New York: Harper and Row, 1979], p. 38). But see also Roberts (1984):31, f.n. 15.

23. Roberts, *Supply-Side Revolution*, p. 45.

24. Quoted in ibid., p. 61.

25. Wanniski, personal interview; David Stockman, *The Triumph of Politics: Why the Reagan Revolution Failed* (New York: Harper and Row, 1986).

26. Jude Wanniski, "With Reagan in California" (Morristown, N.J.: Polyconomics, 5 January 1980, photocopy).

27. Wanniski, personal interview.

28. Blumenthal, *Rise of the Counter-Establishment*, p. 198.

29. Reagan, *Reagan*, p. 231.

30. William F. Buckley, Jr., personal interview, 11 October 1986. Buckley went on during this interview to compare Reagan to Jesus Christ on this account!

31. See Garry Wills's complementary comments about Reagan's ability to "will his own innocence" (*Reagan's America*, p. 161). Cf., however, the argument of Lou Cannon, "The Real Reagan," in *Modern Presidents and the Presidency*, Proceedings of the Second Thomas P. O'Neill, Jr., Symposium on

American Politics, Department of Political Science, Boston College (Lexington, Mass.: Lexington Books, 1985).

32. Excerpts appeared in the *New York Times*, 14 December 1980.

33. Ture, personal interview; see also Ture's essay, "Department of the Treasury," pp. 647–94 in *Mandate for Leadership: Policy Management in a Conservative Administration*, ed. Charles Heatherly (Washington, D.C.: Heritage Foundation, 1981), published just in time for Reagan's 1981 transition.

34. Hugh Heclo, "Executive Budget Making," in *Federal Budget Policy in the 1980s*, ed. Gregory B. Mills and John L. Palmer (Washington, D.C.: Urban Institute Press, 1984), p. 263.

35. Stockman, *Triumph of Politics*, p. 110.

36. Ibid., p. 111.

37. See Chester A. Newland, "A Mid-Term Appraisal: The Reagan Presidency," *Public Administration Review* 43 (January–February 1983): 4–5.

38. Joseph Wholey, "Executive Agency Retrenchment," in Mills and Palmer, *Federal Budget Policy in the 1980s*, p. 301.

39. Ibid., 306–8.

40. Robert Pear, "3 Key Aides Reshape Welfare Policy," *New York Times*, 26 April 1982.

41. David R. Beam, "New Federalism, Old Realities: The Reagan Administration and Intergovernmental Reform," in *The Reagan Presidency and the Governing of America*, ed. Lester M. Salamon and Michael S. Lund (Washington, D.C.: Urban Institute Press, 1984), p. 430. See also John William Ellwood, ed., *Reductions in U.S. Domestic Spending: How They Affect State and Local Governments* (New Brunswick, N.J.: Transaction Press, 1982), pp. 297–304; and R. Kent Weaver, "Controlling Entitlements," in *The New Direction in American Politics*, ed. John E. Chubb and Paul E. Peterson (Washington, D.C.: Brookings Institution Press, 1985), pp. 307–41.

42. See Aaron Wildavsky, *The Politics of the Budgetary Process* (Boston: Little Brown, 1984); and Bruce E. Johnson, "From Analyst to Negotiator: The OMB's New Role," *Journal of Policy Analysis and Management* 3 (Summer 1984): 501–15.

43. Stockman, *Triumph of Politics*, p. 82.

44. These individuals are named in ibid., p. 84. Their names also came up in interviews with Ture, Roberts, Wanniski, and Lehrman.

45. Ibid., pp. 46, 93.

46. Hugh Heclo and Rudolph Penner, "Fiscal and Political Strategy in the Reagan Administration," in *The Reagan Presidency: An Early Assessment*, ed. Fred I. Greenstein (Baltimore: Johns Hopkins University Press, 1983), p. 36. Cf. W. Bowman Carter, "The Presidency and Economic Policy: A Tale of Two Budgets," in *The Presidency and the Political System*, ed. Michael Nelson (Washington, D.C.: CQ Press, 1984), p. 471.

47. Stockman, *Triumph of Politics*, p. 123.

48. Ibid., p. 159.

49. Thomas P. O'Neill (with William Novak), *Man of the House: The Life and Political Memoirs of Speaker Tip O'Neill* (New York: Random House, 1987), p. 344.

50. Quoted in Anthony King, "The American Polity in the 1990s," in *The New American Political System*, ed. Anthony King, rev. ed. (Washington, D.C.: American Enterprise Institute, 1990), p. 300.

51. John Burke, "Presidential Influence and the Budget Process: A Comparative Analysis," in *The Presidency and Public Policy Making*, ed. George C. Edwards III, Steven A. Shull, and Norman C. Thomas (Pittsburgh: University of Pittsburgh Press, 1985), pp. 80–82.

52. James P. Pfiffner, "The Carter-Reagan Transition: Hitting the Ground Running," *Presidential Studies Quarterly* 13 (Fall 1983): 623–45.

53. Stockman, *Triumph of Politics*, following p. 118.

54. This, Stockman reports, was Reagan's "mantra."

55. Roberts, *Supply-Side Revolution*, p. 110. Roberts was very conscious of the role of the media, having been an editorial writer for the *Wall Street Journal*.

56. Ibid.

57. Stockman, *Triumph of Politics*, p. 199.

58. Even among Reagan voters, a balanced budget was preferred to a tax cut almost 2 to 1 in 1981 (*New York Times*/CBS poll, cited in James Q. Wilson, *American Government*, 3d ed. [Lexington, Mass.: D. C. Heath, 1986], p. 472).

59. Stockman, *Triumph of Politics*, pp. 266–67, 214.

60. John William Ellwood, "How Congress Controls Expenditures," in Ellwood, ed., *Reductions*, p. 25.

61. Paul Peterson, "The Rise and Fall of Special Interest Politics," *Political Science Quarterly* 105 (Winter 1990–91): 550–51.

62. Weaver, "Controlling Entitlements," p. 325.

63. Personal interviews, Roberts and Ture; see also Stockman, *Triumph of Politics*, pp. 74, 135, 272–74. Also of relevance is Martin Anderson's extended discussion in *Revolution* (San Diego: Harcourt, Brace, Jovanovich, 1988), pp. 152–63.

64. See, e.g., Jude Wanniski, "The Burden of Friedman's Monetarism," *New York Times*, 26 July 1981; Alan Reynolds, "Reaganomics in Retrospect" (Morristown, N.J.: Polyconomics, 30 August 1984, photocopy); and Jack Kemp, "Supply-Side Economics: Success or Failure?" *Human Events*, 25 February 1984.

65. The most recent sympathetic evaluations of the supply side are offered by Paul Craig Roberts, "Why Supply-Side Will Stay in Demand," *Wall Street Journal*, 12 July 1988; idem, "'Supply-Side' Economics—Theory and Results," *Public Interest* 93 (Fall 1988): 16–36; and Lawrence Lindsey, *The Growth Experiment: How the New Tax Policy Is Transforming the United States Economy* (New York: Basic Books, 1990). See also the evaluation of George Bush's CEA chairman, Michael Boskin, *Reagan and the Economy: The Successes, Failures, and Unfinished Agenda* (San Francisco: Institute for Contemporary Studies, 1987).

66. *Weekly Compilation of Presidential Documents* 20, no. 12 (1984): 400, as quoted in James Ceaser, "The Theory of Governance of the Reagan Administration," in Salamon and Lund, *The Reagan Presidency*, pp. 56–87.

67. *New York Times*, 6 February 1986.

68. Reagan, *Reagan*, p. 232.

69. Stockman, *Triumph of Politics*, p. 68.

70. Ibid., p. 133.

71. Tom Wicker, "In the Nation: A Deliberate Deficit," *New York Times*, 18 July 1985; and Daniel Patrick Moynihan, *Came the Revolution: Argument in the Reagan Era* (San Diego: Harcourt, Brace, Jovanovich, 1988), esp. p. 154.

72. David Stockman to the author, 18 March 1991.

73. Buckley, personal interview. Even Paul Weyrich, a conservative critic of the former president, does not believe that Reagan intended for his fiscal policy to result in huge deficits. Rather, he suggests, Reagan was simply temperamentally incapable of making the requisite "tough choices" (see Weyrich's comments in *National Journal*, 18 March 1989, p. 678).

74. Anderson, *Revolution*, pp. xx–xxii.

75. See Alan Murray, "Downward Curve: Supply-Siders Suffer a Decline in Demand for Their Policy Ideas," *Wall Street Journal*, 18 August 1987. Murray's analysis belies his article's title.

76. See the figures in Paul Krugman, *The Age of Diminished Expectations: U.S. Economic Policy in the 1990s* (Cambridge: MIT Press, 1990), pp. 19–25.

77. Kevin Phillips, *The Politics of Rich and Poor: Wealth and the American Electorate in the Reagan Aftermath* (New York: Random House, 1990).

78. Krugman, *Age of Diminished Expectations*.

79. Stockman, *Triumph of Politics*, p. 353.

Chapter Six   The Radical's Dilemma and the Future of American Politics

1. James Allen Smith, *The Idea Brokers: Think Tanks and the Rise of the New Policy Elite* (New York: Free Press, 1991).

2. Michael E. Lind, executive editor of *The National Interest*, suggested this idea to me.

3. Perhaps the most influential elaboration of this theme has been Theodore J. Lowi's *The Personal President: Power Invested, Promise Unfulfilled* (Ithaca: Cornell University Press, 1985).

4. Erwin Hargrove and Michael Nelson, *Presidents, Politics, and Policy* (Baltimore: Johns Hopkins University Press, 1984), p. 68.

5. Ibid., p. 82.

6. Jimmy Carter, *Keeping Faith: Memoirs of a President* (New York: Bantam Books, 1982), pp. 73–74.

7. Paul Light, *Domestic Policy Choice: Kennedy to Carter, with Notes on Ronald Reagan* (Baltimore: Johns Hopkins University Press, 1982).

8. David McKay, *Domestic Policy and Ideology: Presidents and the American State, 1964–1987* (Cambridge: Cambridge University Press, 1989), p. 131.

9. Dilys M. Hill, "Domestic Policy," in *The Carter Years: The President and Policy Making*, ed. M. Glenn Abernathy, Dilys M. Hill, and Phil Williams (New York: St. Martin's Press, 1984); William M. Lunch, *The Nationalization of American Politics* (Berkeley and Los Angeles: University of California Press,

1987), p. 4; "Doctor's Degree," *New Republic*, 20 October 1986, p. 11, on Joseph Duffey, whom Carter appointed to chair the National Endowment for the Humanities. Also, as Roger Brown notes ("Party and Bureaucracy: From Kennedy to Reagan," *Political Science Quarterly* 97 [Summer 1982]: 279–94), Carter expanded his predecessors' White House liaison program to include an outreach program to intellectuals (p. 292).

10. For a brilliant retelling, see Nicholas Lemann, *The Promised Land: The Great Black Migration and How It Changed America* (New York: Alfred A. Knopf, 1991), pp. 118–68.

11. Hargrove and Nelson, *Presidents, Politics, and Public Policy*, p. 67.

12. Probably the best single source on the Family Assistance Plan, showing that its historical roots extend not to Daniel Patrick Moynihan's influence but directly to Sargent Shriver's OEO under President Johnson, is Vincent J. Burke and Vee Burke, *Nixon's Good Deed: Welfare Reform* (New York: Columbia University Press, 1974). On Rockefeller's vice presidency, see Michael Turner, *The Vice President as Policy Maker: Rockefeller in the Ford White House* (Westport, Conn.: Greenwood Press, 1982).

13. Richard E. Neustadt, *Presidential Power* (New York: John Wiley, 1960), pp. 10, 36.

14. Peter W. Sperlich, "Bargaining and Overload: An Essay on Presidential Power," in *Perspectives on the Presidency*, ed. Aaron Wildavsky (Boston: Little, Brown, 1975), pp. 419–20.

15. Barbara Kellerman, *The Political Presidency: The Practice of Leadership* (New York: Oxford University Press, 1984).

16. Ibid. pp. 42, 256.

17. Daniel Bell, "The Problem of Ideological Rigidity," in *The Failure of a Dream? Essays in the History of American Socialism*, ed. John H. M. Laslett and Seymour Martin Lipset (Garden City, N.Y.: Doubleday, 1974); idem, *Marxian Socialism in the United States* (Princeton: Princeton University Press, 1967).

18. Aileen Kraditor, *The Radical Persuasion, 1894–1917* (Baton Rouge: Louisiana State University Press, 1981).

19. Quoted in *Report of the Congressional Committees Investigating the Iran-Contra Affair* (New York: Times Books, 1988), p. 50.

20. Ibid., p. 64.

21. As quoted in ibid., p. 44. For a highly critical account of this office and its activities, see Robert Parry and Peter Kornbluh, "Iran-Contra's Untold Story," *Foreign Policy* 72 (Fall 1988): 3–30.

22. Martin Anderson, *Revolution* (San Diego: Harcourt, Brace, Jovanovich, 1988), pp. 402–3.

23. Ibid., p. xxii.

Epilogue: People of Ideas in the Bush Administration

1. For a sampling of journalistic dismissals of Bush's domestic policies, see: Lawrence J. Haas, "Pleading Poverty," *National Journal*, 15 September 1990, pp. 2192–96; Julie Rovner, "On Policy Front, Home Is Not Where Bush's

Heart Is," *Congressional Quarterly Weekly Report,* 2 February 1991, pp. 292–98; David Rosenbaum, "Wanted in Domestic Agenda: Unity That U.S. Had in War," *New York Times,* 20 March 1991; and "Nothing," *New Republic,* 25 February 1991, pp. 7–8. The incentive-oriented domestic initiatives proposed by the ideologues in this administration were lampooned by Richard Darman, director of OMB, in a speech he delivered before the Council for Excellence in Government in Washington, D.C., on November 16, 1990. White House Chief of Staff John Sununu, meanwhile, is on record as saying that "there is not a single piece of legislation that needs to be passed in the next two years" (from a speech delivered in the fall of 1990, as quoted in "Outflanking the Democrats," *Boston Globe,* 10 February 1991, p. 82).

2. Fred Barnes, "Bush's Big Government Conservatives," *American Spectator,* April 1990, pp. 14–15.

3. George Bush, Inaugural Address, *Congressional Quarterly Almanac, 1989* (Washington, D.C.: CQ Press, 1989), pp. 7–9 C.

4. Rhodes Cook, "Turnout Hits 64-Year Low in Presidential Race," *Congressional Quarterly Weekly Report,* 21 January 1989, pp. 135–38.

5. Burton Yale Pines, "Bull Moose Roosevelt," *Policy Review,* Winter 1991, pp. 2–5.

6. On Quayle's election to the Senate, see Richard Fenno, Jr., *The Making of a Senator: Dan Quayle* (Washington, D.C.: CQ Press, 1989). In a midterm evaluation of the Bush-Quayle administration, *Policy Review*'s team of conservative evaluators gave Quayle far higher marks than the president (see Martin Anderson et al., "Sophomore Slump: Mid-Term Grades for the Bush Administration," *Policy Review,* Winter 1991, p. 35).

7. Burt Solomon, "White House Notebook," *National Journal,* 21 January 1989, pp. 142–43.

8. Chase Untermeyer, personal interview, 15 April 1991.

9. David Mason, personal interview, 16 April 1991.

10. Susan Chira, "Bush Presses Bill Allowing Parents to Choose Schools," *New York Times,* 19 April 1991.

11. Untermeyer, a member of the original White House senior staff, was one of four persons whose ties to Bush extended to the Texas GOP (see Burt Solomon, "White House Notebook," *National Journal,* 30 September 1989, p. 2419).

12. Untermeyer, personal interview.

13. See James P. Pfiffner, "Establishing the Bush Presidency," *Public Administration Review* 50 (January-February 1990): 69.

14. See "Outflanking the Democrats," p. 65.

15. William Kristol, personal interview, 14 May 1991.

16. Robert Pear, "U.S. Laws Delayed by Complex Rules and Partisanship," *New York Times,* 31 March 1991.

17. Kristol, personal interview.

18. "The New Paradigm," remarks by James Pinkerton to the Reason Foundation, Los Angeles, 23 April 1990, p. 1.

19. James Pinkerton, personal interview, 15 April 1991.

20. "The War in the Gulf, The War on Poverty, and the New Para-

digm," remarks by James Pinkerton to the Institute of Politics at the Kennedy School of Government, Harvard University, 19 March 1991.

21. Pinkerton, personal interview.

22. Pinkerton, "The War in the Gulf."

23. Pinkerton, personal interview.

24. Nicholas Lemann, "Fighting the Last War," *Atlantic Monthly*, February 1991, p. 31.

25. Carol Steinbach, "Kemp's Crusade," *National Journal*, 9 December 1989, p. 2996. See also "A New War on Poverty," remarks by HUD Secretary Kemp to the Heritage Foundation, 6 June 1990, p. 1.

26. Thomas Humbert, personal interview, 16 April 1991.

27. Lemann, "Fighting the Last War," p. 30.

28. "Homeownership and Opportunity for People Everywhere," remarks by HUD Secretary Jack Kemp to the National Press Club, Washington, D.C., 15 November 1989.

29. George Bush, 28 November 1990, *Weekly Compilation of Presidential Documents* 26, no. 48 (1990): 1929.

30. U.S. Department of Housing and Urban Development, Office of Public Affairs, "1992 Budget for HUD Represents Dramatic New Direction for Housing Policy," news release no. 91-06(A), 4 February 1991.

31. Humbert, personal interview.

32. S. Anna Kondratas, personal interview, 17 April 1991.

33. "101st Congress Leaves Behind Plenty of Laws, Criticism," *Congressional Quarterly*, 3 November 1990, pp. 3683–3709.

34. *Housing Affairs Letter*, 2 February 1990, p. 1.

35. Kondratas, personal interview.

36. Fitts was driven from HUD in 1990, in any event, by the conservatives within HUD (*Housing Affairs Letter*, 17 August 1990, pp. 3–4).

37. Supplemental appropriations requests for fiscal year 1991 are detailed in HUD's fiscal year 1992 Budget document, "New Directions in Housing: Empowering Low Income Americans with Choice, Opportunity, and Homeownership," 4 February 1991 (Washington, D.C.: HUD Public Affairs Office, photocopy).

38. Humbert, personal interview.

39. Daniel J. Monti, personal interview, 1 May 1991.

40. George Hager, "Bush's Success Rate Sinks to Near-Record Low," *Congressional Quarterly Weekly Report*, 22 December 1990, pp. 4183–94.

41. Maureen Dowd, "Bush Visits a Project to Back Tax Cuts," *New York Times*, 4 May 1991; Andrew Rosenthal, "Bush Accuses Congress," ibid., 13 June 1991.

A Note on Sources

Interviews

Personal interviews were an important source of information on the Johnson and Reagan presidencies. Interviews were conducted with the following individuals (unless otherwise indicated, titles reflect occupational status at the time of the interview):

John Aughton, telephone interview, 8 June 1987. Treasury Department, senior civil servant.

Gary Bauer, Washington, D.C., 24 November 1986. Undersecretary of education.

Brigitte Berger, Brookline, Mass., 16 October 1986. Professor of sociology, Wellesley College.

Peter L. Berger, Brookline, Mass., 16 October 1986. University Professor, Boston University.

Richard Brookhiser, New York City, 26 October 1986. Managing editor, *National Review*.

William F. Buckley, Jr., Stamford, Conn., 11 October 1986. Editor, *National Review*.

Bernard J. Frieden, Cambridge, Mass., 7 July 1987. Co-director, Johnson administration's Model Cities Task Force staff.

Thomas Humbert, Washington, D.C., 16 April 1991. Deputy assistant secretary, HUD.

E. Pendleton James, New York City, 15 December 1986. President Reagan's first director of presidential personnel.

S. Anna Kondratas, Washington, D.C., 17 April 1991. Assistant secretary, HUD.

Irving Kristol, New York City, 16 December 1986. Editor, *The Public Interest*.

William Kristol, Washington, D.C., 14 May 1991. Chief of staff to the vice president.

Lewis Lehrman, New York City, 20 November and 16 December 1986. Founder, Lehrman Institute.

Carl Leiden, Austin, Tex., numerous conversations, 1984–86. Retired professor of government, University of Texas.

Leslie Lenkowsky, Washington, D.C., 3 November 1986. Director, Institute for Educational Affairs.

Lawrence E. Levinson, telephone interview, 9 July 1987. Deputy assistant to the president in the Johnson White House.

Paul Light, Washington, D.C., November 1986. Director of academy studies, National Academy of Public Administration.

Michael Lind, Washington, D.C., numerous conversations, 1985–91. Executive editor, *The National Interest.*

G. Calvin McKenzie, Waterville, Maine, 17 November 1986. Professor of government, Colby College, and authority on the presidential appointments process.

David Mason, Washington, D.C., 16 April 1991. Director of executive branch liaison, Heritage Foundation.

Adam Meyerson, Washington, D.C., 24 November 1986. Editor, *Policy Review,* Heritage Foundation.

Daniel J. Monti, Boston, Mass., 1 May 1991. Professor of sociology, University of Missouri, St. Louis, and authority on urban affairs.

James Piereson, New York City, November 1986. Director, John M. Olin Foundation.

James Pinkerton, Washington, D.C., 15 April 1991. Deputy assistant to the president for policy planning.

Lucian Pye, Cambridge, Mass., numerous conversations, 1984–86. Professor of political science, MIT, and former associate of Robert Wood.

Alan Reynolds, Morristown, N.J., 5 November 1986. Supply-side economist, associate of Jude Wanniski.

Paul Craig Roberts, Washington, D.C., 11 June 1987. Assistant secretary of the treasury in the early Reagan administration.

John P. Roche, Medford, Mass., 19 June 1987. Special assistant to President Johnson.

Marco Rosenbaum, New Haven, Conn., numerous conversations, 1986–87. Yale University conservative activist.

William Rusher, New York City, 26 October 1986. Publisher, *National Review.*

William E. Simon, New York City, 4 December 1986, and telephone interview, 5 December 1986. President, John M. Olin Foundation, and former secretary of the treasury.

Norman Ture, Washington, D.C., 26 December 1987. Undersecretary of the treasury in the early Reagan administration.

Charles Untermeyer, Washington, D.C., 15 April 1991. Director of presidential personnel.

Jude Wanniski, Morristown, N.J., 5 November 1986. Supply-side author and activist.

John Weicher, Washington, D.C., 17 April 1991. Assistant secretary, HUD.

Robert C. Wood, Middletown, Conn., 2 June 1987. Chairman of the Model Cities Task Force, and former undersecretary and secretary, HUD.

The transcripts of Oral History Interviews with the following individuals were obtained from the Lyndon Baines Johnson Library (unless otherwise indicated, titles reflect responsibility in the Johnson administration):

Matthew B. Coffey (personnel aide)

James Farley (political friend of President Johnson, director of presidential personnel in the Franklin Roosevelt administration)

Dan Fenn (personnel aide in the Kennedy administration)

James C. Gaither (White House aide)

Kermit Gordon (budget director)
Charles Haar (assistant secretary, HUD)
Harry McPherson (special counsel to the president)
John Macy (civil service commissioner and director of presidential personnel)
Mike Manatos (legislative liaison)
Richard Neustadt (professor of government, presidential adviser)
John P. Roche (special assistant to the president)
Arthur M. Schlesinger, Jr. (historian, presidential adviser in the Kennedy administration)
Charles L. Schultze (budget director)
John Sparkman (U.S. senator from Alabama)
Robert S. Strauss (Democratic party leader)
James L. Sundquist (deputy undersecretary of agriculture, author)
H. Ralph Taylor (assistant secretary, HUD)
Benjamin Wattenberg (presidential speechwriter, author)
Robert Weaver (secretary, HUD)
Lee White (White House aide)
Robert Wood (undersecretary and secretary, HUD)
Whitney Young (president, National Urban League).

Published interviews with other policy makers also were consulted, as indicated in the notes.

Archives, Special Collections

Numerous archival materials were consulted at the Franklin Delano Roosevelt Library, in Hyde Park, New York, and the Lyndon Baines Johnson Library, in Austin, Texas. For the relevant collections, see the notes to the appropriate chapters.

Congressional committee transcripts and reports relating to the Tennessee Valley Authority were consulted in the social science and law collections of the Library of Congress, in Washington, D.C.. Materials relating to the Model Cities program and the Reagan administration's fiscal policy were found in, respectively, the libraries of the Department of Housing and Urban Development and the Department of the Treasury. The former contains a microfiche collection of the speeches of all HUD officials, as well as extensive documentation of individual grants under the Model Cities program. The Treasury Department library, which offers only highly limited access to visitors, contains useful compilations of mostly unpublished documents, including all public statements of Treasury Department officials.

Index

Designed by Julie Burris
Composed by The Composing Room of Michigan, Inc.,
in Baskerville
Printed by The Maple Press Company, Inc.,
on 50-lb. M. V. Eggshell Cream